"*Bravery is not a mystical attribute that some adventurous souls are given but the rest of us lack. Being brave is about saying 'Yes' to God and to others; it is about facing our internal obstacles and making tough choices in a crisis. Nathalie has chosen to live by faith and not by fear, and her life so far has been extraordinary as a result. You will be encouraged and challenged by the wisdom she shares and you will, in turn, undoubtedly dare to dream more about what God can do through you. Having visited Liberia and the Ebola hospital, I know that sharing this story has been costly, but this bravery will also be rewarded as we each say a bigger 'Yes' to God as a result of all that is shared in these pages.*"

Cathy Madavan, speaker, writer, author of *Digging for Diamonds* and part of Spring Harvest Planning Group

"*In Dare To Trust, Nathalie MacDermott shares her own compelling story, but her story and my story will forever be intertwined. She shares in accurate detail the trauma we witnessed together during the Ebola outbreak in Liberia in 2014, including my own near-death experience with the dreaded disease. So much of Nathalie's story resonates deeply with me, especially this truth: 'Being a Christian does not make us immune from difficult situations, but it does mean we have a God who stands by our side…' Thank you, Nathalie, for standing by my side in my darkest hour.*"

Dr Kent Brantly, American Ebola survivor and co-author of *Called For Life: How Loving Our Neighbor Led Us into the Heart of the Ebola Epidemic*

"Courageous, remarkable, compassionate and selfless all describe who Dr Nathalie MacDermott is. Her book, Dare to Trust, challenges us to 'go beyond our comfort zones to radically love the person in front of us – no matter their background. We reach out because we are all sinners, saved by grace.' She answers the question that so many of us are asked: 'Would you really go back and put yourself through it all again?' Dare to Trust is a reflection of the mandate that we as Christians have to demonstrate Christ's love to the world. Nathalie exemplifies that call. It was a privilege to serve alongside Nathalie in Liberia."

Nancy Writebol, Serving in Mission (SIM), Liberia

"This book is a breathtaking account of what God can achieve through somebody who is totally dedicated to him and his purpose. My friend Nathalie has learned that her faith in Jesus is more valuable than her own life; in fact, Jesus has become her life. Her story is a challenge to us to take our discipleship seriously, and be radical in our commitment to the Lord."

Dr Roger Aubrey, All Nations Church Cardiff and author of
Discovering God

"It has been my privilege to get to know Nathalie over the past 5 years as she has deployed with Samaritan's Purse into disaster situations around the world. She has put her faith to the test serving Jesus in extreme conditions such as the Samaritan's Purse Ebola hospital in Liberia – and she has found God to be faithful. As you read her inspiring story, be inspired and then go and do likewise!"

Simon Barrington, CEO Samaritan's Purse UK

DARE TO TRUST

CHOOSING A LIFE OF RISK

NATHALIE MACDERMOTT

MONARCH
BOOKS

Oxford, UK and Grand Rapids, USA

Published by Monarch Books
an imprint of
Lion Hudson plc
Wilkinson House, Jordan Hill Road,
Oxford OX2 8DR, England
Email: monarch@lionhudson.com
www.lionhudson.com/monarch

ISBN 978 0 85721 803 2
e-ISBN 978 0 85721 804 9

First edition 2017

Acknowledgments
Scripture quotations marked "NLT" are taken from the Holy Bible, New Living Translation,
copyright © 1996, 2004. Used by permission of Tyndale House Publishers, Inc., Carol
Stream, Illinois 60188. All rights reserved.
Scripture quotations marked "NKJV" are taken from the New King James Version®.
Copyright © 1982 by Thomas Nelson. Used by permission. All rights reserved.
Scripture quotations marked "NIV" are taken from the Holy Bible, New International
Version Anglicised. Copyright © 1979, 1984, 2011 Biblica, formerly International Bible
Society. Used by permission of Hodder & Stoughton Ltd, an Hachette UK company. All
rights reserved. "NIV" is a registered trademark of Biblica. UK trademark number 1448790

Throughout the book, the names of patients have been changed to preserve their anonymity.

A catalogue record for this book is available from the British Library

Printed and bound in Great Britain by
Marston Book Services Ltd, Oxfordshire

DEDICATION

For the healthcare workers who fought valiantly for their patients, but lost their lives to Ebola.

For Bobby and all the patients of ELWA2 – I am sorry I was not able to do more for you.

May your memories live on in the hearts of all who knew you and may the lessons of the 2014–2016 West African Ebola epidemic never be forgotten.

CONTENTS

FOREWORD

This book is a cameo of a young doctor's life of helping others. It could not be more timely. In a world where the church struggles against its own inertia and seeks an identity, Dr Nathalie recalls some of her adventures, which helped her find herself and give her purpose.

These adventures show her qualities of boldness, courage, tenacity, perseverance, and above all her faith in her Lord Jesus Christ. Her book challenges the apathy and lethargy so often found in ourselves. It sets us on an adventure of daring, danger, and deliverance. Dr Nathalie has been on numerous adventures that have been hazardous and extremely challenging, but shining through it all comes her compassion and love for her fellow man.

A gripping tale, with the evidence of the providence of God helping the good young doctor achieve her goals and destiny.

A must read, but not for the faint hearted.

Enjoy the adventure!

Keri Jones
Ministries Without Borders
2016

ACKNOWLEDGMENTS

Many people have contributed to the writing of this book and the events that led up to it. I hope to acknowledge everyone here, but if I miss anyone, I apologize and hope you know that you are greatly appreciated.

I would first like to thank Mum, Dad, Ben, and Callum for your support, patience, and understanding of the work that I do. I know it has cost you many sleepless nights and I am grateful for the opportunities you have afforded me that have led to me being able to undertake this work. Your influence has made me the person I am today, even when you may not have realized it. I hope you realize that in this manner you have contributed to the work that I do and are very much a part of it. I know you are not always happy with the risks I take, but I am very grateful that you respect them and allow me to fly – even when it goes against everything a parent/sibling feels they should do to protect their daughter/sister.

I would like to thank my church family and my friends, who have encouraged me and stood by my side through some very difficult times. I would particularly like to thank Keri Jones and the Ministries Without Borders family who have sown into my life and invested their time and finances into growing me in my faith and training me in disaster response. Thank you for investing in the Rapid Response Unit, believing in my ability to develop it, and facilitating the process. I would also like to thank the leadership and members of All Nations Church, Cardiff, for sowing into my life all these years. I am who I am today because of your investment and encouragement.

I would like to thank Sarah Butcher, Richard Renew, Mark and Marjan De Leeuw van Weenen, Roger Aubrey, Maggie Knight, and Gabrielle McGregor for following God's prompting and playing an integral part in leading me to the Lord. My heartfelt thanks also go to Gabrielle McGregor, Esther Coggins, and Bethan Jones: you have stood by my side through some dark times, have listened and encouraged, but also cleaned my apartment, looked after my car, and sorted my post, thus enabling me to do the work that I do. You also showered love on me on my return, when I needed people around me. Without you and the many other ladies who have helped you I would not have been able to do the things I have done.

Thank you to all my friends, extended family, and colleagues who have supported me, encouraged me and prayed for me. You have no idea how much your often timely encouragements have motivated me to continue in the work I have been doing.

Thank you to my supervisor, Prof Michael Levin, for the opportunity and support to undertake an incredible PhD at Imperial College London.

I would like to thank the leaders of King's Church

Manchester and all those who sowed into my life during my year at Covenant School of Ministries School of the Word, including faculty, classmates, and church members. Particularly, I would like to thank Dave Emmett, Principal extraordinaire, Richard Anniss, Gavin White, Roger Aubrey, Ezekiel and Mahongo Shibemba, Matthew Ling, Tony Ling, Trevor Lloyd, David Lyon, Richard Jones, Mick Walford, Andrew and Angela Hughes, Dave and Carol Roberts, Bryan Shutt, David Shutt, and many others who invested time and energy into teaching me, guiding me, and bringing me into the revelation of Christ that I am blessed to walk in today.

Huge thanks also goes to Samaritan's Purse and all its staff in the US, UK, Canada, and Australia who work incredibly hard to support staff working overseas and in disaster response. It truly is a great organization to work with, and one that I know cares deeply about its staff and volunteers, but particularly about the people we reach. There are not many organizations that do international aid and disaster response of this calibre and it is an honour to work with you, witness with you, and pray with you. I would also like to thank all those with whom I have had the fortune to serve in disaster response with Samaritan's Purse – it has been a privilege to work with such incredible, servant-hearted people. I look forward to serving with you again in the future.

To the Samaritan's Purse and Serving in Mission Ebola response team members: I am sorry I could not name you all in this book, but I want you to know you all hold a very special place in my heart. Thank you for your service, courage, strength, and loyalty through some of the darkest moments we have known. Particularly the team of the summer of 2014: Kent and Amber Brantly, John and Beth Fankhauser, Nancy and David Writebol, Eric and Pam Buller, Kendell and Bev Kauffeldt, Chris and Wendy Simpson, Debbie Eisenhut, Joni Byker, Lance Plyler, John Freyler, Linda Mobula, Allison Rolston, Dorothy McEachern, Alicia Chilito, Ellen Hanson, Ian Mackay, Christine McCubbing, Karen Daniels, Taya Raine, Kathy Mazzella, Nathan Glancy, Ed Carns, Azaria Marthyman, Mike and Sheila Kerls, and Tim Mosher. Kelly Sites, thank you for being a prayer warrior and soundboard for me during my time in isolation.

To the Médecins Sans Frontières team who supported us at ELWA2: Cokie Van der Velde, Sarah Temmerman, Olympia, Simon Peter, and Lindus. Thank you for guiding us, supporting us, and encouraging us.

To the Liberian staff who worked at ELWA2: thank you for standing in the trenches, for fighting for your people, for placing their care above your own safety, and for your valiant efforts in bringing this epidemic to an end.

To the patients of ELWA2: you have taught me more about courage and strength in the face of huge adversity than anyone else. Thank you for fighting the fight. Eventually we won the battle.

To the Samaritan's Purse team who returned to continue the fight: thank you for your willingness to serve despite the inherent risks. Nathan Glancy, Bev and Kendell Kauffeldt,

Sean Kaufman, Azaria Marthyman, Chris and Wendy Simpson, Kelly Sites, Alisa Buma, Taya Raine, Judith Hoover, Amanda Shettleroe, Keren Massey, Anne Sherome Amirthanayagam, Luke Armstrong, Dave McDowell, Rudy Gonzalez, Tom Comtois, Kathy and Andrew Mazzella, Dorothy McEachern, Alison Herbert, Kyle Husmann, Lisa Ennis, Melissa Edmiston, David Jesson, Mike and Sheila Kerls – you all held me together at times in ways you probably didn't even realize. To the Samaritan's Purse country office staff in Liberia: thank you all for your support, friendship, and hard work during such a difficult time. To the Samaritan's Purse staff at the River Gee, Lofa, and Gbarpolu bases: thank you for your support, friendship, and accommodation. To the Community Care Centre and RITE response staff in River Gee, Lofa, and Gbarpolu counties: thank you for your hard work and willingness to serve.

I would like to thank those who have made this book possible: Tim Pettingale for your patience and understanding while writing this book, particularly for "getting me" and the essence of what I wanted to convey; Tony Collins, Simon Cox, and the team at Monarch Books for making the book a reality; and David Uttley, Joni Byker, and Kate Davey for your incredible photography.

CHAPTER 1

GOD, ARE YOU REALLY THERE?

Is this how I'm going to die? I thought, as I huddled for warmth next to two girls I'd only recently met. We were shielding ourselves from the cold wind in the bend of a dried-up river by a nameless frozen lake. I was only eighteen and I'd just got into medical school. I'd thought that my whole life lay ahead of me, and now this…

These were not the only thoughts that clawed their way through my mind as I struggled weakly against the urge to simply drift off, nor were they the most frightening. What if poachers discovered us before we died and decided to hold us for ransom? If that didn't happen, what would my funeral be like? Would our bodies even be retrievable, or would we end up as food for the packs of wolves that hunted throughout the region?

It's strange, but I had always thought that when a real crisis finally hit me, I'd be the one to fall apart. But that wasn't what happened. Gabriela, Sophie and I had been trekking all day, and I'd been aware of them fighting the ever-increasing urge to panic. To my amazement, I remained relatively calm. Even once my legs became numb, darkness crept down from the sky and a heavy silence lay upon us, I was still thinking straight. I'd been able to make sensible decisions and consider what – if any – options we had.

Now, however, we had come to a halt, and that was bad news. We weren't going to last for long. It was time to face the biggest question of all: *God, are you really there? If so, please help us!*

* * *

I never should have trusted Hubert Lin. But when you're eighteen years old, 5,000 miles from home, and your plans for the next three months of your life start to fall apart, it's natural to want to trust people like him. In his mid-thirties, quiet, and with a near-perfect English accent he'd acquired at Cambridge University, Hubert was the best hope we had of turning a disastrous trip around.

A group of seven of us had gone out to Tibet. Gabriela, Sophie, Gary, and I all wanted to do something exciting before returning home and beginning our university studies. We quickly grew bored kicking our heels in a half-empty hospital in rural China, but now we were on a pre-arranged trek for two weeks, during which we would explore the mountains, temples and forests of one of the world's most enigmatic regions. Hubert was going to be leading us.

On the journey south Hubert was unusually talkative, by his standards at least.

"You are very lucky," he told us as he interrupted one of the many silences coming from the front of the minibus. "No foreigners are allowed to stay where I'm taking you, but I have contacts with the anti-poaching branch of the police. They allow me to bring guests and stay with them."

During the drive we were hit by a blizzard as we climbed over a 16,000ft pass. The snow started to come in through gaps around the doors and at times the bus slowed down and the driver and his colleague had to get out and manually wind up the engine. However, it was exciting to think that we were experiencing something that other travellers couldn't access. When we arrived in the dark we happily followed Hubert into the first of three small red trailers, all interconnected, none of them bigger than a shipping container. We exchanged excited glances when we saw three police officers sitting around a table and didn't worry too much when Hubert sat down beside them and seemed to forget that we existed.

The next day it took a while for things to deteriorate, but the trip started to look like a bit of a disaster. That morning Gary had developed a bad headache. By the afternoon he had become increasingly confused and it was clear that it was something more than a headache. He decided to go for a sleep, but by evening we were unable to wake him. Unfortunately, Hubert had spent this time drinking the local liquor, barley spirit. He wasn't completely drunk, but he'd had enough to cloud his judgment and it was difficult to get his attention as we tried to wake Gary.

Having grown up in Switzerland I was comfortable with the way the air started to thin out at about 12,000 feet, but my own sore head told me that we were higher than that. As we fussed around Gary, one of the police officers came over to see what was the matter. He didn't speak any English and looked at us blankly as we fired frantic questions at him. The officer crouched down and prodded Gary, then tried to lift him, but he just flopped like a rag doll. At this point the policeman jumped up and started yelling at Hubert. He scrambled around for a canister and began giving Gary oxygen.

Within a few minutes Gary had been bundled into one of the police jeeps as we looked on, confused.

"Where are you going?" I asked.

"Back down to Golmud," said Hubert, who was looking grouchy, but was at least sober enough to help carry Gary out. Golmud was the last place we had stopped at before arriving at the trailers, and it was eight hours' drive away. The air was better down there, but I was concerned that Gary might not get the level of medical attention he needed. Leaving him in Hubert's care didn't feel good, but what option did we have?

We stood and listened in the darkness as the noise of the jeep was swallowed by the silence. There was nothing to see, just a solid wall of night that I knew covered mile upon mile of nothing. All day I had been captivated by the views across the plateau. Wherever I turned, I had seen only flat, dusty ground extending into the distance: no buildings apart from our trailers, no valleys, no trees and no hills within easy reach. We were surrounded by a carpet of frozen brown and grey, flat and desolate. Somewhere on the horizon I knew there were what looked like snow-capped mountains, but even in the day they were so far off that they could almost have been clouds.

We stood outside for a while, but the cold wind started to bite through our clothes and we shuffled back towards the trailers. We looked through our guidebooks, but they didn't cover the region we were in.

"Where are the temples?" said Gabriela.

Sophie scrunched her face up and pointed to another page. "In Lhasa. About a day's drive away."

"I guess there aren't any forests here either."

"Nope. It says here that the Wudaoliang region is nearly 16,000 feet above sea level. Nothing grows here."

The next day drifted along. The two officers who had stayed behind spoke no English, but we'd pieced together enough information from Hubert to understand that they lived up here for most of the year with only occasional trips back to see their families. The rest of the time they were trying to keep a lid on the trade in wild yak. The guys were nice enough, and used to Hubert bringing the occasional traveller. Since there was nothing to do, and nowhere to visit without a vehicle, our only occupation was playing cards with the policemen. We took occasional walks around the trailer, just to keep moving in the bitter cold, but due to the altitude we never strayed far.

We waited. One day stretched into two and then became three. We were all worried and frustrated. When Hubert turned up on the fourth day we were very glad to see him. He told us that Gary was finally getting better.

"I thought he was going to die at one point, though," he confessed as nonchalantly as if he was telling us what he'd had for breakfast.

Hubert had brought a visitor with him, who he introduced as Lin, a journalist from Beijing. They spent a lot of time talking and Hubert seemed to have forgotten the very reason he'd brought us to the trailer in the first place.

"Can we go trekking now?" I asked.

"Hmm," he said, looking typically distracted. "We could possibly go the day after tomorrow, which might be preferable as the following day I shall be taking Lin back to Beijing. I won't be back for another week."

What on earth was he thinking? The three of us exploded with frustration but he just shrugged it off as if we were overreacting and went back to his conversation. It was clear that there was no use arguing. The discussion was over.

By day seven in the trailer we'd finally had enough and so Hubert told us we were going trekking up to one of the frozen lakes. He said nothing about what we might need to take with us. He was less than communicative and implied we might only be gone for a few hours. It wasn't entirely his fault. While I at least had basic appropriate clothing,

Gabriela's and Sophie's was less than adequate for the weather conditions. One of the police officers drove us to the start point with Hubert sitting next to him up front.

After two to three hours bouncing along a half-made track the jeep stopped and we followed Hubert as he walked off, calling for us to keep up.

The landscape had a strange beauty to it. We reached the edge of the frozen lake, which stretched away from us like a dusty mirror. It was still and peaceful, but with no sign of life anywhere it was as inhospitable as it was quiet.

Hubert fell silent too as he led us around the edge of the lake and over towards another one. Ahead of us was another stretch of ground leading to another frozen lake, with more beyond. We walked in silence, partly out of reverence for the view and partly out of breathlessness due to the altitude. We'd been up on the plateau for just one week – it was clear that we were not yet fully acclimatized.

We walked past a third lake and then out into a dry expanse of flat earth, still walking in silence behind our guide. For three hours we wandered away from the lakes, content to let Hubert march on ahead of us without taking much note for ourselves of where we were going. But when Hubert stopped and stared back at the way we had come, it was clear something was wrong.

"We should turn back to the lake now," he said, pausing and scanning the horizon. We had not walked in a straight line and there were a number of lakes just visible that he seemed to be weighing up. Finally, he pointed at one of them.

"That's the one," he said and started walking.

"I'm not so sure," I said. I was convinced that he was heading for a lake that was too far to the south, but he just looked back, shrugged and carried on walking. After about an hour we had a close enough view of the lake. It was bigger than any of the three we had seen so far that day, and there was no way we were heading in the right direction. Hubert froze, clearly perplexed.

"I told you this wasn't the right lake," I said. I pointed to where it looked as though there were some smaller lakes, side by side, "We need to go in that direction." Hubert dismissed me.

"No, we should go back the same way."

He set off again with us tailing behind. By now we were desperate to get back to the jeep, warm up and return to the conservation station. It was clear that he hadn't got a clue where he was going. But as we continued on and couldn't find the lake, Hubert just kept walking faster and further away from us, beginning to leave us behind as we struggled to keep pace. Nothing looked familiar.

As the distance between us grew Sophie began to get distressed.

"Where are we?" she cried. "I can't go on. I don't think I can walk any further."

Gabriela and I tried to rally around her and get her to pick up the pace, calling to Hubert to wait, but to no avail. I put an arm around Sophie and told her that she could make it, but no matter what we said or did, she just got slower and slower.

I always assumed that I would react like Sophie. I'd never really faced a crisis like this before, but when my dad left when I was ten, I'd become familiar with the ache of feeling out of control. I had cried on the plane on the way over to China, feeling overwhelmed by the fact that I knew nothing about what to expect when I arrived. But this was different. I felt calm, peaceful even. The more distressed Sophie became, the clearer it became to me that if I added to the panic it would achieve nothing.

I know now that this calmness came from God. Even when I didn't know him, he chose to guide me, and he did it in a way that I would allow him to. I've always been headstrong, but I believe he gently took control in a way that I barely noticed. Years later I came to appreciate the beauty of this grace and tenderness. Despite my denials of him, he broke through in the only way I would allow.

Why me? Others have died in similar circumstances. I don't know why God chose to intervene, but I guess that he had plans for my life, so he helped to bring peace into the chaos of that moment.

"We *will* get out of here," I told the girls. "We'll be fine. We'll find the jeep."

I scanned the horizon and spotted Hubert in the distance. He had stopped. Was he going to come back and help Sophie? It was more likely that he'd just stand there and wait for us to catch up, I thought. What I didn't expect was for him to turn around and carry on walking, effectively abandoning us.

"Hubert!" I yelled, but the sound was swallowed up by the vast tundra.

Sophie's fear turned to panic.

"Oh my goodness," she gasped, "we're all going to die!"

"What are we going to do now?" Gabriela asked, her own eyes widening. She wasn't panicking, but she was clearly looking to me to do something.

Oh, OK then – this is all on me then, is it? I thought. We were lost and Hubert was gone – despite me telling him that we'd been going in the wrong direction all along. I still had an idea of the way we should go, so we changed direction and set off at a trudge. The trek was supposed to take about three hours and we were into the sixth. At Sophie's pace, by the time we reached the first of the three lakes we would have been out for nearly eight hours. April on the Tibetan plateau is still winter, and though the sun had been shining all day, the wind had beaten the temperature down. As the sun began to dip, the cold was becoming more severe, and having had nothing to eat apart from a few cookies since breakfast, we were slowing down.

I was still sure that the jeep was one more lake ahead of us, but I knew equally well that at our pace there was zero chance of covering those final few miles before nightfall. Finding somewhere to shelter was the only option, but that was not as simple as it seemed. The plateau was flat and exposed to the wind; there were no trees at all to hide beneath. The best we could find was a bend in a frozen river, which might block out the worst of the wind as it whipped at our backs.

None of us had spoken for a while. We stopped to look for something to burn, but very little grew at that altitude. We managed to scrape together a few shrubs and found some yak dung we hoped would act as coal.

I was sure that if we made it through the night we would be able to find the jeep, or if not the jeep then the main road across the plateau, from where we might be able to flag down a passing vehicle. The cold was my biggest concern. We may have found enough materials to start a fire, but we didn't have enough to sustain it. Gabriela and I split up to go to look for more things to burn. The light was ebbing away all the time. Eventually we found a few bits and pieces and tried to get a fire started. It wasn't simple. We had some toilet paper to use as kindling, but no matter how we tried to block the wind, it whipped around us and extinguished our matches until we'd gone through most of the box. The third to last match managed to get it going!

It was a short-lived victory. Though the yak dung we'd found burned well enough, the sun had set. During the day the temperature hovered at around –5°C, but after sundown it often dropped as low as –20°C. We huddled around the pathetic fire and I prayed inwardly. *God, if you're there, please do something…*

The glimmer of a headlight in the distance immediately caught our attention. It dipped out of sight for a while, but then returned. It was tiny, way off in the distance. But it was clearly a vehicle. Instinctively we got up to try and wave it down, knowing full well there was no way we could be seen.

But could they see our fire? We waved and shouted; then I had a thought.

What if it's not our jeep? What if it's a poacher?

The jeep's lights arced away from us and it was gone again. We tried to keep each other talking. In desperation we did anything to keep the conversation going, firing off questions at random, discussing our funniest or most embarrassing moments. We sang songs, even nursery rhymes, but none of us could remember the words. We lapsed back into silence. This time it was Sophie who broke it.

"I'm never going to see my parents again."

She paused and the words echoed around my head. In truth, my main thought at this point was: *I've worked really hard to get into medical school – will I ever get the opportunity to go now, or is this it?* Then I too thought about my family and felt sad at what I would put them through if I never returned from this bleak place.

Then I knew it was time to think about God again. With Irish ancestry on my father's side and an Italian mother it was hardly surprising that I was raised as a Roman Catholic. We went to church every Sunday when my father lived with us, without fail. But as soon as he left, things started to change. Mum felt unsupported and hurt by the church and my dad stopped going too. My brother bailed on it and I was the one left trying to persuade Mum to go. Something always drew me towards church. I definitely believed in God, I just didn't have any kind of relationship with him.

The English language service of the Catholic church

we attended was held in the crypt, and I would sit on the wooden chairs and gaze about me, taking in the low ceiling, the simple whitewashed walls and the exhortations of the priest. An American priest came for a few years and I liked him a lot; his words always made me listen. That was church, and it was good enough. But what of God? Was he real? Did he exist, and if he did, was he real enough to be there after I died? I had nothing against the church, but as the cold from the Tibetan rocks numbed my legs, it struck me that all that Sunday activity had not brought me to a place where I knew for myself whether God was real or not. Just like the frozen lakes we had stared at for so much of the day, I was at the edge of something unknown and unfamiliar that dared me to step out on to it and test it for myself. The more I worked through these thoughts, the more I felt a heaviness within me, a weight that was filling me up. My sadness at the idea of never seeing my family again was overwhelming.

My eyes were blurring but by the light of the dying fire I could see that Gabriela and Sophie were still awake, just. Their heads were hanging heavy on their shoulders, arms bundled tight in a desperate attempt to retain the last of their body heat.

In the end, it wasn't the cold that finally pulled me down, it was the pain. My skin and bones ached. I had nothing left. I hadn't realized how difficult it would be to stay awake. My shivering had stopped and I felt strangely detached from the pains in my body. The urge to close my eyes and sleep was just too strong. If I gave in, then all the pain would drift away. It was logical, inevitable. I had lost the fight and was faced with only two options. Either I stayed conscious and experienced more of the pain that accompanied the sadness, or I could drift away. I took one final glimpse at the fire at our feet, its embers barely visible, then looked up to the darkness beyond us. I saw a faint glimmer in the distance. I shut my eyes and started to drift off.

I knew so little about Jesus back then. Today I know beyond doubt that he knew me then. I thought I was in control, that I had led the way, but I had no idea of the truth that it was he who had led me all along. I was clueless to the fact that all the events of that day – as well as so many days before – had brought me to the place where I was finally ready to take my first ever risk and dare to trust God.

"Just for the record, God," I barely whispered, "I do believe you exist. I really do."

It never occurred to me that these words might carry the weight of a real prayer to God.

I drifted and allowed my body to give in to sleep. I didn't hear Gabriela move, but her shout broke into my consciousness.

"The jeep! It's the jeep! It's coming towards us!"

Startled awake, my body somehow marshalled some adrenalin and I was on my feet again, waving my arms. The jeep was coming in our direction. We ran forward screaming as it started to snake its way towards us.

Later, when we asked the driver why he had turned and begun driving towards us, he said, "I saw the glimmer of a reflection of the torch on the reflective strip on your trousers and I took a chance on it." Gabriela had been shining a torch on me to try and get attention, since I was wearing waterproof trousers with reflective strips. The chances of such a strategy succeeding were so slim that this seemed sure evidence of God's hand in our rescue.

CHAPTER 2

READING THE BIBLE SO I CAN DISMISS IT

Sarah catapulted the ball towards me and I moved to intercept it. At full stretch, I managed to fire it over the net at the opposition. It was a good shot, catching the girl on the other side off guard, but somehow she scrabbled to deflect it. It span off towards a teammate who propelled it back over the net. What a shame – that point might have won us the game!

I loved volleyball. I'd played it from the age of twelve. Volleyball was one of the extra-curricular activities I'd most enjoyed at the international school I attended in Zurich, and I kept it up when I finally landed at Cardiff University. Sarah and I met when I joined the university team during my first year, and had been good friends ever since.

After the game, Sarah chatted to me as we got changed.

"So, Nathalie, can I finally get you to come along to the Alpha Course?"

Alpha – for the last year this had been a recurring theme in our conversations. I knew Sarah was a Christian and that she attended a local church in Cardiff. She had invited me to attend the church's Alpha course several times now. Each time I'd given her a 'holding' response:

"It sounds interesting … I *might* come sometime."

That line was wearing a bit thin, and I didn't want to offend her, so finally I said,

"Yes, OK, I'll come."

I was twenty and approaching the end of my second year at Cardiff University's medical school when I began attending the Alpha course. In truth, I didn't really know what Alpha was. When Sarah had mentioned it to me, I'd thought it was perhaps a lecture-style meeting with someone at the front talking about Jesus. Or maybe it was about the history of Christianity? I didn't know. I was actually telling the truth when I said that it "sounded interesting", but it hadn't been enough to motivate me to action – so I procrastinated. Now, however, I'd agreed to go.

When I walked through the door to attend the first session it wasn't anything like I'd thought. Quite a few people were sat around tables in small groups. Two ladies – Gabs and Maggie – seemed to be looking after our table. We shared some food, chatted about all sorts of normal things, and then a guy called Mark got up to talk about Jesus.

My family, whilst not deeply religious, had definitely observed the Catholic faith as I grew up. I knew how to say my Hail Marys and Our Fathers, but that was just religious rhetoric. I can't recall a time when I *didn't* believe in Jesus, but I had no concept of the possibility of having any kind of personal relationship with him. Yes, I'd always had some level of belief, but it didn't affect my daily life in any way.

It's interesting that out on the plains of northern Tibet, when faced with the reality of my mortality, I had instinctively called out to God. Back then, whether or not he was real had become a matter of great and immediate importance. After the rescue life carried on as normal, but I'm nevertheless certain a seed was planted during that encounter. Before then I'd believed in God in my head. After I'd called out to him, I began to sense his presence, albeit dimly. I guess that was the start of my journey to faith.

Immersed in my medical studies, thoughts about God had faded, but that first Alpha session left me intrigued. I had lots of questions about God and especially about parts of the Bible, but I decided I couldn't honestly say that I didn't believe it was true unless I had actually read it, so I made up my mind to do so.

Shortly after beginning Alpha, Sarah gave me a Bible and I began reading it. I dived in at the beginning and set about reading from Genesis to Revelation – not something Christians in the know recommend, but to me it seemed logical. I was about to go travelling again, so I would have plenty of time to read during the summer break.

While travelling that summer, I read my Bible daily and was about halfway through 2 Chronicles when I got back to Cardiff to begin my third year of studies. On reflection, I'm not sure how I made it through Deuteronomy and Leviticus and kept going, although I don't recall finding it that difficult to plough through the long passages about the Law. Perhaps that was because it was the first time I was reading them, and I was fascinated by how much logical sense they made, particularly from a medical perspective, when it came to the management of, for example, skin diseases.

TRAVELLING AGAIN

Having just completed my second year of studies the summer holidays beckoned with a sense of anticipation. This would be my last set of long holidays at medical school and I wanted to make the most of them. Following my trip to China during my gap year – and despite the traumatic events that had occurred there – I'd been bitten by the travelling bug and was hungry to experience more. The whole world was out there. I wanted to see and explore as much of it as I could, while I was still able.

Consequently, I didn't attend the rest of that particular Alpha course, and planned to pick up where I'd left off when I began my third year. For a while I'd really wanted to visit Vietnam, so I planned to go travelling through Southeast Asia. At the time, I didn't have anyone from university to travel with, so I decided to book myself onto an overland group tour – effectively with a bunch of strangers – which would last six weeks and thread its way through Vietnam,

Cambodia, Thailand and Malaysia, ending in Singapore.

On my way to Vietnam I had an overnight stopover in Singapore by myself. I was due to travel to Vietnam the next day to rendezvous with my travelling companions and begin the tour in earnest. My Singapore hotel turned out to be really quite rough. It was a low budget, no-frills affair, more motel than hotel. My bedroom door didn't lock very well. It had one of those push button mechanisms that needs pressing in to prevent the door handle being turned from the other side. I fiddled with it for a long time but it was temperamental and didn't want to cooperate. The room smelled musty and was quite dirty. I didn't feel very safe.

My room window backed on to the kitchen of an all-night Tandoori restaurant, so it was soon filled with the smell of fried onions and garlic. I was treated to a constant soundtrack of chattering conversation, punctuated by voices occasionally raised in argument. This, combined with my fears about not being safe and the sweltering heat, meant that I didn't get much sleep. The only thing that kept me calm that night was reading through my Bible. The words brought a sense of peace. I prayed a not very eloquent prayer that no one would break into my room.

The next day I travelled on to Vietnam, met up with my group and our tour guides, and the adventure began. We started by trekking through the north of the country, with its vast, rolling mountains and steep valleys covered by the rice paddies so familiar from nature programmes. These pond-like paddies form a network of pools that highlight the contours of the hills and look unlike any other landscape. At least fifty different ethnic groups make up the hill tribes who live there – each with their own distinct dialect, culture and traditions.

Our trek traced its way along a sinuous, verdant path through numerous little hamlets. On one of the days we were caught in a monsoon-style downpour which completely soaked us and everything we were carrying – which for me included my Bible. Later I did my best to dry it out and kept on reading. The trip continued from the hill tribes of the north and Ha Long Bay – a UNESCO World Heritage Site – down to the old town of Hanoi and the beautiful beaches of the east coast, then to the Mekong Delta and the hustle and bustle of Ho Chi Minh City (which many still refer to by its former name, Saigon).

From Vietnam we crossed into Cambodia. After the beauty of Vietnam, this was an altogether different, even harrowing experience. Although Cambodia shares many geological similarities with its neighbour, Vietnam – such as the sculpted, contoured hillsides, and some truly stunning beaches – I found that the general atmosphere in the nation, and that of its people, was quite different. As we passed through the countryside I was shocked to see how malnourished many of the children were. At that time the nation was still struggling to recover from the devastating rule of Pol Pot and the Khmer Rouge. It was going to take a long time before some sort of normality returned.

One of our days included a trip to the notorious "Killing

Fields" – the collective name for a number of sites in the region where more than 1.3 million people were slaughtered by the Khmer Rouge over a four-year period following the end of the Cambodian Civil War. We began by visiting the Tuol Sleng Genocide Museum in Phnom Penh, which commemorates the genocide.

The museum is housed in a former secondary school, which under the Khmer Rouge regime became the infamous Security Prison 21, or simply S-21. "Tuol Sleng" means "hill of the poisonous trees" and this place was one of 150 execution centres across the country. It was here that the educated classes of Phnom Penh were murdered in large numbers. There were numerous photographs of people who had died there, and in places I could still see bloodstains on the floor and wall.

After looking at the many exhibits our group went to see the fields themselves – the site of unimaginable bloodshed. One of the first things that confronts visitors is a monument – a glass structure containing thousands of skulls. It is a stark reminder, if one were needed, of what happened there.

Some fields were now being used for crops, while others had been fenced off for viewing by tourists. Essentially they were simply nondescript green fields, but looking across them it was disturbing to think of the sheer scale of what had happened there. Fields grow and change with the seasons, but the memory of the events in that place lives on.

As we arrived at the Killing Fields we were stormed by a gang of young children who came rushing out of the local village, excited to see the foreigners. They were used to visiting tourists and clearly hoped that we'd give them some sweets. It was a strange contrast, being greeted by this group of lively, happy kids just a short time after seeing the tower of skulls that spoke of this place's painful history.

Phnom Penh, the capital of Cambodia, was like a ghost town. There were people, but very few businesses or shops were open. We stayed in a hotel for a couple of nights and ate in one of the few open restaurants, before moving on with our tour, but it was deathly quiet. Although there had been a civil war, the buildings hadn't been bombed or the city destroyed – everything was intact – but it was as if the city had been robbed of its soul.

From Phnom Penh we travelled to Siem Reap, near the border with Thailand, and visited the striking temples of Angkor Wat. We passed through Thailand to Bangkok and down to the beaches of the island of Kho Pha Ngan. Back then, very few tourists knew about this place (though today it is frequented by vast numbers). It was a secret, unspoiled paradise. We then made our way south to Malaysia, where we visited Penang, the Cameron Highlands, Kuala Lumpur and the historic city of Melaka.

Melaka was beautiful and I really enjoyed the history, but evidently it had a problem with criminal gangs. One evening four of us – an older couple, another girl, and me – were making our way back to our accommodation via a pedestrianized area. We knew enough to avoid walking along the roadside, as there were lots of motorbike-riding thieves – people who would drive by at high speed and try to snatch a bag, camera, or any accessible item. They would often swoop in and use a knife to cut a victim's bag straps, making it easier to take. We were being careful because we'd heard about an incident in Ho Chi Minh City where a thief had grabbed a tourist's bag. He didn't have a knife, so had just tried to snatch it, but the tourist had clung on. She ended up being dragged behind the motorbike for a long way and later died of her injuries.

As we walked through the pedestrianized area, which was well-lit and had CCTV, we became aware of two groups of men, one on either side of the street. As we walked by I became a little uneasy, but it was too late by this point. I shot a glance at one of my companions.

"Just be careful, Emma," I said in a stage whisper.

I was a few metres ahead of my companions. We didn't even hear the sound of the bike until it was too late. Suddenly it was upon us and a man grabbed hold of Emma's camera, which was still hanging around her neck and over one shoulder. He didn't have a knife and initially she couldn't let go. In what seemed like an awful repeat of the recent incident, she was dragged along for a short distance, but thankfully managed to unravel herself and had the sense to let go. Miraculously she suffered only a couple of minor grazes.

The thief, however, also let go and zoomed away. Whilst very distressed by the incident, Emma still had her camera and the would-be thief left with nothing. We left the area as quickly as we could and made our way to the road. There was no pavement, so we had to walk on the other side of the gutter that separated us from the road. Shortly before we reached our hotel, unbelievably, another motorcyclist made a beeline for me and attempted to grab my bag. Only too aware of the danger by this point, I had switched my bag away from the roadside and it was too difficult for him to grab. The thief moved on to look for an easier target.

Back in my room I sighed with relief as I re-lived the events. To this day I don't understand why I wasn't the target of the first attack, since I was on my own and well ahead of our group. I was a much easier target. Looking back, I can only conclude that God protected our little group. The worst thing that happened was Emma getting a few grazes, but we'd not lost any property, and it could all have been so much worse.

PRAYING THE PRAYER

It was just before I'd left to go on this trip that God nudged me into taking the next step on my spiritual journey. It was the third week of Alpha when Mark spoke on "Why did Jesus die?" In the accompanying literature there was a suggested prayer of commitment to Jesus. I prayed that prayer silently to myself, but initially didn't tell anyone that I had done so, and then shortly after I left to go travelling.

I recalled the confirmation classes I'd taken years earlier.

There was little talk about having any kind of personal relationship with Jesus. In my class we studied the book of Genesis, and didn't get very far with it. One of the gospels might have been a better choice! But the fact was, I had no concept that I could know Jesus *personally*, and at that point I still didn't fully understand the need to "get saved". So I prayed – more an expression of wanting to get to know Jesus better – but I didn't understand the significance of what I'd done.

When I got back from my trip and started the new university term, I rejoined the Alpha course as I'd planned. When I saw Mark, I told him that I'd been reading my Bible. He suggested I might find it helpful to read some of the New Testament, but I was adamant that I was reading from Genesis to Revelation. He pointed out that I could still do that, but encouraged me to read some of Matthew's Gospel too.

I didn't understand it at the time, but I felt elated at the thought of attending each Alpha session. In retrospect I realize that I was experiencing something of God's presence. I was keen to find a local church to attend so that I could carry on feeling that way every Sunday, knowing that Alpha would come to an end in due course. After my chat with Mark, I did begin reading some of Matthew. I reached Chapter 3:16–17 and read about Jesus being baptized. As I read the description of the Holy Spirit resting on him in the form of a dove, and the Father speaking from heaven, "This is My beloved Son, in whom I am well pleased" (verse 17,

NKJV), it was like a light turned on. Suddenly, I knew for sure that this was all true – that Jesus really was who he said he was. It was an incredible feeling.

Not long after this I began attending the church the Alpha course was being run from. On my second Sunday morning there Roger, one of the leaders, made an appeal saying, "Is there anyone here who would like to know Jesus more?" Although I still had lots of questions, and still didn't quite understand what salvation was all about, I remember thinking,

Well, everyone should want to know Jesus more!

I waited a little while for others to respond, but no one did. Yet I couldn't deny the feeling that was pulling me forward. Despite no one else responding, I took a deep breath, got up and walked to the front.

My decision was witnessed by many of my friends at the Alpha course who attended the church. Mark came over for a chat, clearly very excited.

"Great!" he exclaimed, bounding up to me, "Now you can get baptized and be filled with the Spirit."

I just looked at him.

"Whoa!" I said. "One thing at a time. Slow down!"

When the meeting wound up, I went with Gabs to Maggie's house. She had invited all of our Alpha table to lunch. While we were there, Patricia – a friend of Maggie's I hadn't met before – arrived and we were chatting in a group when Gabs turned to me and said:

"Tell Patricia what you did this morning."

I didn't know what she was getting at.

"Err, I don't know," I began, "I walked forward to the front?"

Gabs gave me a funny look and prompted:

"You got saved!"

"Oh!" I replied, "OK … all right then."

All I knew was that I had said "yes" to wanting to know Jesus better. I had no frame of reference for "getting saved". I didn't really know what that terminology meant. But once Gabs had said it, the penny dropped. *So that's what getting saved means*, I thought.

After this Gabs and I chatted more about what my decision meant and I decided that I would in fact like to get baptized. Despite being baptized as a baby in the Catholic church, I felt that baptism was a decision I needed to make for myself; no one could do it for me if it was to mean something. So only a few days later, on a Wednesday evening, I was one of a couple of people baptized at my new church. The midweek group leaders prayed for us to be filled with the Holy Spirit and then we were baptized. At this point I found myself beginning to speak in tongues, but frankly I was quite confused by it all.

The following Sunday I spoke about it with Brian, who led the church, telling him that I wasn't sure if I was making it up. He prayed for me and I felt reassured that it was all real. Later that evening I was walking home and noticed that the sky was beautifully clear. It was one of those nights where the moon is shining really brightly and lots of stars are visible. I suddenly felt overwhelmed. The sky spoke to me of the beauty of creation and I was overawed by the wonder of what God had made. Spontaneously I began speaking in tongues. When I arrived home I went straight to my room, sat on my bed, and spoke in tongues for about two hours! For the next month or so I was on cloud nine; I had fallen into the greatest love relationship of my life.

CHAPTER 3

"YOU WANT ME TO GIVE UP MEDICAL SCHOOL?"

"I *want you to give up medical school."*

The words came to me so clearly that I knew for sure it was God who had spoken. I'd spent lots of time praying and reading my Bible, sitting in God's presence, and I was getting to know how to hear his voice – which is why I was really confused.

I'd been a Christian for about a month now. It was around the beginning of December 2002, part way through my third year at medical school. On this particular Sunday evening I'd attended Alpha again, and walked home reflecting on what we'd discussed. Back in my room, I continued thinking about Jesus' sacrifice on the cross, and talking to God about my decision to surrender my life into his hands. That's when I heard him speak, asking me to lay down medical school – and presumably my whole future as a doctor.

My initial reaction was one of bemusement.

"Is that really you, God?" I asked. "Why would you want me to give up medical school?"

I sat in silence and waited, listening carefully. After a moment, God spoke again into the silence, as clear as can be, but he only repeated himself:

I want you to give up medical school.

In reply I got into a lengthy debate with him about all the reasons why it was a bad idea to give up medical school, and I questioned him about why he would ask me to do that. But allow me to backtrack a little...

FOOTBALLER OR SPY?

Up until the age of ten, if someone asked what I wanted to do with my life when I grew up, I would give the predictable response, "I want to be a teacher like my mum." But when I was a little older I harboured secret ambitions of either becoming a professional footballer or, more likely, a spy.

I liked playing football and I was a competent goalkeeper for our school team. At the international school I attended in Zurich, there were plans to enter the boys' football team into a tournament against the international school in Berne. Then our school discovered that they could also enter a girls' team. There was no girls' team at the time, but one was hastily assembled.

Girls were picked for various positions, but no one wanted to go in goal. I was shoved into that position –

because I was tall and couldn't run very fast! But I grew to really like it. Once I had overcome the fear of being smacked in the face by the ball, I came to love the thrill and pressure of a penalty shootout, and of stopping attacking players. Our scratch team did pretty well, going on to compete in the Swiss Group of International Schools' league.

Back then, women's football was not as well established around the world as it is now, and in truth I probably wasn't good enough to compete at a very high level, so I had to admit that my ambitions to play professional football were perhaps unrealistic. Alternatively, however, there was being a spy. I always read a lot of books and was a fan of John Grisham and Tom Clancy, and I loved watching the *James Bond* movies. So I conceived a plan…

The sciences were never my strong subjects at school – I was always better at languages and humanities – so I decided that I would go on to study French and history at university and, after qualifying, apply for a job at MI6. Definitely not MI5, because I wanted to be international. I spoke fluent German, and my French was already pretty good, so I figured I would learn further languages while being trained to be a spy.

Funnily enough, what put a stop to my ambition to become involved in international espionage was the fact that, after due consideration, I decided I wouldn't actually be prepared to kill someone. Thinking through the implications of being a spy I concluded that it could entail having to take another person's life. At the very least, I would find myself in situations where I'd have to make such a judgment call. In the end, I decided that I would rather do something to *give life back* to people, rather than take it away.

As a child I had often seen harrowing footage of malnourished children in Africa on television. The terrible famine in Ethiopia was prominent in the media during the 1980s, and the Band Aid song, "Do They Know It's Christmas?" was played every Christmas. I remember wondering why some children in the world didn't have enough to eat and thinking that I wanted to do something to change that – but what?

Then I recall one time overhearing a conversation between my mother and her friend. At one point Mum said,

"What happened to the days when we were going to change the world?"

I remember thinking naïvely, as children do:

That's what I should do with my life – something that will change the world!

* * *

It was around the time when I'd just chosen the subjects I would take for my International Baccalaureate (IB), that my older brother, Ben, came back from a universities fair with a couple of prospectuses – one of which was for King's College London. I flicked through the prospectus and took an interest in the section about their medical school. I noticed that there was a one-year pre-med course for those students who had taken the "wrong subjects" at school but wanted to move into medicine. I thought then that even if I stuck with languages and humanities, if one day I decided to study medicine, I would still be able to.

A career in medicine... some kind of doctor... that would be a role in which I could have a positive impact on the lives of others. Over the next few weeks I thought about it constantly and it quickly became the only option I wanted to pursue. I decided that if I was thinking like this now, what was the point of going around the houses to study medicine? I might as well choose the right subjects now, rather than trying to keep my options open.

So from the age of about fourteen onwards, my heart was set on a career in medicine, and my entire focus shifted towards how I might achieve this goal. It's easy to see why God's words to me later were such a shock, coming as they did years into my university studies – but more of that later. I was convinced that becoming a doctor was the way in which I might be able to provide help to those who were poor, or suffering the consequences of natural or man-made disasters. Maybe that was how I could help to change the world?

Looking back, I firmly believe that God was at work in my life during this time. Even though I didn't know him yet, and certainly hadn't prayed about the direction my life should take, he was nevertheless guiding me, opening doors, gently prodding me in the right direction – all towards the goal of bringing about his purposes for me in the future. I think he knew gentle prodding was probably the best approach to take with me. While I was never rebellious, I was certainly stubborn. I've always been a staunchly independent person and like to do things my own way and make my own decisions!

OBSTACLES

There was just one hindrance to these great plans of mine: the small fact that I wasn't very good at science or maths – and to qualify for medical school one typically needs chemistry, biology and maths or physics (sometimes both, depending on the university).

The fact is, my early school life was a struggle. Our family had moved from the UK to Switzerland when I was just five years old. My dad was a physicist doing post-doctoral research and he had applied for, and been awarded, a research post at the technical university in Zurich. Originally the plan was that we'd live there for a couple of years then return home, but as things turned out, we never left.

I remember my parents telling me that we were moving to Switzerland. I had only been at school for six months or so when we packed our bags and left. At the time we lived in a quiet little close where there were lots of children my age. We knew each other and were all friends. As we were about to leave, I remember going around knocking on each door with my brother, Ben, saying, "Goodbye, we're going to Switzerland now!" – having absolutely no idea where

Switzerland was or what it really meant.

Arriving in Zurich, there was no space in the international school's kindergarten, so I was placed in first grade. Normally, children in Switzerland enter kindergarten at four or five and go on to first grade aged six. I was only five. As a result I struggled in subjects such as maths and science for a long while. I didn't come into my own at school until I was about thirteen. Our ability for abstract thinking doesn't develop until puberty, and I found that I didn't have that ability when others in my year group did. It meant that some of the more difficult mathematical concepts (such as calculating the volume of a cylinder, I recall) were quite baffling to me. I trundled along near the bottom of my year group until the eighth grade, when at last I began to improve academically, finding that I had a natural affinity for languages, literature and humanities. Maths and physics were still my nemeses though; I did better at chemistry, but I was far from achieving the grades I would need to get into medical school.

I had already chosen the subjects I would study for my IB, so when I decided to pursue medicine instead I needed to change tack. I would need to persuade my teachers to help me. Mum was always very supportive and told me to go for it.

It was never going to be easy. I knew that I wasn't capable of achieving a higher level grade in maths or physics, but I thought I might be able to scrape through in biology, even though I'd not studied it at IGCSE. To get the necessary points to qualify for medical school I needed to get a grade six in chemistry, which seemed unlikely, and the same in biology. My chemistry teacher was sceptical when I chatted to him about it, and told me,

"If you work really hard you can definitely achieve a grade five. But a six? I don't know… "

Over the next few weeks, I changed all the subjects I'd planned to take and set myself on a course of tackling higher level sciences without a clue as to how I would achieve the required grades. But in a short space of time I had become passionate about studying medicine, so I made up my mind to give it my best shot. I thought I might fail trying, but I had to at least try to pursue my new dream.

My mum would no doubt have supported me, no matter what I wanted to do – and was probably quite happy that I wanted to study medicine – but I don't think she thought for a moment that I was capable of achieving it, just like my teachers. In fact, everyone was encouraging – probably because they didn't want to crush a young girl's dreams – but I don't think anyone at any point thought I would actually get into medical school.

I threw myself into my IB subjects and enjoyed biology, but struggled with chemistry. I did OK, but my grades were not on target to achieve a six. Meanwhile, I applied to several medical schools, even though my predicted grades were borderline. I was motivated to keep trying and keep pushing, even if that meant studying for another degree first and then reapplying to medical school later. I would keep trying until there was no longer any hope of me going. I was fortunate to get two interviews for medical schools and, following those, two offers.

The IB is based on a numerical grading system and it's all about getting the appropriate number of points for a particular course. At the time, Scottish universities didn't seem to understand the IB system, and compared to other universities their points requirements were astronomical. This ruled out some possibilities. Welsh universities had a much better understanding of the IB, probably because the organization's headquarters are in Cardiff. Of the twenty-six possible medical schools that existed at the time, I could apply to thirteen, based on my predicted points. I'd heard good things about Cardiff University's medical school from friends of our family, whose son had qualified there, so I applied to Cardiff, as well as King's College and Imperial College London. Though the London universities claim they don't talk to one another, I received a rejection letter from Imperial on the same day as an offer letter from King's.

Cardiff had been my second choice, and because their points requirement was lower than my third choice, King's, I decided to accept the offer from Cardiff. I had already begun revising for my final exams. The IB was not modular, so all of the marks (except those contributed by coursework) would rest on my final exams that May. I worked hard every weekend, making lots of revision notes. I was so concerned about chemistry that I summarised almost the entire textbook!

LOSING CONTROL

During this time, I was driven by my desire to get into medical school and it consumed every moment of every day. In my desperation, afraid of failure, I think I was quite depressed and I started to develop an eating disorder. In retrospect, the stress and pressure of having to perform were definite catalysts for this, but other circumstances contributed as well and, in fact, the seeds had probably been sown much earlier.

Compared to me, most of the girls at my school were quite petite. I had always been very tall and maybe a bit on the heavier side, especially as a teenager. I wasn't overweight, but I certainly wasn't petite. It was something that constantly played on my mind.

I didn't have many friends at school either. The classes were small – there were just twenty-three people in my graduating year – and there were only five girls, including me. My friends, therefore, were not chosen for the usual reasons, but because they were the only people around. I didn't dislike any of them – they just weren't my best buddies.

Then there was the fact that my mother taught at my school. It's difficult being a pupil at a school where one of your parents is a teacher. You have two choices: you can either keep your head down, do the work, make your mother's life easier with her colleagues, and not have too many friends. Or you can be the rebel, make your mother's life a misery by not getting good grades and causing her colleagues grief, and be popular and have friends. I was never going to be in the latter group.

Looking back, being uprooted at five after just a few months of school, and being planted in a new school in an unfamiliar country had its challenges for all of us. My brother and I didn't speak German and none of the children we met in the local community spoke English. Joining an international school meant that we didn't have the community aspect to our lives that we'd had in the UK. When you attend an international school that tends to become your community, but the pupils come from all over the city. It was quite a drive from our new home to the school, so when I did make friends, they might live on the other side of Zurich. It meant being driven places by my parents, rather than popping around the corner.

There was also some family turmoil between my parents around the time I was revising for my IB exams and that left me feeling insecure. I began to feel as though nothing in my life was under control. Applying to medical school then working like mad to achieve my grades certainly exacerbated my eating disorder, even if it wasn't the root cause.

I couldn't control most things in my life, but I could control my food. That's how it started. Then the problem was fuelled by low self-esteem and body issues. I started to eat less than I normally would. I was still living at home, and my mum noticed that I was eating less, so she kept a watchful eye on me. But I went to live with my dad for six months during my gap year, before my trip to China, and during that time my problem became more extreme. When I lived with Dad I never ate breakfast, always skipped lunch, and only ate in the evenings because my boyfriend at the time made me. Even then, I didn't eat a lot.

This was to continue throughout my first year at university, where I further reduced my food intake, and tried to survive on less than 500 calories per day. Things continued to be difficult between my parents. They had separated when I was ten years old, spent two years talking about getting back together, and then the next decade getting divorced – and it wasn't amicable. By the time I was going to university, Ben had almost graduated and would no longer be financially dependent on my parents. I, however, was dependent and would be for some time, as medical school lasts for six years. The big argument during the divorce was about money, and unfortunately that meant I was dragged into the argument.

I'd left home, my family were overseas, and there were questions and uncertainty about who would help to support me financially.

Why am I in the middle of this? I wondered.

I still felt my life was out of control. I starved myself, surviving on a minimal amount of food – to the point where I couldn't walk up a flight of stairs at university without feeling faint. Then, at the end of my first year, I developed labyrinthitis, an infection of the inner ear that causes dizziness and disturbs balance. I would stand up and the world would spin and I'd fall over. I began to suspect that

I had done some kind of damage to myself. I later found out that it was just an infection, but it was a wake-up call. I chastised myself:

"Stop being an idiot and pull yourself together!"

From then on, I returned to a relatively normal diet and exercised a lot instead. I began playing volleyball and swimming several times a week.

Thankfully, over time, things settled down and I wasn't quite so obsessive about exercising all the time or being really thin. When I became a Christian, God mercifully helped me with my control issues. I realized that I had a Father in heaven who loved me and accepted me just as I was. I had a revelation that I didn't need to be in control any more, because God was in control, and that was OK.

LEARNING TO TRUST

The day I received my exam results I was in Italy with my mother, who was attending a course there. We were staying in a small apartment. I was alone, waiting for Mum to finish for the day, when one of my teachers called with the results. I couldn't believe the outcome. I had made all the grades I needed to get into medical school – including the higher level 6 in chemistry. I left the apartment to go to find my mother at her course. She was just leaving the building as I came running down the street towards her. She saw the look on my face and knew I had got in. Later that day she confessed that she hadn't believed I would do it. She had done an extremely good job of pretending that she believed I could!

* * *

Fast forward to year three of medical school. I had become a Christian and, looking back, could see the hand of God on my life as he helped me to get over one hurdle after another, bringing me closer to achieving my dream of being a qualified doctor. Now he was asking me to give up the one thing that had defined my life for the last six years – something that meant everything to me.

I fought with God as I struggled to understand what was going on, never doubting that it was he who was speaking to me. It felt like a tug of war. On the one hand, I desperately wanted to be obedient and do what I heard him asking me to do. On the other hand, I wished he wasn't asking me to throw away everything I'd dreamed of and worked for. At one point the feeling was so intense that I thought I might be torn in two.

Some hours later, with tears streaming down my face, I finally conceded.

"OK God," I said, "If this is what you're asking me to do, then I'll do it."

I knew he had the best intentions for my life and, ultimately, if medicine was not a part of that, then I concluded he must have something better for me. I prayed that he would show me what lay ahead soon, and most importantly that he would help me find the words to tell my family, who I knew would not understand. Decision made, I suddenly felt God's peace wash over me. It was late at night by this time. I went to the bathroom, washed my tear-streaked face and got in bed.

When I woke up the next morning, the sense of peace was still there, even though at the same time I felt sad to be leaving medical school and wondered how I would tell my family. That morning, as I sat eating some breakfast and reading my Bible, God met with me again.

"My child," he said to me, "I don't want you to give up medical school. I just wanted to know that you would if I asked."

It was then that I realized: I had allowed medicine to be my god for a long time. It was the most important thing in my life. While I had given my life to Jesus, this was the one thing I had been holding back. I had not been ready to relinquish my ultimate dream to God's control and allow him to guide it. I now think of this time as my "Abraham and Isaac moment". God needed me to realize that he was more important to me than anything else and that he could restore to me anything that he chose to take away. It was the beginning of my learning how to truly trust God, come what may.

CHAPTER 4

HE'S DEAD – GOD ANSWERED MY PRAYER

The medical school at Cardiff University had a charity called BACCUP – the Belarusian Aid for Children Cardiff Undergraduate Programme. One of its main purposes was to support an orphanage for children with learning and motor disabilities located just outside the city of Minsk. During the summer holidays, teams of healthcare professionals would travel to the orphanage to work with the children and staff, providing basic equipment and helping to care for the kids. Our group was made up of students who were all studying some aspect of healthcare – some training to be doctors or nurses; others to become occupational or physiotherapists.

I first visited Belarus in 2001. Our team was based in Minsk, and we had a daily 45-minute drive to reach the Novinki Orphanage, in a small village on the outskirts of the city. I found Minsk to be a city of contradictions. The buildings were stark and cold, yet somehow there was still a beauty to them, in a communist Russia kind of way. Novinki was more remote, removed from the hustle and bustle of the city.

Under the communist regime, if you were not a valuable member of society you didn't carry any worth. This culture still exists in modern-day Belarus to some degree, but when we were there it was an accepted part of life. Society's attitude to disability was particularly shocking. No one wanted to accept or confront it, so disability was locked away, hidden and forgotten about. Thus, arriving at the orphanage for the first time, it was hard not to be appalled by the conditions we found. The austere building was bland and lacking facilities to care for children with disabilities. It was woefully under-resourced and under-staffed. Many of the staff it did have lacked the basic skills and competency to properly care for children. During that first visit, it was plain to see that even a few miniscule improvements would dramatically raise the standards, but the task was so daunting – would our efforts make any difference?

CAN WE MAKE A DIFFERENCE?

In the beginning there were many odd practices at the orphanage. For instance, it is well known that children with cerebral palsy often have difficulty swallowing, yet these kids were fed lying flat on their backs. I don't have difficulty swallowing, but even I would find it a challenge to eat with someone shovelling food into me whilst lying down. A further complication of this bad practice was that many of the children contracted pneumonia from aspirating their food.

There were so many tragic cases in the orphanage that I initially asked myself searching questions about what difference I was making, if any, by being there. We were in Belarus for just a few weeks over the summer months, and for the rest of the year Novinki would be left to its own devices. During the first two years of our charity working there, change was painfully slow. It was all pretty discouraging.

Many of the staff at the orphanage were not ideal people to look after children with disabilities. They were paid so little money that many who worked there were those who couldn't get a job anywhere else. In other words, some were virtually unemployable – but no one cared because of the culture of shame that sought to brush things under the carpet. The staff would sometimes hit the children in an attempt to control their behaviour. It was a shocking environment.

Gradually, however, the situation did begin to improve. Over time our team was able to take simple measures to improve the children's quality of life. With help from us and another charity, their diet improved and the kids began to grow plumper and look much healthier. Providing some toys to play with and spending time interacting with the Down's syndrome or autistic children made a huge difference. Many of them began to walk and talk for the first time, just because they'd finally had some stimulation.

Our charity didn't have much cash to spare, but we did manage to employ a couple of extra staff to provide further support. We also employed a play therapist to use the toys to engage with the children. The more we went back to Novinki, the more the staff understood there was another approach to managing these children. We tried not to show our disapproval, but rather to demonstrate a different way, by loving and caring for the children and interacting with them. It had an effect. Over time, perhaps out of embarrassment as much as anything, the worst staff were removed and replaced with better trained, more caring staff. Towards the end of our time with the project, there were many people there who clearly loved these children and cared for them well.

Going back year after year I began to see such an improvement in the children, and I knew that although it had taken a long time, our efforts had significantly improved their lot in life. It was always a challenge being there – but it was more challenging to walk away from the many children I'd bonded with, wondering if they would still be cared for properly after I'd gone.

What was particularly sad was that most of the parents of the children who occupied Novinki didn't want them to be there. They were left at the orphanage because there was simply no provision in society for them to be cared for.

The state of the economy in Belarus meant that couples

couldn't afford to pay their mortgage or rent unless both were in full-time employment. If a couple had a child with higher level needs, there was nowhere for them to be looked after during the day. It was a classic catch-22 situation: either you stayed at home to care for your child, but couldn't afford to live, or you worked to live and couldn't afford to keep your child.

One positive difference that was relatively simple to make was to set up a kindergarten for children with special needs, which was done by a Belarusian couple who themselves had a severely autistic child. This made it feasible for parents who wanted to keep their children to do so. Sad to say, while some parents were committed to their children, and would visit them at weekends, others simply dumped them at the orphanage. Sometimes it was because they couldn't afford to keep their children, but others didn't want the stigma. One cute little boy with Down's syndrome had been left there, even though both of his parents were doctors. There was still a great stigma in society attached to having a disabled child, and they didn't want that.

DIMA

During my first visit, I really bonded with a little boy called Dima, who had a heart defect. One of the saddest aspects about so many of the children in Novinki was that their problems could have been treated, if only they'd been addressed earlier. Dima's heart problem would probably have been treatable by surgery in its early stages. But he didn't get the treatment he needed because at that time in Belarus children were only entitled to emergency healthcare from the state, not to elective procedures. Later on, Dima developed a condition known as Eisenmenger's syndrome, where, due to the heart pumping incorrectly, the blood doesn't mix as it should, and pressure is put on the lungs. People with this condition are essentially in cardiac and respiratory failure. As a result, Dima was literally blue all of the time.

I saw little Dima for two consecutive years, but by the time I returned for a third time, he had died. Exactly how he died was debatable. I was told that they had tried to operate on him and that he had died on the operating table due to complications from his condition. I knew, however, that once a person has Eisenmenger's it is basically inoperable. The only hope for a cure is a heart and lung transplant, which Dima certainly didn't get. It is more likely that he simply died and the staff wanted to make it sound as if they had tried to help him.

As with so many children in that place, one year Dima was there and the next he was gone. I said goodbye to him and never saw him again. He was a smart little cookie. Despite the fact that he never, ever spoke, he understood exactly what was going on. He hated goodbyes. He knew that when people said goodbye, they didn't come back. When I tried to say goodbye to him he literally held up his hand in a stop motion and looked the other way, refusing to accept that I was leaving. I still went to give him a hug, but he pushed me away.

EMILIA

When we first arrived at Novinki it was clear to see that the children had been grossly neglected to the point where most were malnourished. They were simply not fed adequately. There were many children with Down's syndrome there, who have a tendency to be quite stocky, but these children were emaciated. Children were routinely tied to their beds if they were perceived to be "difficult" and others were put in straitjackets. All that some children did was sit on their beds and rock for hours on end. There were no toys, nothing for them to play with, and so they became ever more insular through a lack of interaction.

The worst cases were those children with cerebral palsy – like Emilia. They were typically left permanently lying on their beds, hardly ever moving, and this added to their disability. They would develop contractures (a shortening of the muscles or tendons which leads to deformity or rigidity of joints) and so they had what is known as the "windswept" look, which develops when the hips begin to rotate to one side.

Emilia couldn't lie flat because her body was permanently twisted. Her sternum and spine both stuck out, making her body look as if it was being blown backwards in the wind and was twisting away from her legs – hence the term.

Emilia had severe contractures and couldn't straighten out her arms or legs properly. She was covered in pressure sores. The staff would try to turn her over, but it was extremely uncomfortable for her and she would cry in pain. I tried to take her out of her bed a few times to give her some stimulation, but she cried the whole time. She wasn't used to it and it made her afraid. I saw Emilia each year and looked after her from the age of thirteen to seventeen. Like many of the children in Novinki, given her condition, it was amazing that she had survived for so long.

MAXIM

Maxim was another of the little ones who had been left to develop horrific contractures. I met him properly on my second visit to Novinki. I had been aware of him the previous year, but hadn't directly cared for him until now. He was born with hydrocephalus and cerebral palsy and had been in the institution from early in his infancy. This little boy had been left in bed for most of his life, so just like Emilia he was "windswept". Access to basic physical therapy and support aids could have improved his condition so much.

Due to his contractures he had awful pressure sores on both his hips, which were close to revealing the bone. Without the right equipment it was difficult to position him in such a way as to prevent these from getting worse, and to relieve his pain. Whenever we removed him from his cot to try to bring him some comfort, or help him experience some of the activities the other children were doing, he would simply cry in distress and pain.

Even though he was eight years old, Maxim was the size of a toddler. Since he'd suffered with a swallowing problem all his life due to his cerebral palsy, he was severely malnourished and could only consume a puréed diet from a bottle – and he would often choke on that. He could have been treated by having a feeding tube inserted directly into his stomach to help with nutrition, but as this fell under the category of an "elective procedure" rather than an emergency, it was not state-funded.

During that second year at Novinki we'd been able to bring with us some special dressings for pressure sores, and these helped a great deal. But such dressings were expensive and weren't available to the orphanage unless donated. By the time of my third visit, Maxim's pressure sores had deteriorated and he was in constant agony. He was in such a poor state that I thought he was not far from death.

One afternoon as a colleague and I were changing Maxim he vomited on his bed. I cleaned him, picked him up in my arms and walked around cuddling him so that my colleague could change his bed. As I held him I prayed over him. I had only been a Christian for nine months at this point, so I didn't really know what to expect, but I believed that God could do anything. As I prayed, I cried over this frail little boy.

"Lord, I ask that you would either restore Maxim to full health, so that he can be a normal eight-year old little boy with a good quality of life, or take him to be with Jesus."

Looking back, I don't think at that point I really believed the former could happen. But neither did I believe that it was God's will this child should continue to suffer in the manner he was. I questioned God about why this fragile boy continued to be in such distress. Surely it wasn't fair that he should continue to live his life in constant pain?

I finished by asking God that when I returned to the orphanage the next day, Maxim would either be a healthy child or safe in Jesus' arms. Even as I prayed this "options open" prayer, I knew in my heart that he would go to be with the Lord.

There isn't the scope here to debate the many viewpoints on Maxim's eternal home that Christians from different backgrounds will have. Personally, I believe that to those who are unable to confess Jesus as Lord, God extends great mercy. He loves the little, defenceless ones – they are his children. Knowing my Father, I am sure that he would never abandon them and has great compassion for them.

I laid the matter to rest in my mind as my colleague finished changing Maxim's bed and I gently placed him back in his cot. A short while later we left for the day. The following morning the vehicle that normally picked us up to take us to the orphanage was late, and when it did turn up I remember it was full of flies, which seemed really odd.

On arrival at the orphanage I was informed that Maxim

had died in the early hours of the morning. I was stunned. For a moment I felt really guilty that I had prayed as I had. Who was I to make a judgment call about Maxim's life? But then I realized that, at last, this little boy was running around in heaven and was no longer in pain. I was grateful that God had answered my prayer. I told one of my team members about my prayer, but she just laughed and informed the rest of our team that I thought I was responsible for his death. This did however lead to many interesting conversations with team members about how God heals, how he gives life and takes it away, and I was able to share my faith with them. I'm not certain what impact those conversations had, but I do believe that God used them to sow seeds in people's lives.

Conditions gradually got a lot better at the orphanage. With the help of our, and other organizations', intervention it eventually became a prime example in the nation of how an orphanage should be run. We can't take all the credit for that. The fact is, it received so much international attention that it became an embarrassment to the government, who didn't want visitors to see such an awful place. It eventually galvanized some action.

During the years that I visited Novinki significant improvements were made. One summer I returned to find that many of the kids had had the operations they'd needed – procedures they would never have been allowed before. I wondered what had happened and discovered that the law regarding medical care had been changed. Gradually, even if it was painfully slowly, things were changing and society was becoming more accepting of disability.

Looking back, I don't know why God responded to my prayer for Maxim in the way he did. What I do know is that God always hears the prayers of his children, and he answers them in the way that he knows is best. He has compassion on all those who suffer, and he gives us compassion for them too. I learned that day that our Father cares deeply for every one of us. I also learned about the power of prayer, and what can happen when we take a moment to pour out our hearts to God about the injustice in the world. He hears and acts, even if it is not necessarily in the way we expect. Many don't view death as a form of healing, but I believe it is. Really, it is the ultimate healing, as we are released from our frail vessels to live with Jesus in freedom. If God chooses to heal someone by taking them to be with him, I'm OK with that.

"'For my thoughts are not your thoughts, neither are your ways my ways,' declares the LORD. 'As the heavens are higher than the earth, so are my ways higher than your ways and my thoughts than your thoughts'" Isaiah 55:8–9 (NIV).

CHAPTER 5

GOD MULTIPLIED THOSE BIBLES FOR A REASON

My heart was in my mouth as our bags were loaded on to the conveyor belt. One by one they passed through the X-ray scanner and were examined on screen by inscrutable Belarusian security staff. I was expecting to see raised eyebrows, frowns, questions being fired back and forth amongst the staff – but it didn't come. Not a murmur: not even a blink! Surely the huge, shrink-wrapped packs of Bibles were easy to spot on the X-ray machines? They could hardly be missed. Yet, seven times, as each bag passed through... nothing.

* * *

Another summer came and I travelled to Belarus again, this time as project coordinator, looking after a team of students who had volunteered to help at Novinki. We were returning to put our medical training to good use in the orphanage, but this time I also wanted to bless the workers there. I spoke with the leaders of my church in Cardiff and they agreed to fund the donation of 200 Cyrillic Bibles – one for each member of staff. I had to make it clear that these were a gift from my church, and not supplied by the BACCUP charity, which wasn't a Christian organization. All of this was made clear in a letter translated into Cyrillic, a copy of which would be inserted in each Bible in due course.

My medical studies kept me busy and life was hectic in the run-up to the trip. I was doing what is known as an intercalated BSc that year (taking a year out from medical studies to complete what is essentially the final year of a BSc degree, so that you receive a BSc as well as a medical degree on completion). Mark, who had led the Alpha course, had ordered packs of mini-Bibles and New Testaments with Psalms for us to take. We needed 200 copies, but he'd only been able to get hold of 180. I popped round to the church to pick them up and counted them off – 180 in total – but the person in the office, who was clearly on the ball, had already printed 200 letters in anticipation, so I ended up with twenty more letters than Bibles. I was disappointed and annoyed at myself for not having organized things better. Because of that some of the staff would go without. However, I resigned myself to the fact that I'd just have to give away what I had.

There were nine packs of Bibles and seven of us going on the trip. Everyone agreed to take one pack in their luggage; another team member and I took two each. We packed them into the bottom of our bags then crammed other supplies on top.

It was normal for us to take some supplies into Belarus. Usually it was nappies, which are very expensive in Belarus – a luxury, in fact – and the orphanage was only allowed a meagre supply.

The security at Minsk airport were used to this – they'd seen us before and knew we were working at the orphanage. None of our team spoke Russian, and the security staff hardly spoke any English, so if any of them appeared to protest about the supplies we were bringing into the country, we would just say, "Novinki" and typically they would dismissively wave us through. We took so many supplies into Belarus that we would regularly go out with two bags stuffed to capacity, and come back with one that was pretty empty. Only on one occasion did we have any real trouble, when we'd sent some supplies ahead with another organization. The supplies were in a truck loaded with equipment which was stopped at the border and everything was impounded. After a great deal of lobbying and pleading the authorities eventually agreed to release the nappies to the orphanage, but in an act of pure bureaucracy did so at the rate of three nappies per week per child.

Despite the fact that we were used to this brazen "smuggling", taking Bibles into the country in plain sight was an entirely different matter. Belarus was the last communist dictatorship in the former Eastern Bloc, and while formal and more traditional Orthodox Christianity was tolerated in the country, evangelism and the importing of large numbers of Bibles was not – hence my concern.

The atmosphere at Minsk airport was fairly strict and stern. I would stop short of describing the staff as intimidating, but they made sure visitors knew they were not to be messed with. Unlike most other airports, visitors to Belarus had to go through passport control, collect their bags, and have them X-rayed before being allowed to leave the airport. As our group reassembled after passing through immigration, we began to load our bags one by one on to the machines, which look identical to the ones found in European airports for scanning cabin baggage, except much larger.

As the bags went through I held my breath. I knew there was no way the Bibles would not be spotted by the security personnel. *Please, Lord…* I prayed silently. No one batted an eyelid or asked any questions. The customs officers didn't seem to notice the large packs of Bibles at the bottom of everyone's bags. We were waved through.

I have found that, when God is "in" something, it often seems that things that would normally be an issue just aren't. It doesn't always happen this way, but sometimes it appears that God has his hand on a situation, and he goes ahead of us to open doors and remove hurdles that we thought would be major obstacles. Looking back, I find it remarkable that not a single colleague objected to smuggling Bibles into a communist country. They could easily have done, but it was a complete non-issue.

The following day we stacked all the Bibles in the

Portakabin that doubled as our office in the grounds of the orphanage. This was our HQ during the trip and as project coordinator I was busy there during the first few days, arranging contracts for the support staff we were employing at the orphanage and signing off official agreements for our continuing work there. Whenever we went to Belarus we would work in partnership with the medical school in Minsk. A handful of their senior students would come and work for us as translators, and we would stay in spare rooms in their halls of residence for our accommodation.

One day, knowing that we had these Bibles to give away, and that each one needed a letter putting inside, my team spontaneously took this task upon themselves in their lunch break without me asking.

"Oh, we'll help you with that," one of the girls said. "We know you're busy."

"Wow! Thanks, guys!" I said, surprised and grateful. "Just to say, there are more letters than Bibles, so eventually you'll run out – but that's fine."

They set up a production line and began preparing the Bibles. I went back to my admin and continued to plough through paperwork, eating a piece of bread on the go. After some time, Melissa, the girl who'd volunteered her services, came over.

"Nathalie, we've run out."

"Yes, I know," I responded, still engrossed in my paperwork. "I said you'd run out of Bibles; we were about twenty short."

"No," she said, "we've run out of letters – we've got plenty of Bibles."

I looked up, puzzled.

"You can't have," I said. "You've used all the letters?"

"Yes."

"So how many Bibles do you have left?"

"One and a half packs."

I stopped short of saying, *I don't believe you, I counted them myself… twice!* Instead, I got up to go and have a look.

There they were: several piles of Bibles, neatly stacked, each one with a letter sticking out, and then a single, unopened pack and another half empty one. I quickly ran my finger down the piles of Bibles – 200 copies. Then I counted the "leftovers". There were fifty spare Bibles! I was in a state of shock. How could this be? I'd counted the Bibles before we left and knew exactly how many we'd had. It's possible that I could have miscounted a small amount, but I certainly wasn't out by nearly 30 per cent!

"Oh, I don't know how that has happened," I said.

It took a while for the truth to sink in: for some reason God had multiplied the Bibles and we had fifty left over.

"You must have a plan for these Bibles, Lord," I prayed. "Who are they for? Show me what to do with them."

The answer came the next day. There was a knock on the door of the Portakabin. I opened it to find a member of staff and her husband standing there. I'd had my suspicions that she might be a Christian, just from the way she spoke and how she cared for the children. Plus, her husband, who had a full-time job elsewhere, would often stop by the orphanage in the evening or at weekends and volunteer his time, spending it interacting with the kids. Certain children had a great connection with him and he would play with them or walk around cuddling them. Through our translator, the woman said,

"My husband and I are running the Sunday school in our church and the children don't have any Bibles. Would you have any spare copies at all?"

I could barely believe it myself, but was delighted to be able to tell them I had fifty spare copies that they were welcome to take.

I handed them over and the couple expressed their deep gratitude and thanked me. They didn't show much emotion. It's often hard to read Belarusians. Similar to Russians, they contain their emotions and tend to be quite stoical. If you ask someone how they are, they will rarely say, *Khorosho,* which means "Good". Instead they will reply, *Neplokho,* which means "Not bad". This is the standard response, which says something about the people's mindset. Things are never "good"; they are either *plokho* – "bad" – or *neplokho* – "not bad".

I'd love to be able to report that this couple had been praying and asking the Lord for the miraculous provision of Bibles for months, and now here they were… They may well have been, but I'm afraid I don't have that part of the jigsaw puzzle. I could work out, however, that they must have been running a charismatic church, because Orthodox

Christian churches there don't tend to have Sunday schools. Orthodox Christianity is permitted and tolerated in Belarus, but the charismatic churches have faced much persecution and the government have continually tried to shut them down. Under such a regime, I imagine that Cyrillic Bibles were both hard to come by and expensive. What God had done for this couple hit me more when I got home and stood up to tell the congregation what had happened. Then the full impact struck me: God had done a miracle.

This increased my faith, but it also amazed me that God had done a miracle without me even asking. I had been quite accepting of the situation: *We haven't got as many Bibles as we need, but never mind.* It never occurred to me to pray, *Lord, would you multiply the number of Bibles for me?* and I wouldn't have had the faith for it.

But our generous Father had other ideas. He had a plan and a purpose. God took my rather disorganized plan and turned it into a miracle. It wasn't that I didn't think he could do such a thing, it's just I never considered it. Multiplication miracles appear throughout the Bible – such as the loaves and fish multiplying when Jesus prayed so that 5,000 people could be fed with just five loaves and two fish; and the story of the widow of Zarephath, whose oil miraculously never ran out. There are also many modern day stories of God multiplying food, as has happened a number of times in Heidi and Rolland Baker's ministry in Mozambique. But I never thought that God might want to multiply Bibles as well!

It shows how good and kind our God is, that he cares about us and wants to provide for our needs. He is interested in the small (and not so small) details of our lives. Through this God showed me that when we are obedient to his call, he goes before us and can use us in ways we may never have imagined. Every day with him can be an adventure and we can trust that, in accordance with his will, he will remove any obstacles that hinder us and open the doors he wants us to walk through.

As a young Christian I was impacted by John Ortberg's book, *If You Want to Walk on Water, You've Got to Get Out of the Boat*. At the end of the chapter entitled, "Crying out in fear" he writes, prophetically:

> *In the vast eternal scheme of things, your life is*
> *briefer than you could possibly imagine.*
> *But whatever you do in faith,*
> *Every time you trust me,*
> *Whenever you act in risky obedience and jump in*
> *response to my invitation–*
> *That you will have forever.*
> *Go ahead and jump.*[1]

When I read this I had a revelation: *I had a choice.* In life, I could either give in to my fears and remain safe in the boat, or, like Peter, I could get out of the boat and take some risks (Matthew 14:29). Yes, I might sink, but there was also the

---

[1]   John Ortberg, *If You Want to Walk on Water, You've Got to Get Out of the Boat,* Grand Rapids, MI: Zondervan, 2001

possibility of a miracle occurring as I kept my eyes on Jesus and obeyed his command to come. One thing was for sure: if I stayed in the boat, nothing would happen. God wouldn't condemn me, but neither would we go on a great adventure together. I decided that, whenever I could, I would get out of the boat and trust that no matter what, Jesus had my back. If I did, then who knows what might happen? Whatever it might be, it would be incredible, because I would be partnering with Jesus.

I'd only been a Christian for five months when I decided that I didn't ever want fear to limit me. That desire to take a risk and to trust has never left me. I want to trust God and be willing to go wherever he asks me, to do whatever he wants me to do. That doesn't mean I don't falter at times, because I do. Neither does it mean that I am never afraid, because I have been very afraid at times. Rather, I acknowledge that it is Father God who is in control of me, not my fear. Trusting God is a daily choice and I refuse to allow fear to dictate my decisions in life.

I continue to pray that those Bibles have sown seeds in the lives of the children who received them, and that they are strengthening their walk with God.

CHAPTER 6

LIFE AND DEATH IN AFRICA

I was sitting playing the piano, eavesdropping on a conversation between my mum and her friend when I heard her make reference to the days when they'd planned to "change the world". It was a light-hearted comment and a throwaway exchange, but the words arrested me. Later I asked Mum what they had meant.

"Well, it's just that we had ambitions, you know?" she said. "We both wanted to do something with our lives that would really impact the world. But life moves on... "

I was twelve at the time and I didn't know that people thought like that.

Does that mean I could do something that will change the world? I wondered.

I was taken with the idea of doing something useful and impactful to make the world a better place.

I was born in 1982, and a couple of years later Band Aid's "Do They Know It's Christmas?" came out. I grew up with it, since it was played every Christmas thereafter for a long time. Its accompanying video showed images of small, malnourished children in Ethiopia who were dying of hunger. I recall asking my mum when I was quite small,

"Why is it like that? *Why* don't they have any food?"

It was one of those questions that can't be answered simply, if at all.

Years later, as a medical student, although I chose mainly to travel through Asia when I had the opportunity to go overseas, in my head I was always going to work in Africa at some point. Through the Band Aid video, and a host of other influences, God was sowing seeds in my life that would come to fruition in the future.

I didn't have any concrete plans – more ideas that were floating around – but I did have the desire, once qualified as a doctor, to spend time doing aid work in Africa. People did their best to put me off:

"Don't do it, it will ruin your career."

"You won't be the same when you come back and you'll struggle to fit in… "

After I became a Christian, however, I just concluded:

"Well, God has a plan for me and he'll take me where he wants."

I believed that if I did go to work in Africa, and at some point returned to the UK, God would pave the way for that to happen at the right time and in the right way.

A VISIT TO ZAMBIA

In my final year of medical school I had to take a medical elective (a work placement a student can choose themselves) and decided to work at a hospital in the North-West Province of Cameroon. Term had just finished and I had four weeks' holiday to use before my placement began, so in July 2005 I decided to explore southern Africa.

I flew out to Zambia to begin with, because I had links with a project there. The BACCUP charity which supported the orphanage in Belarus had grown into a bigger umbrella organization called Students for Kids International Projects, or SKIP. My friend Rahail Ahmed, Raz for short, had the idea of launching projects similar to the Novinki project in medical schools all over the UK. I stepped up to become the fundraising coordinator and eventually a few of us formed a national committee. By the time I'd qualified and needed to hand over my responsibilities to others, there were thirteen such projects running across the country.

The first project established after Novinki was run by Birmingham University students and based in the Kanakantapa resettlement area just outside Lusaka, Zambia. They were supporting a community school, helping to fund school meals for children and their teachers. The school aimed to help those children whose families could not afford to send them to government-run schools.

At that time in Zambia, while primary education was free, parents had to pay for their children's uniforms, shoes, pens and pencils, and textbooks. Plenty of families simply couldn't afford to do that. Most of the kids who came to the community school had few clothes to speak of, and most didn't have shoes. A few had flip flops, but most would burn the soles of their feet on the hot sand as they walked several miles to and from school each day.

This was my first time in sub-Saharan Africa, apart from a brief holiday I'd had in Cape Town almost a year earlier. This was a far cry from the big city feel of Cape Town. I met up with the students who had already travelled out, and we were picked up from our accommodation for a hot, dusty, bumpy ride into the bush.

The school was in the middle of nowhere. After leaving the main road to travel the rough, potholed dirt tracks, you couldn't see anything much but miles of arid, savannah-like grassland; there were few villages on the way, and even those were just a scattering of huts, and no real landmarks. The school eventually emerged, set in a clearing. The only other building was a nearby house, which belonged to a local pastor called Lazarus. Although the school wasn't specifically Christian, it had been developed by Lazarus and his church, and he acted as headteacher and helped to oversee it.

The school "building" was roughly constructed. The walls were made from wooden poles – more like branches, really, since they were all odd angles and lengths – with straw woven in between. Similar "walls" of poles and straw designated the classroom areas. A better quality metal frame held up the roof, which was made from corrugated tin. Although it protected everyone from the sun, it acted rather like a pressure cooker, so that it was as hot inside as out, although the design permitted the breeze to flow freely, bringing some relief.

The school had Zambian teachers, but volunteers from Birmingham University medical school went out for the summer to offer support and do some teaching of English and maths to give the teachers a break. I spent some time going around the classrooms, listening to the children having their lessons and trying not to be a distraction. Then, with the other students, I spent time playing with the children, doing fun activities. At lunchtimes I would sit on the dirt floor with the teachers and eat "nshima" (a staple food made from maize flour and water), beans, and cabbage with my hands – with the noise of joyful children in the background. Every now and then I would get a mouthful of nshima and grit, because the wind would whip up the sand.

I remember one little girl. At one point I noticed her being picked on by a group of older kids – I don't know why. I bent down and picked her up, just to remove her from the situation. She didn't mind being picked up, but she squirmed in my arms, trying to pull her clothing down, which had ridden up just a little. She was wearing an adult-sized shirt as a substitute for a dress. I realized then that she had nothing on underneath it. Underwear was a luxury. It struck me how much we take simple things for granted. This was real poverty: no shoes and an old shirt for a dress.

I could only stay at the school for a couple of days before I had to move on with my planned trip, but although this environment was a world away from my life in Cardiff and all that I was used to, I felt completely at home. It was a glimpse into what working in Africa might look like in the future. I was totally at peace with the idea of calling this place – or somewhere similar – "home" for a period of time, knowing that it wouldn't faze me.

God has since taught me that this sense of peace is a useful indication of the rightness, or otherwise, of situations I find myself in. I've learned that when it comes to making decisions, it's not just what I hear from the Holy Spirit, but also how I feel about a situation that guides my decisions. Sometimes I find myself desperately wanting to say "yes" to something that I would normally be averse to – or the opposite, feeling strongly averse to something I would usually jump at the chance to do. These nudges from the Spirit are important and have been a guide through extremely challenging circumstances. Nowadays I know that when I receive a phone call or an email asking me to respond to a disaster, if I feel that sense of peace alongside an overwhelming excitement to go, it is a pretty good indication that I should go. I still take time to pray, to make sure I am not caught up in the whims of my own desires, but I also allow these nudges to guide me.

CAMEROON

Following my time in Zambia I travelled down to Victoria Falls and then through Botswana, Namibia and South Africa, ending my trip in Cape Town. From there I boarded a plane to Cameroon, to travel to Kumbo in the North-West Province. It was here that I would be undertaking my medical elective, in Banso Baptist Hospital. Cameroon was my first proper experience of practising medicine in a low-income nation.

Even though I still had ten months of medical school left to complete, I was allowed to see patients independently in the outpatient clinic, which also functioned as an emergency department and general practice clinic. So many situations I faced in Cameroon struck a chord with me that it's hard to be selective, but two cases in particular will stay with me forever. After experiences like these I was certainly well prepared for my first few months as a junior doctor. They helped to make me the doctor I am today.

Ada

I was working in the obstetrics department one day when a newborn baby was brought in. Information was scant about the birth. All I knew was that this little girl, Ada, had been born at a rural health centre. She had begun to have seizures and the health centre couldn't deal with her, so she had been sent to us. She was only a couple of hours old.

From what I could gather, it seemed that the labour had been prolonged and it was likely that Ada had been starved of oxygen prior to her birth. Prolonged oxygen starvation will typically result in damage to a baby's brain, a condition called hypoxic-ischaemic encephalopathy. In its most severe form, the child may develop seizures. In UK hospitals this condition can be treated proactively, as it is usually identified during delivery or immediately after a baby is born, rather than becoming evident when the child starts having seizures. Limited facilities mean this is often not the case in Cameroon.

I was working alongside a local doctor who gave Ada some diazepam to try to stop the seizures, but seconds later we had a crisis on our hands.

"Quick, we need to do something, she's stopped breathing!"

We used a bag and mask to breathe for her until she started breathing on her own again. There were no proper ventilators available at the hospital, or for that matter anywhere in the town. Unfortunately, though, her seizures did not stop and there was no other medication we could give this tiny girl. We left her for a while to attend to a patient who had arrived needing emergency surgery, and returned later to see how she was doing. During a prolonged seizure she had stopped breathing again and this time no one had bagged her, because this was not a long term solution; neither were there enough staff available to constantly breathe for this baby.

Ada passed away a short while after this. She was a casualty of the lack of resources in a low-income nation. So many similar stories could be told every day in such countries. What struck me most about this case was when I walked past the ward later and spotted Ada's mother sitting on the steps outside, crying. This was her first child, gone before she'd barely arrived. I was about to go over and comfort her when her own mother arrived, so I held back. I listened, shocked, as she told her to get over it:

"Babies often die. There will be other children."

How was this young girl supposed to simply move on after losing her child a couple of hours before? But then I thought about the fact that her mother would probably have lost several children herself. In her mind, no doubt she felt that she was helping her daughter by telling her: "This is how it is… We just have to go on."

Lelato

About a week later a lady called Lelato arrived at the hospital in labour. She too had been referred to us by an ill-equipped rural health centre. By the time she reached us she had already been in labour for 48 hours. Now her contractions were beginning to subside and she had not yet delivered her baby.

We examined Lelato and found that the baby, a girl, was a "hand presentation". In other words, instead of the baby's head presenting itself to be delivered, she had twisted around and one hand and arm had come into the birth canal first. The result was that she was stuck, due to the angle of her head and body in relation to her mother's pelvis. We quickly discovered that, sadly, Lelato's baby was already dead.

Faced with this tragic news, the surgeons began discussing how they would remove the baby.

"We may have to do a caesarean, or something else," one of them informed me.

"Like what? What other option is there?" I wondered.

"Sometimes we have to dismember the baby so that it can be delivered normally," he told me matter-of-factly.

"What?" I was horrified.

"Yes," he continued, "in a case like this it is sometimes easier to cut the arm off in order to allow the head to come out."

I had never heard of anything like this. Fortunately, they decided to perform a caesarean section to remove Lelato's baby girl. I don't think I could have tolerated witnessing the alternative, let alone thought about what the mother would have to go through.

I assisted with the caesarean and it turned out that Lelato had what is called a "placenta praevia". This is where the placenta has developed in the wrong location in the uterus and is either partially or fully covering the cervix. It prevents the baby from being born normally and may cause the mother to haemorrhage profusely. This was the cause of the hand presentation as there wasn't enough room for the head to come through. It was fortunate that Lelato had not bled heavily or she may have died as well.

The surgeon removed the baby and handed her to me. She was slippery and it felt as if she moved in my hands. For a split second I thought she might be alive and my heart jumped, but she wasn't. When I saw her perfect little face I realized that she was never going to take the breath she should be taking right now. I looked around to see where I should place her, but there was nowhere. Then a theatre assistant arrived with a bucket. I prayed for the little girl and then placed her in the bucket. I wondered – did her mother not want to see her?

Around the world, women face similar circumstances in childbirth every day. We often forget how fortunate we are in high-income nations to have the healthcare provision we do, where the risk of fatality in childbirth is so low. Many pregnant women in other nations know only too well the significant risk that they, their baby, or both of them will not survive the birth. Around this time, Sierra Leone had the worst maternal and perinatal mortality figures in the world with approximately 2 per cent of pregnant women and 4 per cent of infants born dying each year as a result of pregnancy related complications (data courtesy of World Health Organisation). That is what happens when there is inadequate medical care during pregnancy and at the time of delivery. I have come across many women in the UK who feel like failures because their baby was born by caesarean section, rather than through a "normal" delivery. Truly all that matters, in the end, is that there is a healthy mother and a healthy baby.

A few hours later, I went to visit Lelato as she was recovering on the ward. It was such a traumatic event that I wondered how she was doing. She was resting in bed with her head tilted back. I sat down next to her.

"Are you OK, Lelato?"

"Yes," she said simply.

"Are you sure? Would you like to talk about it?" I asked.

She looked me in the eyes and smiled.

"I am fine, sister," she said. "Are *you* OK?"

It turned out this was her fifth child. She clearly felt fortunate to have four children who were alive and healthy. In her view, it was completely normal to lose a child, since this was the experience of so many women in her country. She was sad, of course, but resigned to what had happened.

"This is the way it is here," she told me. "It happens and life goes on. It is expected."

It shouldn't be expected, I thought.

A DIFFERENT VIEW OF DEATH

That day I learned how far removed my Western understanding of life and death was from the African mindset. In a way, it was refreshing that people were more ready to accept the inevitability of death, unlike in the West. But at the same time, I was outraged that women should accept the death of a child so easily, just because for them it was "normal". It felt so unjust – it should *never* be normal.

Once we accept situations because, "this is the way it is here," things will never change.

In many African countries, when a person dies their family and friends are sad – they grieve openly, much more vocally than in the West, with wailing and crying – but once the mourning is done, they quickly move on with life. They do so because life *must* continue. In richer societies if a person chooses to do so, they can take time off and grieve for a couple of weeks, and may receive some form of support. This is not an option in most of Africa. If you don't carry on, then your family doesn't eat.

In high-income nations we frequently struggle to accept the death of elderly relatives. That is not to say we shouldn't provide optimal healthcare for all, and endeavour to treat people of all ages, but we also need to realize when we have reached the limitations of what is possible. Death is as much a part of life as birth. Somehow we have nurtured a mindset where it is no longer acceptable for people to die, even when they are very old. Because of this, we are far more susceptible to getting stuck in our grief; yet death is inevitable and comes to everyone at some point.

When I was working as a junior doctor in a hospital, I recall my consultant surgeon telling me to arrange a CT scan for a patient. The gentleman in question was in his nineties, had end-stage dementia, severe cardiovascular disease, chronic obstructive pulmonary disease, and other issues too. I questioned what we might do with the results of the scan – which in his confused state wouldn't be pleasant for him – since he was unlikely to survive any resulting surgery. Wasn't it better to allow him to be with his family and enjoy the time he had left?

As Christians, we no longer need to fear death, because Christ has conquered it and, for believers, death has lost its sting. We may grieve for those we have lost, but we have hope. Though we may miss them, we know we will have the joy of one day seeing them again. I hold on to this truth. Although as a doctor I frequently come face to face with the fragile and fleeting nature of life, I don't want to lose sight of the bigger picture. Our short time on earth is but a brief prelude to an eternity with Jesus. As A. W. Tozer once said, "We must meet the uncertainties of this world with the certainty of the world to come."[2]

---

2   A. W. Tozer, *Of God and Men*, Camp Hill, PA: Christian Publications, 1960, p. 132

CHAPTER 7

MISSION 193

I was sitting with a cup of coffee and my Bible, absentmindedly gazing out of the window when God broke into my thoughts with what seemed like a change of plan.

"Nathalie, I want you to move to Manchester."

"Oh, OK," I responded. I was getting used to these divine interruptions. I began to think about how this news would affect my current plans.

* * *

After my medical elective in Cameroon I had returned to the UK and finished my last year in medical school. I then became a house officer at the University Hospital of Wales, where I would spend the next year as a junior doctor, learning the ropes, facing the challenges that healthcare professionals encounter every day, and working the long hours that junior doctors always put in.

The second year of my on-the-job training would be

in Merthyr Tydfil. During this second year I would apply for further training posts for year three and beyond. These were to focus on a specific discipline, and could take place anywhere in the country, depending on the specialism. When God spoke to me about moving to Manchester, I initially wondered whether it had something to do with that – perhaps I would be training in Manchester? At the same time, however, I'd long had a desire to take some time out to attend our church movement's Bible college, which ran a 10-month course. At the time, the UK Government were changing the training structure for junior doctors, and conditions were set to become more rigid, making it increasingly difficult to take time out in the future. I had begun to think, "Perhaps now is the right time to pause my career and go to Bible college?"

However, the college was based near where I lived, in Cardiff, and God had just told me to move to Manchester.

I decided to go to see the college's principal, Roger Aubrey, just to talk things over. At one point during our chat he said,

"Well, the college is actually relocating to Manchester next year. We've just decided that in the last week."

"How interesting!" I replied, as pieces of the puzzle fell into place.

Until then I had been quite settled in Cardiff. I think this was God's way of graciously introducing the idea of moving to me, so that it wasn't a complete shock. After praying about it some more, I received a great sense of God's peace that this was his will for me and I began to prepare for the move to Manchester.

The end of July 2008 came around and I finished my second year of junior doctor training. Bible college would begin the first week of September. But before then I had some more travelling to do. Our church network was running an initiative called Mission 193, which aimed to get copies of the Bible into every nation on earth, in its indigenous language. (The UN recognized 193 nations as independent nations or states at that time and the plan was to reach every country officially recognized as a nation). The idea was to travel in pairs to a nation carrying a few Bibles, pray for that nation and then pray that God would supernaturally connect you with the Christians who needed them.

My friend Ceri and I decided to do this and planned a trip that would take us to Laos and Myanmar. At the time Myanmar was ruled by a military junta and was being called to account for its human rights abuses. The UK Government had put in place sanctions, which included a number of trade embargoes and a ban on flights. It meant that we couldn't purchase our flights in the UK. But after praying about it, we felt that this was definitely where God wanted us to go.

We considered a number of options, including the possibility of travelling into Myanmar overland from Chiang Rai in Thailand, but that would have left us stranded at the border town in Myanmar, making traveling further a problem. The military had decreed that foreigners were not permitted to travel on the roads in that region, nor to go outside the border town without special permits. Eventually we decided to buy return flights to Bangkok, with an additional return flight from there to Luang Prabang in Laos. We would arrange to stay with friends in Bangkok on our return from Laos for a few days, and during that time we would purchase flights to Myanmar and obtain our visas.

Ceri and I embarked on our journey each carrying three Bibles – one Arabic copy, one in Lao and one in Bamar, the most common language in Myanmar. I also packed a large Bible concordance, which was destined for some Christians we'd already managed to make contact with in Myanmar. We prayed that God would guide us and go ahead of us, placing the adventure securely in his hands.

En route to Bangkok, we had a 24-hour stopover in a Middle Eastern nation. In this country it was forbidden to proselytize or hold church meetings. It was also forbidden to carry Bibles into the country, other than a single copy for personal use. As in Belarus, our bags were X-rayed on the way out of the airport. Ceri and I exchanged nervous glances as we approached security, with the exit to the airport just metres away, and I had to stop myself from holding my breath and try to look as normal and relaxed as possible.

My bag went through the scanner and the conveyor belt stopped while it was scrutinized. Then it was Ceri's turn. When our bags came out the other side the security guard looked me in the eye knowingly. I'm sure I didn't imagine that. He gave a slight smile, then waved us away, allowing us to collect our bags and leave the airport.

We travelled to our hotel and checked in. It was still early and we were tired from the flight, so we caught up on some rest. Later that morning we decided we would go outside for a brief walk to orient ourselves and find somewhere for lunch, but the hotel staff wouldn't let us walk outside – they insisted we take an air-conditioned taxi, since the temperature was currently 50°C. I went over to a window to look outside and could feel the heat radiating off it.

Given the intense heat, we decided to eat lunch at the hotel, but time was running short to locate those whom God intended to have the Arabic Bibles. Ceri and I prayed about it in our room, then went to the front desk to make some enquiries. All of the hotel staff were foreigners, so we concluded it would be safe to ask a few questions without getting into any trouble. The man we spoke to said that we shouldn't discuss things further right then, but he would find a particular member of staff and bring her to us.

It turned out that this lady was part of an underground church that organized prayer meetings across the city. Visiting the church was out of the question, as it moved location constantly to avoid being discovered, but we were able to pray with her and bless her with the gift of Arabic Bibles. She was thrilled and grateful.

The following day we returned to the airport and caught our flight to Bangkok, where we stayed the night before flying to Laos. Laos was beautiful and we saw a lot of Luang Prabang before travelling down to the capital, Vientiane, stopping in Vang Vieng on the way. The whole time we kept our eyes open to see if we came across any churches or bumped into anyone who looked as if they might be a Christian.

Laos is predominantly Buddhist, so we struggled to encounter any Christians in Luang Prabang. We thought we may have more chance in the capital, Vientiane. We didn't have long there, however, arriving late on a Thursday afternoon. We were due to leave that Saturday morning to travel back to Luang Prabang to catch our flight back to Bangkok on Sunday. We spent all of Friday walking around Vientiane, but didn't find anyone to pray with and bless with the Bibles.

Time was running out when we spotted a sign for an aid organization called Norwegian Church Aid in the town centre. We knocked on their door and asked if there were any Christians in the office we could speak with. To our surprise, all of the staff were either Buddhist or Muslim, but they directed us to the nearby office of World Vision. There we were introduced to a local man named Lae. We chatted to him about his church and prayed with him. He was very grateful to receive the Bibles as they were nearly impossible to source locally in the Lao language.

Two days later we arrived in Bangkok. It was here that we had to obtain the visas we needed to enter Myanmar and book our flights. We connected with friends and stayed in their apartment block. At the bottom of the apartments there was a travel agent, so we provisionally booked our flights to Yangon, Myanmar. We then had to visit the Myanmar embassy in downtown Bangkok to secure our visas. We already knew that this could prove difficult because of the UK's strained relations with Myanmar – and we were not disappointed.

GOD'S FAVOUR

Arriving at the embassy we were greeted by a lengthy queue. This first queue was simply to collect our visa application forms, then there was another long queue to submit them. We were informed that since we were from the UK we would also need to provide details of five former employers, but neither of us had been working long enough to have five previous employers.

We stood in line with our completed forms and watched what happened to the people ahead of us. We saw one man being directed to the next window along. When we finally reached the official we were told to go there too – we would need to be interviewed before our visa applications could be approved or rejected. It was evident that it was only Brits and Americans who had to have interviews, no doubt because of the sanctions both countries had imposed on Myanmar.

As we waited we could clearly hear the conversation between an official and an American tourist. It wasn't going well. In fact, it was a masterclass in how *not* to approach a visa interview. We sat down to wait our turn and I leaned into Ceri.

"That is how not to do it," I whispered.

The stern-faced official eyed the US tourist.

"Why do you want to visit Myanmar?" he snapped.

"I am a tourist and I would like to see your country," the American replied.

"What do you want to do in Myanmar?"

"Well, I just want to travel around and see as much of it as I can."

(Much of Myanmar was out of bounds to foreigners at this time – special government permission was needed to go anywhere significant outside Yangon.)

"What else do you want to do in Myanmar?"

"I've heard your country is very beautiful, so I'd like to take some photos," the American smiled.

(The government were wary of foreign journalists who might cast the country in a bad light. Taking photos of many areas was forbidden, especially if there were government buildings there.)

The official persisted ...

"What else do you want to do in Myanmar?"

Searching for a response the American replied,

"Err, I'd also like to take photos of the children."

"Really?" the official responded, making a note. "And what else do you want to do in Myanmar?"

"Well, I guess I might teach some of the children some English..."

The government was fearful of any kind of Western influence coming into their nation, so a short while later the interview concluded and the man had his visa application denied. He stormed out of the embassy. All this time I had been praying silently that the Holy Spirit would guide our conversation and give me the right words to say. Then it was our turn.

"Why do you want to visit Myanmar?" the official began predictably.

"We are tourists," I replied, "and we have heard your country is very beautiful, so we would like to visit it."

"Yes, but *why* do you want to visit Myanmar?" he said irritably.

"We are tourists and we have heard your country is very beautiful, so we would like to visit it," I repeated.

He looked at our paperwork.

"You have flights booked. You will only be there for seven days. Seven days is not enough time in which to see Myanmar."

"We know seven days is not enough time, but we both work and we must return to our jobs, so we only have seven days."

"Seven days is not enough time in which to see Myanmar!" he insisted.

"We know this, but we both must return to work and so we only have seven days in which to visit."

"What is your job?"

"I am a doctor."

"A doctor? What kind of doctor?"

"A medical doctor."

"Are you sure you are a medical doctor and not a PhD doctor?"

"Yes, I am a medical doctor, not a PhD doctor."

"You are not a journalist or a politician?"

"No, I am not a journalist or a politician."

Turning to Ceri:

"What is your job?"

"I am an auditor," she replied.

"Ahh, auditor, OK."

Turning back to me:

"Why do you want to visit Myanmar?"

"We have heard your country is very beautiful. We would like to visit it."

"Why else do you want to visit Myanmar?"

"We would like to visit because we have heard your country is very beautiful."

"But seven days is not enough time in which to see Myanmar!"

"We must return to our work, so we only have seven days to see Myanmar."

"You have flights booked to Myanmar leaving in 48 hours, but it takes 48 hours to issue the visas."

"We can change the flights. They are provisionally booked and we can travel a day later."

I thought we might go around in circles like this forever, but then the man's face softened.

"No, it is OK," he said. "I have decided I like you. And because I like you, I give you visa. And I give you visa in 24 hours, not 48 hours. But I only charge you standard visa fee, not express visa fee – because I like you!"

We thanked the man profusely, glancing at each other only briefly, then held our composure until we were outside the embassy and a little way down the street. Ceri and I looked incredulously at each other and exploded with laughter. This was definitely the favour of God. We almost didn't dare believe what had happened until we collected our passports and visas the following day.

We flew to Myanmar the next day and were met at the airport by our contact, Amos. A few months earlier Amos had contacted my home church in Cardiff when Myanmar had been hit by Cyclone Nargis. It had caused widespread destruction to the south of the country and our church had sent Amos funds to support his relief efforts. Amos was a pastor and oversaw multiple churches in Myanmar.

Christianity is not forbidden in Myanmar, and Christians are allowed to gather for worship, but it is not permitted to try to convert others. Previously Amos had spent time in prison when another Christian denomination claimed he was speaking against them. In fact, he was just preaching about the Holy Spirit. He was jailed for several years. It made me sad to think that even in the face of many forms of persecution, there could be divisions amongst the church that would result in further persecution.

Amos took us to our hotel and then for some food. He explained that we were welcome to come and preach at some of the churches he oversaw in Yangon over the next couple of days. After that we could travel to Kalay in the north west of the country, where there were more churches. This was one of the areas that we'd need special government permission to travel to, since it was out of bounds to foreigners.

After a couple of days of preaching and encouraging the church in Yangon, we were granted permission to travel to Kalay and left the following day. In Kalay there was only one hotel which foreigners were allowed to stay in. It had power most of the time, but they often turned off the generator in the early hours of the morning, causing the fan in our room to stop working. In no time at all the intense heat would invade our room and make it difficult to sleep. We preached at a few churches in Kalay, but were not granted permission to leave the town to speak in some of the more rural churches.

On the first day we were picked up by local pastors and travelled around on the backs of their motorcycles. The following day, however, we were picked up in a tuktuk. We asked why we were no longer travelling by motorcycle and our new friends told us that the government had informed them it was not safe. That's when we realized that the government was watching our every move. Then we discovered that while we'd been in Yangon our hotel had reported daily on our activities. In Kalay Amos also had to write a daily report saying where he had taken us, which restaurants we'd been to, and even what we'd eaten.

Despite such intense scrutiny, it was wonderful to pray with and encourage the believers in Myanmar. At the time

I was reading Bill Johnson's book, *When Heaven Invades Earth*[3], as one of the preparatory texts I had to read for Bible college. It was a book that in many ways changed my life. It wasn't that I didn't believe that the miracles written about in the book were possible – because I did – and I also believed in a God of miracles, a God who heals. But when I read that book, something in me clicked. The potential of the supernatural power of God in me suddenly became real. I realized that God wanted to use me, that he might even use little me to bring about healing in others.

The passage in John 14:12 took on new significance and meaning – that we are called to do the same things that Jesus did while he was on the earth, even greater things, and that we could see God's kingdom in action, here and now. I think this was reflected in my preaching during my time in Myanmar and I hope it encouraged the church there. In the last few years the government of Myanmar has opened its doors to the West again and it is now much easier for people to travel there, and for Myanmar's citizens to travel outside the country. I pray that this will be an increasingly fruitful time for the church in Myanmar, but also that there will be unity and a breaking down of denominational walls.

---

3   Bill Johnson, *When Heaven Invades Earth*, Shippensburg, PA: Destiny Image, 2003

ANOTHER GOD-INTERVENTION

It was around 10.30 p.m. and I had just finished packing the last of my things. I was staying with my friend Tina before travelling up to Manchester the next day for my induction – the first day of Bible college. Then the phone rang. It was my mum with news about my grandfather.

"Nathalie, it's your Nonno. He was admitted to hospital last night and we thought he was going to die. He survived the night, but it doesn't look good."

I had a decision to make.

I didn't want my grandfather to die without seeing him and saying goodbye, but I also didn't want to miss the first week of Bible college. In my heart, at that moment, I felt that despite my mother's assessment of the situation, Nonno was going to be OK. I believed that he wasn't going to die yet and that I would have an opportunity to see him. I just had to trust God. I felt that the timing of this crisis could actually be a sign of spiritual opposition to me going to Bible college. I told my mum that I would still go to Manchester, but would travel down to London to visit Nonno the following weekend.

Morning came and my friend Hayley arrived; we were greeted with torrential rain as we tried to load up our cars. We were going to be travelling in convoy. The rain continued and the drive to Manchester, which should have taken three and a half hours, instead took five and a half hours. The rain was so heavy I could only see a few feet in front of me. I kept rebuking the rain and telling it to stop in the name of Jesus. For about half an hour it would, before returning full pelt.

At the end of that first week at Bible college a member of the church, Sarah, prayed with me before I set off for London. She specifically asked God that Nonno would be saved.

When I arrived at the hospital Nonno was doing much better and was completely lucid. I went into the ward accompanied by my mum and grandma. Mum said,

"Right Nathalie, why don't you and I go and get everyone some drinks, so that Nonna and Nonno can have some time together?"

I said "OK," but then my grandfather began talking to me, so I turned my attention to him. I glanced around only a second later and Mum and Nonna were both gone. My grandma couldn't move very quickly at the time, so it gave me the impression that they'd both just disappeared. I believe it was God opening a door for me. Nonno looked at me and asked,

"So what are you doing with your life now, Nathalie?"

"I'm at Bible college," I told him.

"That's a rather strange thing for someone your age to do, isn't it?" he commented.

"Not really," I replied, "I just wanted to know more about Jesus and the Bible."

"Do you know," he said, "I've been thinking… "

Around six months earlier I'd been having dinner with my grandparents. Although Nonno didn't have a firm faith at the time, he was very well read, and we'd had an interesting conversation about what the Christian symbol of the fish meant. He had been raised as a traditional Roman Catholic, growing up in rural Italy in a context where only priests would read the Bible, since it was supposed that lay people would misinterpret it. In fact, reading the Bible was actively discouraged.

"Do you remember when we were talking about the symbol of the fish?" he said. "Ever since that conversation I've been thinking about it, and you know what? I've decided – I think I believe in Jesus."

I was amazed.

"Can I pray for you then?" I asked.

We prayed together. A second after we'd finished my mum and Nonna returned with the drinks.

A short while later Nonno was discharged from hospital but a few weeks after that he developed severe dementia and it became very hard to communicate with him. He was moved to a nursing home where he lived for a few more years, but I was incredibly grateful for God's timing. A few weeks later and it would have been impossible to have that conversation with him. It was wonderful to know that he had put his trust in Jesus.

I had a great year at Bible school and it was a privilege to be able to spend time studying the Bible, praying, spending time with God, and being taught by some exceptional Bible teachers. In many ways it prepared me for the next part of my journey.

We get so caught up in the busyness of everyday life that it's easy to lose sight of spending time in God's presence and hearing him speak. Yet it is amazing what God will do through us when we choose to lay down our lives for him.

CHAPTER 8

IF I TALK, HE DIES

"**E**veryone, get down – *now!*"

The soldier screamed the order and I was about to comply. He didn't give me a second to obey, however, before kicking my legs from under me; I hit the ground with a bang. I never saw it coming because I was blindfolded. Grenades exploded nearby and the clatter of automatic weapons discharging filled my ears.

I was glad at that moment that this was a training exercise and not happening for real in some remote part of Africa. But the fact was that our instructors were working very hard indeed to make this as real as it could be – and they were succeeding.

* * *

Towards the end of my time at the Covenant Ministries Bible college, one of the apostolic leaders, Keri Jones, asked if I would be willing to help the church movement set up a disaster response unit. He said that when disaster struck around the world he wanted us to have teams of people ready and willing to respond.

For some time I had been thinking about becoming involved in disaster relief, but although I had a fairly good idea of what it entailed, my knowledge of managing such situations was very limited – and there is a big difference between the theory and the reality. Keri and I talked about whether Covenant Ministries should partner with another organization or go it alone. He commented that if we ended up partnering with any organization, he wanted it to be Franklin Graham's Samaritan's Purse. I tried to contact them at the time, but didn't get very far with it.

I began to learn more about disaster relief and bought a book that is considered one of the go-to texts on the topic: *A Framework for Survival* by Kevin M. Cahill, M.D.. Through his book I became aware that Cahill had helped to create a month-long course which awarded delegates the International Diploma in Humanitarian Assistance, recognized by the United Nations.

I knew there were plenty of gaps in my knowledge, so I approached our leaders to tell them about this course and they were willing to pay for me and another girl, Michelle, who was based at an associated church in Ottawa, to go on it. It ran three times per year and the next one would be held in New York fairly soon.

It was amazing that the ministry leaders were willing to pay for me to receive appropriate training, but I also needed another miracle – I would have to be granted a month off work to do it.

At the time I was working in neonatal intensive care, a very busy department. In medicine we do six-month rotations, spending half the year in one department and half in another. We are required to split our leave between the two rotations, and no one is allowed to take all their leave during one six-month period. I had to try to get around this with my clinical director. I would need special permission for that length of time off as my out-of-hours shifts would need to be covered. We talked about me taking some paid leave, some unpaid leave, and some study leave to do it. In the end it still didn't quite work, but I badgered my director so much that in the end he said,

"Do you know what? Just go!"

I recall working many long shifts in the run-up to going away, and doing the same when I got back, but at least I secured the time off that I needed.

It was late May 2010 when I arrived at Fordham University in New York, where Kevin Cahill himself had helped to set up the Center for International Humanitarian Cooperation – the organization that ran the diploma course.

Fordham's Lincoln Center campus is located impressively in central Manhattan. Fordham was founded in 1841 by Jesuits to enable people from poorer backgrounds to attend university, and the Lincoln Center campus is located just off Central Park, within walking distance of Broadway and Times Square. I would be here for the next month. The course would be a combination of lectures, practical work, and training in humanitarian assistance, designed to foster cooperation between organizations which found themselves working side by side in humanitarian crises.

The course was very intense. We were in lectures from 8.30 a.m. until 5.00 p.m. virtually every day, but then we were given a group project that had to be completed and presented each Friday. By Monday morning there would be a gruelling assessment based on our efforts during the previous week. In other words, we had precious little time to get the group project work done – it had to happen during evenings and weekends, grabbing time wherever we could. This was OK to begin with, but as the course became more involved we were surviving on about four hours of sleep per night.

All of this was deliberate. The course sets out to replicate, through its intensity and the use of subtle sleep deprivation, the conditions one might face in a real disaster setting. The organizers were constantly trying to push us to mimic a typical disaster scenario, where you find yourself working in a team with people you don't know very well, having to take important decisions whilst under duress, and generally feeling exhausted.

The first couple of days were all about team building and working together, and were run by an expert on the psychology and dynamics of teams. But then we were split into four teams for the group work, and the course tutors deliberately put us into groups with clashing personalities, where they knew there would be conflict. They wanted as much friction as possible. It's safe to say that we all learned a great deal about each other over the next few weeks.

LIFE AND DEATH SCENARIO

One of the course's most notable features is its "security training day", which in this instance was run by US Army cadets and officers and took place at Lake Frederick, a training ground for the renowned United States Military Academy at West Point.

We weren't told what would happen that day – only that there would be some kind of "incident" that would help prepare us for security situations overseas. The night before I'd sat in my room praying about this day and what might happen. Even though it was a mock exercise, I realized that I needed to make some decisions in advance about the potential situations I might face. Should fear set in, I wanted to have settled in my mind, in advance, a default position that I could fall back on. That way, I would hopefully avoid making any stupid, panic-driven decisions in the heat of the moment that I might later regret. This is a principle we often use in medicine, and is why we regularly practise emergency procedures such as cardiac arrest scenarios. Preparing for such occurrences over and over again programs in an algorithm that becomes so ingrained that when a real emergency occurs, our response is automatic. When the adrenaline is pumping and there is no time to think, you are able to revert to your training and provide the best standard of care possible under the circumstances.

One might reasonably ask at this point: how can such a training exercise be effective if everyone knows it is a deliberately constructed mock scenario?

First of all, we were told to pretend in our heads that it was real at all times in order to get the most out of the exercise – so mentally you make an effort to go along with it. Second, we had no idea what was going to happen, so we couldn't completely prepare for how we might react. But also, all of us were involved in humanitarian aid in some way and had been to a number of unstable countries around the world. It was likely we'd be going back to them or to other volatile places. We could certainly face a scenario like this one day, so it was in all of our interests to learn how to deal with it. We wanted to cooperate in order to get the most out of it.

One of the focuses of the day was to work out how we might respond in a real situation. I realized I might be faced with the decision to save my own life at the cost of giving up someone else's. I decided there and then that I never wanted another person to lose their life as a direct result of my actions or decisions, even if it cost me my own. I would rather die and be with Jesus than live with the knowledge that I had sacrificed another person to save my own skin. I didn't want fear to dictate my decision-making; rather I wanted my choices in life to glorify God. I decided that in any emergency I would do my utmost to put the lives of others before my own. The events that unfolded this day helped me to consolidate that decision.

The morning began with our arrival at Lake Frederick and a bag search. We spent some time learning about radio communications, map reading, first aid in the field, various weapons and improvised explosive devices (IEDs). In the afternoon we were sent on a long walk along a path up a hill that overlooked the lake.

Just as we entered a densely forested area we were stopped, checkpoint-style, by a group of soldiers acting as "local militia" would in another nation. They tried to rough us up a bit, yelling at us and demanding our IDs.

"Where is your ID? Anyone without ID will be taken away!"

At first, it was tempting to risk a little laugh, but the soldiers took the exercise extremely seriously and had very big guns. Eventually they allowed us through and we carried on walking. We were supposed to eat some lunch en route, but of course events were engineered so that we didn't have time for that.

We had been told at the beginning that we didn't have to take part in this exercise if we didn't want to. One girl who was pregnant wisely opted out. There was one guy who said he wasn't going to do it, then changed his mind at the last minute. During the day I began to wonder if he had been planted by our instructors. I noticed that his ID didn't have his name displayed in the same way as ours, and there was no photo. He was acting suspiciously too. Were the organizers playing mind games with us?

The fact is, when you are working overseas you have to operate alongside local staff who you don't know well. It made me think… although most situations are relatively safe and the local staff are wonderful, what about that one day where someone calls in sick and you suddenly have a new driver? You don't know anything about that person, who they are, or what their motives are…

We walked a few hundred metres beyond the checkpoint when suddenly all hell broke loose, gunfire shattering the silence. Grenades exploded and the ground under my feet shook. Seconds later people were running in every direction and there was a huge amount of noise, yelling, and more gunfire. We were surrounded by guerrilla-type militia. They ordered us to take off our shoes and lie face down on the ground. Our hands were then cable-tied behind our backs. I tried to remain calm as the ground still shook underneath me.

I looked up and tried to orient myself. There was a mound of dirt and some trees in front of me. I could see a large number of small crawling insects swarming around – there must have been some sort of nest nearby – and they looked like the biting sort. Seconds later I was blindfolded and thought, *Well, at least I can't see those insects anymore – and if I can't see them I can't worry about them!*

I prayed that God would keep me calm, so that however the exercise developed from here I would remain rational and not get sucked into any hysteria. This was what they were trying to do, to push people to their emotional and physical limits. At that point a peace washed over me as I lay there, despite the continuing gunfire and grenades. I had a friend who I played volleyball with back home who was a psychologist, and I recalled her saying,

"Nathalie, whenever I feel stressed or there are people

getting stressed around me on the court, I just play music in my head."

I liked that, so in the midst of this chaos I tuned out the mayhem and began to play music in my head. It helped to keep me calm. In a real emergency I am usually quite calm; maybe not internally, but externally. I can keep a cool head and continue to function.

Eventually, we were made to stand up and continue walking. When my blindfold was being put on I'd closed my eyes, and the soldier had tied it so tight that I couldn't open them again. We were told the next day in our debrief that we were supposed to try to see through the blindfold, but I couldn't see anything, which is why I nearly walked off the edge of a steep drop a few times and one of the militia had to grab me to stop me from falling. Once we reached a flatter area we were all made to lie face down again. I was at the front as the lead soldier barked for everyone to get down, but he didn't give me the chance to do so and just knocked me to the ground.

More grenades were detonated and blanks fired into the air from US Army semi-automatic assault rifles. Then the soldier in charge began to walk amongst us. They were trying to recreate the dehumanizing techniques that rogue militia would probably use if we were ever captured for real.

The lead soldier stopped and shouted at one of the guys on my team,

"You! Who should I kill? Tell me now!"

"No one, take me," he said.

As I lay there I remembered the decision I'd made the

night before. I knew where I would be going when I died, so I didn't need to be afraid of dying. I couldn't say that of my colleagues. If this were a real life scenario, maybe I would be able to buy them some more time so that, hopefully, they would one day have the chance to make a decision for Christ themselves?

I heard the soldier come towards me. He stood over me and prodded me with his foot.

"You!" he shouted. "Give me a name."

I knew that if I gave anyone up, that person would be taken away and shot (even though I understood it was a mock scenario). This is a standard dehumanizing technique. Hostage takers will convince themselves that the people they've taken are less than human, and to be despised because they gave up one of their own. That makes it easier for them to do inconceivably barbaric things to them. They justify it on the basis that the person is equally capable of atrocious acts if the tables were turned. This technique is also used to invoke a greater level of fear, and therefore a greater level of submission and compliance with requests. I said simply, "No, take me."

"That wasn't what I asked," he yelled. "Give me a *******
name!"

He kicked me in the ribs as he said it. I didn't respond. He walked around the other side of me and shouted again,

"I said give me a name!"

When I refused to respond he kicked me again. This happened a couple more times before he went away to speak to his colleagues. Shortly after this there was another bout of gunfire and then the scenario came to an end.

We had been split into two groups for this exercise. Our group had gone first. I heard that with the second group, the lead soldier had gone to one of the guys and said,

"Give me a number."

Without thinking the guy responded,

"Five!"

This time they had allocated every person a number, so with that, they dragged out "number five" and faked shooting them dead. Then the soldier came back and asked the guy for another number. A second person was dragged away screaming. The guy gave the soldier about five numbers before one of his team mates yelled,

"Shut up, you idiot, they're killing people!"

GOD IS BIGGER THAN OUR FEAR

The organizers came running out of the trees shouting and waving their arms.

"It's over. The exercise has finished!"

They cut our cable ties and set everyone free. People were genuinely shaken up by the experience, but the decision to keep calm, hold my nerve and not endanger my colleagues was a pivotal moment for me. I'm glad that I had the opportunity to make that decision in advance of being thrust into a real humanitarian crisis. It has since served me well and was of particular help during the chaos of the Ebola epidemic in July 2014.

Not long after I'd become a Christian a friend had asked me, "If someone pointed a gun at your head and said that if you didn't deny Christ you would die, what decision would you make?'

At the time I'd not long read the passage in Matthew 10:33 where Jesus says, "But whoever denies Me before men, him I will also deny before My Father who is in heaven" (NKJV). I realized that if I denied my faith in Jesus then my life had no meaning because he is my foundation. I knew right then that I would rather die and be with him than deny him in the vain hope of preserving my life.

I understand that our Father God is endlessly gracious and merciful, and that he understands the choices we are forced to make under extreme pressure. In such a situation if we were to ask his forgiveness it would be readily given. But I would rather obey him in the first place. My view is that our all-powerful, loving God is more than capable of delivering us from every circumstance we face. Whether or not he chooses to do so is his business; ours is to trust him completely and to know that he knows best. Whatever his decision, I win, because I am either delivered and continue to live for him, or I go to be with him in heaven. I have to trust his judgment in every situation. If I can't trust God's judgement in a crisis, then when can I? As Paul writes in Philippians 1:21, "For to me, to live *is* Christ, and to die *is* gain" (NKJV).

I'm not afraid to die because it's a win-win situation.

CHAPTER 9

MEDICINE IN SUN CITY

Cité Soleil is the biggest slum of the Haitian capital, Port-au-Prince. In fact, it is reputedly the largest slum in the northern hemisphere. The sprawling shanty dwellings that spread for miles, punctuated by a water-logged maze of mud alleyways, sit in bleak contrast to the beautiful turquoise ocean beside them. Cité Soleil is infamous for its high levels of crime and violence and the UN has declared it the most dangerous place in the world many times over. The Red Cross has said that "Sun City" represents, "a microcosm of all the ills in Haitian society."[4] At the end of May 2011 I travelled there to help with disaster relief efforts.

The epicentre of the earthquake that struck Haiti on 12 January 2010 was just a short distance from Port-au-Prince, and caused severe destruction to the capital and a wide region surrounding it. In an already poor country, the earthquake left over 100,000 people dead and significantly

---

4   Didier Revol (2006). "Hoping for change in Haiti's Cité-Soleil", International Red Cross.

higher numbers homeless. The nation's infrastructure is limited, so reconstruction efforts were slow and challenging. Approximately ten months after the quake, Haiti reported the first cases of cholera seen in the island in decades. This grew rapidly into a cholera epidemic in which thousands died and hundreds of thousands more were infected.

While the initial surge of the epidemic gradually slowed down over a number of years, Haiti continues to report cases of cholera, with regular flare-ups of the disease. In large part this is due to the poor quality of water and the minimal sanitation infrastructure. Most households don't have running water or private latrines.

I was asked to work with other volunteers from Samaritan's Purse and travelled to Haiti with a medical colleague, John Lippiatt, to work in one of the cholera treatment centres they had constructed. Samaritan's Purse had mounted a large response to the earthquake and had been heavily involved with shelter construction and water and sanitation interventions. Initially, it was not primarily a medical response – until the cholera epidemic broke out. After that they quickly established two large cholera treatment centres, the largest of which was in the Cité Soleil slum. Due to my work schedule, and the difficulty of getting leave, I could only be there for two weeks.

The medical team was driven daily from our accommodation – an old repurposed Baptist mission with dormitories – to a large area of land covered with white gravel. The treatment centre was huge; there were two "buildings" constructed from wood and the distinctive royal blue tarpaulin of Samaritan's Purse, bearing their logo. Due to the colour of the roof tarps there was a constant blue hue inside. The side tarps rolled up like blinds to allow a breeze through, to mitigate the Haitian heat. The inside had been sectioned off to create six wards. Towards the back of the structure was a makeshift morgue, and to the other side were huge chlorinated containers needed to dispose of large amounts of diarrhoea and urine. A cluster of smaller tents formed a triage area to admit patients and treat emergencies. This backed on to a dirt road, so people could just walk in and be treated. If they were not very dehydrated from the cholera they would be sent to the oral rehydration tent to observe if they could tolerate oral fluids. If they could, they would later be sent home.

Outside the centre was a road junction. Because it was one of the main roads into Port-au-Prince, wealthier people would drive that way, and there were often carjackings and muggings. One day there was a gang shootout. I was busy in the treatment centre, and it was noisy, but I could still hear the "pop, pop, pop" of gunfire in the background. Just before I'd arrived at the centre, Tiffany, one of our nurse coordinators, had been in a vehicle that was hijacked and had been robbed. We had to be extremely careful and it was decided that we would arrive at the centre in the early morning, after sunrise, and leave before sunset. No one was allowed to travel that road in the dark.

The start of our trek in Tibet, shortly before we got lost at approximately 4,800m. The Kunlun mountains are visible in the background. April 2000, China.

Community school in Kanakantapa, near Lusaka, Zambia, 2005.

Farewell party at Banso Baptist Hospital, Kumbo, Cameroon, 2005. The man on the far left is Dr Martin Salia, from Sierra Leone, who was doing his surgical training with the Pan-African Academy of Christian Surgeons (PAACS). On completion he returned to Sierra Leone as one of the few experienced surgeons in the country. In November 2014 he became infected with Ebola during his clinical work and died shortly after his evacuation to Nebraska, USA.

In Laos as part of Mission 193, giving a Bible to a local Christian in Vientane, 2008.

Visiting Myanmar during Mission 193 – with Amos and the church in Yangon

Samaritan's Purse medical team outside the Cité Soleil cholera treatment centre, Port-au-Prince, Haiti, June 2011.

Nathalie and the medical team with the dehydrated premature baby at the cholera treatment centre, Haiti, June 2011.

Cubicles in the confirmed patients ward at ELWA2, July 2014. Image courtesy of Eric Buller/SIM.

Cubicle in the suspected patients ward at ELWA2, July 2014. Image courtesy of Eric Buller/SIM.

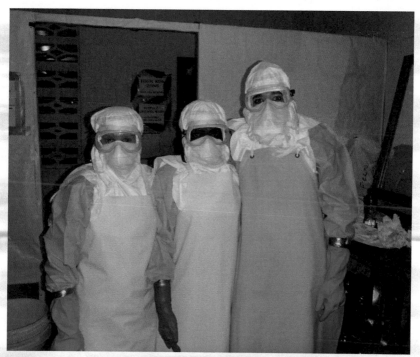

Nathalie (right) with colleagues wearing personal protective equipment.

Moving Ebola patients from ELWA1 to ELWA2. Image courtesy of Joni Byker/ Samaritan's Purse.

Nathalie with Dorothy, Alicia, and William, who was the first patient at ELWA2 to survive Ebola. Image courtesy of Joni Byker/Samaritan's Purse.

Graveyard built by Samaritan's Purse to commemorate those lost in the Ebola epidemic. Image courtesy of Joni Byker/Samaritan's Purse.

Helping to offload children from refugee boats, Lesvos island, Greece, 2015. Image courtesy of David Uttley/Samaritan's Purse.

Assessing patients at Moria migrant camp, Lesvos island, Greece, 2015
Image courtesy of David Uttley/Samaritan's Purse.

Helping a boy with asthma at the Gevgelija transit centre, Macedonia, 2015.
Image courtesy of David Uttley/Samaritan's Purse.

LOST

On my first day there I did a "handover" ward round with the paediatrician who would be leaving the next day. I would then be taking over as the only paediatrician for the next couple of weeks. There were about forty children in the paediatric area, so this took quite a bit of time.

One of the first children I saw was a little girl, around eighteen months old. She was getting better and had improved significantly since she'd been admitted. She hadn't had any diarrhoea for 24 hours, so we had stopped giving her intravenous fluids and were encouraging her to drink normally. I could see, however, that she was acutely malnourished and would need help from a specialist nutrition centre on discharge. We didn't have the facilities for this – we were only set up to care for cholera patients.

As I came to the end of the ward round, near to where I'd begun, this little girl caught my eye. I noticed that she was breathing very quickly. I went over to see her and found that she had developed a fever and crepitations in her chest (a crackling or rattling sound), which suggested she had an infection. She was still drinking well, though, and I wanted to avoid intravenous access. Children with severe malnutrition can't tolerate large amounts of fluid as it can make them go into heart failure. We didn't have any pumps to control how quickly the fluid went through the intravenous lines and sometimes it would flow more quickly than we wanted. I didn't want to endanger this little girl's life, so I gave her some oral antibiotics and watched her closely.

Neither did we have any oxygen or probes that could measure oxygen levels in such a small child. I spoke with Christine, our nurse coordinator, and suggested she be transferred to another hospital that could provide the support she needed. Christine agreed and got on the phone. Minutes later she spoke to me, disappointed.

"Unfortunately, the other hospital refused to take her because of her history of cholera, even though it's settled."

We decided she would keep trying. I left Christine attempting to persuade the hospital to take the child and returned to the ward. I checked on some other patients and kept a close eye on this little girl, who I was very concerned about. Unfortunately, the other hospital still refused to take her.

About two hours later I went to check on her again. She had been asleep, but was now crawling around her cot. Her mother was sat beside her. She told me that she was worried because the little girl was quite floppy. I explained that I was concerned too, but she was sick and we were doing what we could.

As I stood there, however, the girl stopped crawling and suddenly passed out. I caught her as she almost rolled off the cot. At this point I had no other choice but to insert an intravenous line. As I did so, she passed a large amount of cholera diarrhoea – the first in 24 hours. I gave her a small bolus of intravenous fluid, still wary of her malnutrition, and followed the fluid guidelines that the World Health

Organization recommends for children with severe malnutrition. I also gave her intravenous antibiotics as she still had a fever and was breathing quickly.

After this I returned to speak with Christine.

"We've got to transfer her somewhere!" I insisted.

We just didn't have adequate facilities to treat her. Nearly five hours after our initial discussion with the hospital they agreed to take her. Unfortunately, it was a forty-five minute drive away, on the other side of Port-au-Prince.

Another child had just arrived at the centre with a severe infection (not cholera), so I placed both children into one of our vehicles with their parents and sent them off. Around forty minutes later the vehicle returned. They had made it halfway to the hospital when the girl had stopped breathing. The driver didn't know what to do, so he turned around and drove back to the treatment centre. Christine and I rushed out to the vehicle as it pulled up in the entrance to the centre.

"Move back and let me get in," I said, climbing into the car to assess her. I listened to her chest; I couldn't hear a heartbeat.

Christine looked at me.

"Should we start CPR?"

"There is no point. I can't correct what caused her arrest in the first place," I told her.

At this point, CPR would have been futile, particularly given the length of time that the girl had stopped breathing – thirty minutes or more. I turned to her mother and communicated via our translator:

"I'm so sorry, she has passed away."

The mother became hysterical and threw herself from the vehicle on to the gravel, appearing to have passed out. I held the little girl in my arms. Her mother then got to her feet and began to shout at me:

"I told you she wasn't right!"

I tried to explain that I agreed with her, that I had done everything I could to try and save her daughter.

Christine took the mother to one side to sit in the shade and the translator fetched her some water while Christine showed me the way to the morgue tent as I carried the toddler. I looked down at her impassive face and the extreme severity of her malnutrition became even more apparent. She had sores in her mouth and it was clear her teeth had not been developing properly. Her skin was covered in small lesions, as if someone had taken a hole punch to her. The malnutrition had compromised the integrity of her skin and it had started to break down. She weighed almost nothing in my arms, like a doll. I realized then that I had been fighting a losing battle all along.

After I placed the child in the morgue, we supported her mother while she sat with her daughter, then I rushed back to the vehicle to check on the other child. She was only three weeks old and had a fever of 40°C. She was still OK, but her intravenous line had stopped working because it was blocked with a blood clot and no fluid was getting through. I was able to salvage the line, remove the clot and get the fluid running again. Christine and I then sent the vehicle to take her to the other hospital. This little girl arrived safely and was admitted.

It was extremely hard to lose a patient on my first day at the treatment facility. I had not looked after patients with cholera before, but looking after a child so severely malnourished, and with cholera, was always going to be a challenge – particularly in a setting with limited resources. I questioned if I had done everything I could, but I was not sure what else I could have done under the circumstances. Even so, as a doctor you never stop feeling responsible; you always ask yourself, *Could I have done something more?*

SAVED

The next day I had just completed my morning ward round when I was called to an empty area of one of the adult wards. A young woman, just eighteen years old, had arrived in pre-term labour. Even though we were a cholera treatment facility, many people came to our triage area with other complaints and infections, simply because we were nearby and they thought we might have other treatments. We were only set up for treating cholera; we did have a few other supplies but they weren't sufficient to sustain patients for long – just enough to treat them at triage before transporting them elsewhere.

This young mother had arrived and was thought to have malaria, but before we could transfer her she went into labour. Her labour progressed rapidly and it would not have been safe to try to transfer her across the city to another facility. In due course, my colleague Annie delivered the baby girl and passed her to me to check. Although we estimated that she was thirty-three or thirty-four weeks' gestation (six to seven weeks premature), she was a good size and let us all know she had arrived with a loud cry. Following the delivery we were able to transfer the mother and child to another facility. They were both discharged later that evening.

The next day, however, the mother was back at the treatment centre, brought in by family members, and this time it appeared that she did have symptoms of cholera. She was admitted and we began to treat her, but her baby wasn't with her.

"Who is looking after the baby?" I wanted to know. "Who is feeding her?"

Despite my questions, I got no clear answers, so I told the family members:

"Please bring the baby in so I can check she is OK."

They agreed, but didn't return with the child until a day and a half later.

Since the mother was with us at the treatment centre, my main concern was how her baby was being fed. Formula milk was very expensive, but if it was being used, how clean was the water it was being mixed with?

When the baby finally came in she was like a floppy rag doll. It seemed that she hadn't been fed at all, and it had now been forty-eight hours since her mother was admitted. She was wearing the same nappy we had discharged her in and it was bone dry. I rushed her to the paediatric tent and put in an intravenous line to give her some fluid. At the same time, given our difficulties with controlling how quickly fluid went through the lines, I also put in a nasogastric tube, as she was too floppy to feed at this point. We created the right strength sugar solution for such a young infant and ran the fluid as slowly as we could. We also gave her a formula feed down the nasogastric tube.

That night, after the traumatic events of the first day, I prayed that this little girl would do well. I arrived the following morning to find a little bundle all wrapped in blankets lying on top of an adult-sized cholera cot. Both her hands were behind her head and her eyes were wide open. She looked up at me as if to say,

"What was all the fuss about?"

We stopped her intravenous fluids and were able to give her expressed breast milk from her mother down the nasogastric tube. Soon after, her mother joined her on the paediatric ward and the baby was alert enough to start breastfeeding, which she did surprisingly well. Some time later, her father appeared and came to thank me for treating his daughter.

"She doesn't have a name yet," he informed me. "You should name her."

"You should call her Grace," I told him, "because it's truly by the grace of God that she is alive."

A couple of days later, when her mother had fully

recovered from her cholera infection, the little girl went home with her family.

NOW, BUT NOT YET

It was a strange situation to be in – losing a child one day and seeing another born the next. I can't pretend to understand why one child survived and the other didn't. I don't believe it is ever our Father's will for these little ones to die. But we live in a fallen world, and sickness and death are part of that.

It has been said that we live in the "now and not yet" of God's kingdom. In other words, God's kingdom is breaking out on the earth and being established, and at times we see it penetrating the darkness with breakthroughs and miracles. But at other times, we don't see the miracles we hope and pray for. I believe that the more we see God's kingdom advance on the earth, the more we will see heaven released and miracles abounding. But until Jesus comes and restores the fullness of his kingdom, death will remain a part of life.

I am learning that I must simply be where he has called me to be, allowing Jesus to work through my life as he sees fit, as I do my best to provide medical care for others. Sometimes I may be privileged to see an outstanding miracle as the supernatural combines with the natural; at other times I won't, and I have to accept that. It doesn't mean that

I should stop expecting the miraculous or stop praying for all those who cross my path.

I've been inspired and learned much from Heidi Baker's books, especially about Heidi's desire to "stop for the one". In a chaotic world, where there seems to be one catastrophe after another, and there is so much need, it is easy to become overwhelmed. Where does one begin? How can we help everyone who is in need?

The simple answer is that you and I can't. But we can help the one person that God puts in front of us. Loneliness has become the plague of this technology-driven generation. We don't have to leave the house in order to have "friends", and yet we can feel invisible to the world around us. God has called us to love those in front of us, to reach out to them. We can't solve all of the world's problems in one go, but we can show Jesus' love to one person at a time. When I feel overwhelmed by all the need in front of me, I look for the ones that God has called me to stop for; the people he has asked me to serve. Jesus is calling us to be his hands and feet to this generation, and he will place in our path the ones he wants us to minister to. We just need to make sure we are listening for his voice, and responding to the gentle nudges of the Holy Spirit.

CHAPTER 10

EVERY LIFE MATTERS

During my third year of higher specialty training in medicine I began to get itchy feet. I was impatient for new opportunities – to see all I'd learned so far come together, perhaps in a new direction. After praying, it seemed the right time to get some research experience. This would certainly be essential for the next stage of my career, and I was keen to do something on paediatric infectious diseases. For the last six years I had heard God speak very clearly to me about what he had for my future. I felt that now was the right time for it to come to fruition.

However, there were some obstacles to overcome. Even though I sensed spiritually that the time was right, the doors didn't seem to be opening. I continued to pray, frequently telling God, "Father, I'm ready!" but then I seemed to carry on plodding through my training as I had done for the last few years. Looking back, I realize now that God was using that time to prepare me for what lay ahead. At the time it felt like I was standing still, not progressing. In fact, God was busy laying essential foundations. As the author Graham Cooke once said, "God is not holding you back, he's holding you in."

When I first began applying for research posts, not only did I not have any previous research experience, but I didn't know how to approach the applications. I think my first two applications were car crashes and, unsurprisingly, I was rejected. I managed to get an interview for a third post, but following the interview I wasn't successful. After that, I didn't know what to do any more. I wondered if I should still be pushing this door. *Maybe the time isn't right after all?* I thought. Just as I was about to lay the idea down, God confirmed to me that it was right to keep trying.

"OK Lord," I prayed, "it's in your hands."

A few days later I received an email about a one-year research fellowship for projects in global health at Imperial College London. Applicants were invited to submit plans for a specific project, which then may or may not be accepted for funding. I wanted to study paediatric infectious diseases – an area I was very interested in – and specifically tropical diseases or global health. There was one drawback to applying, however. It specified that I would need a supervisor based at Imperial College, and also an overseas supervisor. I didn't have either of those.

I could have written off the opportunity there and then, but by this time I'd decided that if God was in it, then he would make a way. If not, then he would close the door. I contacted the person named in the email and was told that I should submit an expression of interest anyway, even though I didn't fulfil all the criteria. To cut a long story short, God intervened in a miraculous way, opening doors I could never have opened myself. In the weeks that followed I suddenly found myself with a well-respected supervisor based at Imperial College, and another in The Gambia, as well as the makings of a research project looking at the causes of fever in children in The Gambia, examining different ways of identifying the viruses or bacteria involved. I submitted my application, went for an interview, and was then offered the necessary funding.

I find it amazing that, often in life, God will get our attention by slowing us down and taking us through a season of preparation – perhaps allowing our frustration to shape our character. Then, after a time of waiting, as we become willing to place matters in his hands and trust him, he opens up the new horizon we've been longing for. In the space of two months God had engineered the most unlikely of circumstances. Each apparent impossibility became possible. Every hurdle that cropped up, he knocked down, allowing me a clear path. Such was God's favour that I knew without a doubt that this was his will. The post at Imperial College was his gift to me.

I'm still astonished as I look back on this time. Even though I'd had a few adventures up to this point, it was the beginning of the craziest years of my life. But it was also the start of knowing that I was coming into the calling God had placed on my life. After years of standing still, God had finally opened the door – and when he did, it wasn't as if he gently opened it and guided me through; it was more like he kicked the door down and shoved me through it! I found myself in a completely new environment with the most incredible opportunity in front of me. God has continued to place opportunities in front of me that blow my mind. The Gambia was an exciting beginning, but I could never have imagined what would unfold in the coming years.

I started working at Imperial College at the beginning of September 2012 and travelled out to The Gambia in the November. The research project I was doing fascinated me and gave me essential training in conducting research in low-income settings using lab-based techniques – both of which have been key to me in developing the PhD I am currently working on.

I would spend some of my time in The Gambia working at the Edward Francis Small Teaching Hospital in Banjul, the capital city. The government-run hospital was not well-resourced, although its paediatric unit was quite heavily supported by the Medical Research Council, a British institution with a research facility in The Gambia. Even so, the care it could provide was very limited.

During my first six weeks there I spent time in the neonatal unit, which cared for newborn babies and those within the first month of life. It was a challenging environment to work in because the mortality rate was very high. An audit carried out at the time placed it at around 40 per cent. Some children died simply because they'd been born prematurely and there were no facilities to help them breathe. In fact, there were no ventilators in The Gambia, other than those for use during surgery. Other children died because they were born with congenital abnormalities and the expertise did not exist to operate on them. Still others died of infection, as the level of hygiene was poor – in part due to overcrowding, with sometimes three babies to one overhead heater or two to an incubator. That there was often no running water in the unit didn't help with hygiene matters either. It was frequently difficult to work there.

I worked closely with a UK colleague called Helen. We felt as if we were continually firefighting – running from one child to another, all of them in a desperate condition – never properly getting the chance to ensure normal day-to-day management disciplines were in place. We would often arrive on the unit to find a baby who had just stopped breathing, and would then fight to try and resuscitate them – sometimes successfully, sometimes not.

Children were often brought over from the labour ward in a poor condition. The labour ward was located across a busy road, in a different building to the neonatal unit, and there were no staff assigned the job of bringing the babies over. It was a relative's responsibility to bring them in if they were unwell. When babies were delivered the mother was generally the main priority. If her baby was unwell, he or she was simply put to one side until a relative could carry them across to the neonatal unit. By this time the child was often cold and struggling to breathe.

It was heartbreaking to see many children pass away. But then there were the ones who survived, in large part simply because Helen or I were there, looking out for them. I didn't do anything special; I was just in the right place at the right time, with the right skill set. Words can't describe what it is like to know that you are exactly where God wants you at a particular moment, and that God has used you to ensure a child is alive today who otherwise wouldn't have been. Amidst the tears and joy, two children stand out as miracles.

FATOU

Fatou arrived on the ward one day, brought in by her grandmother. During her birth she had been starved of oxygen. It's likely she had hypoxic-ischaemic encephalopathy, and she had constant seizures. This meant that she would periodically stop breathing. Her grandmother looked at me and asked,

"Will she be all right, Doctor?"

"I will do the best I can," I told her, "but I have to let you know that she might not survive; she is very poorly."

When I had an opportunity, I placed my hand on Fatou's head and prayed.

"Father God, I commit little Fatou into your hands. I pray that you would heal her, in Jesus' name."

I didn't think much more about it as I moved on to the next patient. The following day I was busy again and didn't see her. In fact, I didn't see her again for over a week as I was out of the unit a lot of the time developing my research study. Because I hadn't seen her, I assumed that, sadly, she must have passed away.

Around this time we were moving into a new neonatal unit which was more spacious and had new incubators and cots. One day I was caring for another child when I saw a lady I recognized picking up one of the children. I realized that it was Fatou's grandmother – and there was Fatou, looking perfectly well. I hadn't recognized her because she was now dressed and in a cot. Her seizures had stopped and she had begun to breastfeed normally. She was going home that day.

This is not what was expected from a baby with hypoxic-ischaemic encephalopathy and severe seizures, with no proper treatment available. It was a miracle.

"Thank you, Lord. You're so good," I prayed.

OUSMAN

Ousman was rushed over to the neonatal unit from the labour ward by his father. His dad had spent time living in the UK and was well educated. Consequently he had acted quickly to get his son treated.

"Doctor, please help my son," he said.

I looked at Ousman and saw that he was blue and gasping for breath. He was also covered in meconium – the thick, tar-like substance that is the first poo a baby passes when they are born. Sometimes when babies are distressed in the womb they may pass meconium, and there is a risk that they may swallow or inhale it as they are born. If they inhale it, it can block their airway, or cause a severe inflammatory process if it goes far enough down into the lungs. Many of these babies need help with their breathing, sometimes requiring a ventilator. I could see that Ousman's chest was uneven, as if one side was overinflated and the other wasn't inflating properly. It wasn't possible to get an X-ray, so using a light I checked to make sure he didn't have a pneumothorax (air in between the lung and its lining, preventing the lung from inflating properly). It didn't look as if there was, and listening to his chest I could hear air entering both lungs. His chest, however, remained very uneven.

His father looked on anxiously as I did what I could for Ousman, which was to place him on a trickle of oxygen from the only oxygen concentrator in the room, put an intravenous line in and give him antibiotics and fluid. He couldn't be breastfed in his current condition. That was all I could do for him medically, and even with the oxygen he remained blue and gasping.

"Lord, what now?" I prayed inwardly.

At this point, there was nothing more I could do. I was more or less resigned to the fact that he wouldn't make it through the night. I placed my hand on his tiny chest and prayed.

"Ousman, I speak health and life over you – life in all its fullness, in the name of Jesus."

That was it. In all honesty, I wasn't sure if my prayer would achieve anything, but it was all I had. Sometimes our faith is miniscule, and yet Jesus speaks about using faith the size of a mustard seed. I'm not sure my faith matched up to even that at this point.

Then it was evening and time to take our transport back to our accommodation, so I left for the day, leaving the matter in God's hands.

The following day I arrived and was presented with another child who wasn't doing very well, so I was preoccupied with caring for them. I didn't really expect Ousman to have survived to see the morning. Then I saw his father approaching me.

"Doctor," he said, "can I take my son home today?"

I gave him a strange look. I wanted to say, "Take him home? I can't believe he has made it through the night!" Instead I shook my head and informed him politely,

"I'm sorry, Ousman won't be able to go home until he no longer needs the oxygen and is able to breastfeed properly."

He looked at me, puzzled.

"But, Doctor, he is not on oxygen anymore and he has just had a breastfeed!"

He gestured towards his wife and son. I followed his gaze and realized that I had walked right past Ousman and his mother not half an hour ago, but hadn't recognized the normal-looking baby lying peacefully in his cot. I went over and saw that Ousman was breathing normally and was no longer blue. Neither was his chest uneven, with his lopsided breathing. He lay there staring up at me. Ousman showed me that he could breastfeed normally all that day, so the following day he was discharged home with his parents.

Medically speaking, I can't explain how this was possible. Ousman did not recover because of any medical intervention I performed. The only conclusion I can come to is that God intervened. It was a miracle. I often wonder what purpose the Lord has for Ousman's life, because he certainly had his hand upon him.

A TRAGIC INVESTIGATION

Towards the end of my time in The Gambia, an incident occurred at the hospital which shocked us all. Since my study was based more in older children than newborn infants, I'd spent the last couple of months largely based at the Medical Research Council or sometimes on the children's ward or in the emergency/outpatient department. One day I arrived at the hospital quite late because the local police were searching all vehicles arriving in Banjul that morning, and it had caused traffic delays of nearly two hours.

On arrival I walked into the children's emergency room, which was really just a room with some beds where we could examine patients, and saw a young girl lying on one of them. She wasn't moving, but was connected to the oxygen concentrator and receiving oxygen through nasal prongs.

The doctors were sitting solemnly at the table in the middle of the room writing notes.

"What's happening here?" I asked one of the young Gambian doctors.

The atmosphere in the room was tense and the doctors were very quiet. I'd been working with these people for several months and they would normally greet me jovially and we would talk for a bit. The doctor I'd spoken to said simply,

"She is dead."

"What happened?" I asked. "What was her condition like when she arrived?"

I was told that she had come to the outpatient clinic for a check-up, and at that point had been well. She was known to have rheumatic heart disease, but had been doing better and had come for her monthly check-up and injection of penicillin, which helped to prevent repeated infections that could worsen her heart condition.

About two minutes after one of the nurses had injected the penicillin into her thigh, her body had gone completely stiff. Within five minutes she had stopped breathing and gone into cardiac arrest. The doctors had tried to resuscitate her with CPR but it had not been successful. She was twelve years old. The girl did not have any clear features of having had an allergic reaction to the medication; she had been on penicillin for a long time and never had a reaction before. None of this made sense to me.

"Can I see the vial of medication?" I asked.

The doctor handed it to me and I examined it.

Something about it didn't seem right. I didn't recognize the manufacturer's name, but then there are many companies producing generic medication, so it could have been one I'd not encountered before. The strange thing, however, was that the company had a central London address, and pharmaceutical companies, particularly their manufacturing plants, don't tend to be based in Piccadilly. I read on and noticed that the company's email address ended *@yahoo. co.uk*. That worried me a great deal. What kind of reputable pharmaceutical company has a free Yahoo email address? A feeling of nausea crept into the pit of my stomach as the information sank in. I suspected this might be a falsified medical product, or at least a product of dubious quality.

Then I got angry. How dare someone manufacture a fake or substandard product – one that had just cost a twelve-year old girl her life – to make a quick buck! Enough children died every day in The Gambia from preventable causes, without more dying due to someone's complacency and greed.

The Gambian doctors told me that they had checked the vial, but hadn't realized anything was wrong. If medication carries a UK, European or US address, they tend to trust it more than if it comes from China or Southern Asia. Medical products from the West tend to be better regulated, but my Gambian colleagues didn't realize the lengths that the manufacturers of poor quality products will go to in order to hide where a product has been made.

"A reputable pharmaceutical company wouldn't normally have a Yahoo email address," I told them. "I am concerned this may be fake."

At this they shrugged.

"This is The Gambia," one said. "That is what happens here."

"Well, that is not OK!" I protested. "These things should not happen here. We need to try and stop this from happening again."

I was incensed by what I'd seen and heard, but at the same time I didn't know what to do about it. I knew I had to do something though, before more patients died. When I returned to the Medical Research Council that evening I spoke with a consultant colleague to see if he knew what to do. We discussed calling the phone number on the vial, but it was late, so we decided to try to call during office hours the next day. As I sat at my desk processing everything I suddenly remembered the Yellow Card reporting scheme we have in the UK for adverse medication reactions. I tapped "Yellow Card reporting" into Google and up came the website for the Medicines and Healthcare products Regulatory Agency (MHRA), which regulates medicines and healthcare devices in the UK.

As the vial had a UK address on it (I was fairly certain it wasn't actually a UK company), I wondered if it would fall under the MHRA's jurisdiction. On their website was the option for reporting falsified products. I wasn't sure if the product was definitely falsified, but as it promised a response within 24 hours, this seemed the best option. I completed the online form and submitted it. I received an email response by 8.30 a.m. the following morning and had a phone call from one of their intelligence officers before 1.00 p.m.. Their email was also copied to the medicines surveillance section of the World Health Organization and the chief pharmacist for The Gambia. The MHRA undertook a thorough investigation, which involved me shipping samples of the medication to a laboratory in the UK.

It wasn't until the head of paediatrics at the hospital went to the pharmacy where the girl's parents had bought the medication, asking them to stop selling that batch – and they refused – that I began to wonder who this investigation might impact. The fact is, there are high levels of corruption in The Gambia and ongoing human rights issues. The President has been in power for over twenty years and at the time of writing is contesting the results of a democratic election removing him from power. In recent years political opponents and human rights advocates have been imprisoned. Some have simply "disappeared". If some senior person was involved with this product or company, perhaps receiving a cut of the profits, then the investigation would provoke unwanted attention. For the next few weeks I spent a lot more time looking over my shoulder than usual when I was walking down the road. Any time a military vehicle approached I would take a quick detour off the main road.

In due course the investigation found that it was indeed

a falsified medicinal product, though it wasn't possible to identify exactly what was wrong with it. It was penicillin, but it was very poorly manufactured, and the company and its UK broker weren't licensed by the MHRA. Despite its London address, the product was being made in China – where sadly the MHRA and World Health Organization's jurisdiction ends. All they could do was inform Chinese regulators about the problem. But the MHRA made sure that the product could no longer be sold through brokers in the UK.

What was really important about this entire episode though, was for my Gambian colleagues to realize that people do care what happens in The Gambia. They didn't simply have to accept things as they were. In situations like this it was possible to act, and they were able to see others around the world trying to prevent a similar situation from occurring in the future. I was able to show them a way to report falsified products and help them to understand that people would listen to their concerns and take them seriously.

Mortality rates in The Gambia are high, particularly in children under five, so when death occurs it is often simply accepted and people move on. As I talked with local colleagues, I would constantly hear people say, "Oh, that happened to my aunty," or "That happened to one of my patients in Basse." I wondered how many people had died because of falsified or poorly manufactured medicines.

Although in The Gambia many people die from

preventable causes every day, and it can be easy to become accustomed to that as part of everyday life, it is important not to let that kind of thinking take over. Every life is valuable and every life counts – from the moment a person is born to the moment they take their last breath. We should fight for every life, no matter the nationality, culture, faith, skin colour, or gender. Every person is made in God's image and he placed them on this earth with purpose. He called them into being as much as he called you and me into being. They are valuable to him and they should be valuable to us.

We often see in media reports or posts on social media that people respond to atrocities much more passionately when they affect those they see as similar to themselves. While to some extent this is natural – people are more concerned by events they perceive are happening on their doorstep – as Christians we can never allow this to become our way of thinking. We can't shrug our shoulders and say, "What a shame that's happening to them." God created "them" and Jesus died for "them".

Every life is uniquely valuable and in God's eyes counts as much as any other. That is why I don't consider my own life to be any more valuable than anyone else's. If God commands me to run into danger to save the life of another, then I will, because we are both created in his image. I would rather risk my life, and possibly lose it, doing what I believe is right according to God's will, than remain in safety regretting my inaction. The safest place of all is when we are in God's will. As the missionary Jim Elliott famously wrote,

"He is no fool who gives what he cannot keep to gain that which he cannot lose."

At the time of this incident I had been asking God exactly why I was in The Gambia. I knew he wanted me to be there, but I felt there was something more. Then this situation happened. In the book of Esther, Mordecai the Jew approaches his cousin, Queen Esther, to ask her to intercede before the king in order to save the Jews who were due to be exterminated. It meant Esther risking her life, since she was not permitted to approach the king without his prior invitation; she needed to find favour with him in order to submit her request. Esther was afraid, but her mentor Mordecai persuaded her by saying,

"Yet who knows whether you have come to the kingdom for *such* a time as this?" Esther 4:14 (NKJV).

Sometimes we don't know why God has placed us where he has. Sometimes we think we are in a particular place for a specific reason, but God has other purposes for us. When the situation with the falsified medication occurred I could not help but recall this verse. There have been many moments since where that verse has come to me – when I have found myself in unusual or unexpected situations – and I've suddenly realized that this is why God has placed me here at this exact time. Despite the challenges or adversity such a situation might bring, it is a privilege to know that I am perfectly in his will.

CHAPTER 11

WHAT DEVASTATION LOOKS LIKE

At the beginning of November 2013, following my time in The Gambia, I was presenting the findings of my research at a conference in Austria when Typhoon Haiyan made landfall in the Philippines. It remains one of the strongest tropical storms ever to have made landfall, with winds of up to 180mph. It caused significant damage over the Visayas, and particularly to the islands of Leyte and Samar. More than 6,000 people lost their lives and hundreds of thousands were left homeless. As the storm struck the island of Leyte there followed a storm surge with waves five to ten metres high, which added greatly to the destruction and flooding.

Samaritan's Purse was one of the first aid agencies on the ground following the typhoon, known locally in the Philippines as Typhoon Yolanda. Based in the city of Tacloban, on heavily damaged Leyte island, a large scale operation was underway which included the provision of shelter, water and sanitation, and the distribution of hygiene kits and food. Samaritan's Purse also launched a medical response and developed a field hospital in the grounds of the partly destroyed Schistosomiasis Control and Research Hospital in Palo, on the outskirts of Tacloban. The medical team were based here, but the response also operated mobile medical clinics to areas cut off from access to healthcare by the damage to the region.

Within 24 hours of the news breaking, I'd had an email from Samaritan's Purse asking whether I'd be available to help. My gut instinct was that I should go, even as my head filled with all the reasons why I shouldn't: I was working as a doctor; we were currently short-staffed in my department; it would mean missing Christmas with my family and seeing my two young nephews, my brother Ben's boys... Yet I felt the gentle nudging of the Holy Spirit.

I spent some time thinking and praying about the opportunity and decided that, since Samaritan's Purse were only asking for a provisional "yes" or "no" at this stage, I could respond "yes" tentatively, making it clear that this was dependent on my being granted time off. In my heart I felt that if I said no to this opportunity now, I might never get the chance to go.

I'd already taken lots of time out from my training, however, and this trip would require a further chunk of time. That could be tricky. I would need to speak to my clinical director and seek her permission. Personally, I liked my clinical director and got along well with her, but she was known to be no pushover and my mind worked overtime. I assumed that she would be opposed to me taking time off for disaster response work and could think of all the reasons she might put forward to dissuade me from going:

"You should follow your training programme – there's no room for taking time out... you might fail your competencies. How will we cover your shifts as we are short-staffed? What's more important to your career?"

Eventually I put the matter in God's hands. I decided that if it was his will for me to go to the Philippines he would take care of my clinical director and any other obstacles that might stand in my way.

I was back at work shortly after the conference when I bumped into her in a hallway.

"Would it be possible to speak to you about something at some point?" I asked.

"Yes, sure," she said, "just make an appointment with my secretary." Then she added, "Everything's OK, right?"

"Oh yes!" I said. I think she thought it might be bad news, so I elaborated.

"It's just that I've been asked to go to the Philippines in response to the typhoon and I wanted to talk to you about it."

"OK, we'll do that," she said.

A couple of days later I happened to be in her secretary's office sorting out some paperwork. Our official meeting was later that day, but she came in to talk to her secretary and saw me.

"So, the Philippines... " she began.

"Yes," I said. I hadn't planned on bringing the issue up, since we'd be meeting "officially" in due course.

"I've been thinking about this," she told me.

Uh oh, here we go, I thought. She had caught me a little off guard, but I'd already thought about this a lot, so I had my defence prepared and was ready to list all the reasons why I believed I should be allowed to go.

"I've decided that I think you should go," she continued. "It will be a really great experience for you and I'm going to do everything in my power to make it happen."

I was speechless. *But I haven't said anything yet!* I thought. I didn't need to. God had already been working behind the scenes.

Shortly afterwards I got my approval – this time for a month of paid leave, which was remarkable. I worked a week of night shifts in the run-up to going, and as soon as I finished work on the Friday, I went straight to Heathrow and caught my plane. I may sound like a glutton for punishment, but the fact is, I'm used to this kind of travel schedule – it's the only way to do things without losing an additional day, and there is plenty of time for sleep on the plane.

I boarded a flight to Cebu just over three weeks after receiving the initial call from Samaritan's Purse. I was excited to be travelling to the Philippines and felt very strongly that it was where God wanted me to be.

COMPLETE DEVASTATION

When I arrived in Tacloban, the capital of Leyte province and the site of our medical base, I was shocked at how extreme the situation was. Parts of the city were still standing, but much of it had been utterly devastated. Most of the surviving buildings had had their roofs ripped off, or suffered damage from debris.

Whilst the high winds themselves had caused a lot of damage, the real devastation was caused by the tsunami that followed. In the resulting storm surge, huge waves took out two- to three-storey buildings. Waves crashed into the city before being sucked back out, wreaking havoc. As a result, the main causes of death were hypothermia – because people got soaked and had nowhere to shelter – followed by drowning, and finally electrocution – as electricity pylons came down and live cables were immersed in the floodwater.

In Tacloban there was a slum area right by the sea. This entire area had been flattened. The crudely constructed shanty dwellings had been washed away and everything was gone. All that remained was a tangle of splintered wood and bent corrugated tin. Amidst the flattened houses I saw several huge shipping freighters which had been wrenched from their moorings in the harbour, propelled inland, and then abandoned as the water went out. Homes were crushed and destroyed in their wake, and their residents killed in the process. In other places shipping containers were sitting at precarious angles on top of semi-destroyed houses or by the side of the road. There were cars everywhere that had been picked up and deposited elsewhere, often upside down.

As I walked around that area of town with my colleagues I was acutely aware that now, five weeks after the typhoon had made landfall, many people were still missing, buried under the rubble. So many people died there. No one knows exactly how many because this was a slum, and no one knew how many people lived there in the first place. Although reports estimate that around 6,000 people died, it is suspected that the real figure was nearer 10,000. There were large numbers of casualties in this part of town. Entire families and huge sections of the community were lost, commemorated at the time by a simple handmade sign that read, "Welcome to Yolanda village".

Further inland the storm had not been as bad, but it had still caused many difficulties due to trees that had come down and were blocking roads. People were finding it hard to move around – and that meant they weren't getting medical attention when they needed it. They were also beginning to run out of food as crops were destroyed and rice paddies washed away.

A RESILIENT PEOPLE

How the Filipino people responded to this disaster was notable for a number of reasons. Often when disaster strikes a part of the world and aid teams scramble in response it is normal to arrive and find that nothing has been done. There will usually be chaos; the local government may not know what to do, and everything will have fallen apart. Any outside response will have to start with the basics and go from there. Often international military or disaster response personnel will need to come in and perform tasks such as road-clearing.

When I arrived in the Philippines, however, this had already been done. The Filipino military responded very quickly and had soon cleared all the major arterial routes so that aid could be delivered to the worst-hit areas. As a result, aid reached people much more quickly than it would have normally – especially in the larger towns such as Tacloban – and that meant lives were saved which otherwise would have been lost.

The local government were proactive and hands-on. One day we watched a team of men install pylons and re-wire a street that was without power. In a single day they restored power to that particular street so it was up and running again. Having worked in many situations in other disasters, I found this incredible. The people's strong and coordinated response was unique.

Even without the military, I noticed that local people were highly motivated to get back on their feet and get things working again. They never had a woe-is-me attitude; they simply picked themselves up and did their best to sort things out. They were grateful and accepting of aid too, but at the same time more than willing to do what they could themselves.

I joined an incredible Samaritan's Purse team, which was a mixture of international and local Filipino staff. As part of the medical team we spent much time working at the field hospital seeing patients in an outpatient/emergency room-style setting, but with the option to admit people to the local hospital if needed. We also travelled to rural areas to undertake mobile medical clinics. Many of these regions had been cut off from access to healthcare due to the extensive damage to infrastructure. A month had now passed since the typhoon, and there were many people with chronic medical conditions who had run out of their routine prescription medication, as well as those with infections that had gone untreated.

Taking a mobile clinic to a rural location made for some tricky, and at times dangerous, navigation. On our way out of the city it was shocking to see the vast amounts of debris that had been cleared to the sides of the main roads and there was a stench of dead bodies in the air, from those still buried in the rubble. As the roads grew smaller, despite the amazing work the military had done, fallen trees and rubble still blocked what were in some cases essentially dirt tracks leading to villages. Many of the palm trees on the island had been snapped in half like match sticks and those that hadn't had been moulded by the wind so their branches pointed in the opposite direction to which the wind had come, somehow frozen in time from the day of the typhoon. Anywhere you went on the island you could tell which direction the storm had come from just by looking at the palms.

One community we needed to reach in the hills was particularly difficult to access. The track had been partly washed away and a large electricity pylon had come down. We couldn't get around it because of the poor quality of the road, so we had to drive carefully underneath it, avoiding the cables. We didn't have 4x4s to get around in either, just little minivans, and to reach this village we almost got stuck on several occasions.

We saw a lot of severe skin infections, diarrhoeal illnesses and chest infections in the children. In the adults we saw mostly chronic medical conditions – patients with severely high blood pressure, heart disease and gastrointestinal problems. We also saw some cases of advanced cancer where, even prior to the typhoon, treatment had been inaccessible. Severe acute malnutrition was not that common in children in the urban areas of Leyte island, but here in the more rural areas it was more of an issue. We also saw some patients with acute stress reactions secondary to the trauma of the typhoon. The clinics were busy, whether at the field hospital or mobile medical clinics, and it wasn't uncommon for each of us to see thirty to forty patients per morning in the field hospital and a further thirty patients at an afternoon mobile medical clinic.

Yet the Filipino people we worked with were incredible. Many had themselves lost family members, friends, and work colleagues in the typhoon. Even more had either lost their homes or were living in heavily damaged buildings that were barely holding together, never mind serviceable.

Diorie and Jhai were two translators who made a great impression on me. Both had suffered their homes being partly destroyed and were living under makeshift tarpaulin shelters. Yet, despite their atrocious living conditions, they somehow arrived at work each day in clean clothes, having washed. Plus, they were on time, in spite of the complexities of travel at that time, with so much infrastructure having been changed or simply not functioning. Most amazing of all was the fact that they always had smiles on their faces and never murmured a word of complaint. In fact, they expressed their thanks for having a job. Both were teachers at an English speaking school which had been closed until further notice. They were glad to be employed temporarily by Samaritan's Purse during the aid efforts. What resilient people!

The same can be said of the Filipino people as a whole. I have never encountered such gracious, grateful people. It is surprising how frequently in disaster response situations aid agencies are criticized by the people, communities, or local government they are trying to help. The Filipino people were the opposite; gratitude abounded. Everywhere we went locals had erected makeshift cardboard signs saying, "Thank you for your help!" or "Thank you for standing with us."

BACK TO "NORMAL"?

After a month in the Philippines it was time to return to Cardiff and my regular job. After such an experience it is difficult to return to everyday life in the high-income West. The ordinary can seem overwhelming after living amidst poverty and devastation.

People have written about the phenomenon of reverse culture shock and the difficulties associated with returning to regular, day-to-day routine. When I got back from Haiti I experienced something of this shock. I had always assumed that such difficulties only happened to people who had been in a disaster zone or aid response for six months or longer – not a couple of weeks. But when I got back to my apartment, feeling jet-lagged and tired, and looked out of my window over Cardiff, it suddenly hit me.

During the Haiti cholera response I had lived in a dormitory with no air conditioning, and it was always really hot. The only thing that kept me cool were the large fans that whirred constantly and made a lot of noise. I stood staring out of my window in Cardiff and had a moment of panic.

It's so quiet in here! Why is it so quiet? Something's not right…

I suddenly felt like I didn't belong here anymore. I had completely changed, but everything around me had stayed the same. Suddenly, I wasn't sure who I was in Cardiff, in my job. It's hard to describe this feeling, other than to say it was as if I didn't belong in my life any more. For the next couple of weeks I fought off the desire to return to Haiti simply because I thought I knew who I was there. Time passed and I got back into the flow of things. I occupied or distracted myself and gradually began to adjust. I realized then that this feeling never completely goes away, because each time I have been changed by my experiences and am never quite the same as I was before.

I was more prepared for this feeling when I returned from the Philippines, knowing that I was likely to experience it again. I had missed Christmas and returned home on 4 January. Before the trip I had put up my small Christmas tree so that I could enjoy it for a while before I left. Returning to my apartment I found that my church family had been in and left lots of gifts around the tree. There was also a massive bunch of flowers on the table and a card that read, "Welcome home. We're really proud of you!" That was lovely and it meant a great deal.

The next day I was straight back into work and busy again. Because my clinical director had sanctioned the trip and encouraged me to go, she wanted to hear all about it, so a few weeks later I gave a presentation to my department. I also continued to be in touch with many of my Samaritan's Purse colleagues, and so kept up to date with the situation in the country.

By the time I left the Philippines we were close to having addressed the medical crisis and things were getting up and running again. It felt like a good time to leave, and that helped. Leaving with the knowledge that the people were OK was good. If you leave when the situation is still bad, or getting worse, you leave with feelings of guilt.

I tried to imagine what it must be like to leave your house one day and discover that the place you have always lived, the city you called home, no longer exists. How disorienting must it be to no longer recognize your home, your street, the familiar landmarks? Now there is only rubble where you used to buy your groceries, or where you took your children to school. I tried to imagine how I would feel if one day I walked out of my front door and most of Cardiff, or London, didn't exist anymore. How would I feel? How confused and lost would I be that everything physical that had made this place "home" was now gone or devastated? And all in the space of a few hours one morning.

Experiences such as these remind me of the frailty of life. How flimsy are the things that we tend to hold on to on this earth. When they are taken away, we realize what really matters – not the physical or material things we surround ourselves with, but the people we love and want to hold on to; the dreams of the future that we hold in our hearts. Surely this is why Jesus taught us to store up treasure in heaven, not on earth (Matthew 6:19).

CHAPTER 12

I ALWAYS KNEW I WAS SUPPOSED TO DO SOMETHING ABOUT EBOLA

It was March 2014 when I first became aware of cases of Ebola being reported from Guinea in West Africa. Later, media channels across the world would be filled with disturbing images as the virus spread, rapidly developing into the deadliest outbreak since its discovery in the mid-seventies. Initially, however, it didn't receive much press coverage. I was able to follow some brief updates on the World Health Organization's website and I discovered that Médecins Sans Frontières (Doctors Without Borders) had set up a treatment facility in the area of Guéckédou, in the eastern part of Guinea, near the borders of Liberia and Sierra Leone.

THE SPREAD OF A VIRUS

At this point there were only a few cases and these were limited to a rural, forested area of Guinea. But in just a matter of weeks, cases of Ebola had reached Guinea's capital city, Conakry. All previous Ebola outbreaks had been limited to similar, rural areas in central or eastern Africa – this was the first time an epidemic had broken out in West Africa. Critically, it was also the first time Ebola had touched a major city.

Cities are ideal locations for the spread of infectious diseases. The higher population density gives the disease a far greater chance of spreading quickly. Writing in *The Guardian* in February 2014, Sarah Boseley commented:

> *From bubonic plague in the middle ages to bird flu or Sars in the 21st century, infectious diseases have spread horrifyingly fast in cities, where people live in close proximity and sometimes crowded together… citydwellers simply cannot guard their own health independently of their neighbours.*[5]

Major cities are also travel hubs, like Conakry, which has an international airport. Because the incubation period (the time from becoming infected to showing symptoms) for Ebola can be up to twenty-one days, infected people could easily have boarded flights to other places before they realized they were infected.

5   https://www.theguardian.com/cities/2014/feb/26/sick-cities-pandemics-spread-metropolis

The fact that Ebola had reached Conakry so quickly grabbed my attention and I couldn't understand why the World Health Organization (WHO) continued to play down the news, saying that they expected it to burn out, just as other Ebola epidemics had. I felt an urgency about it in my spirit. Perhaps it was the Holy Spirit nudging me? Or perhaps I wasn't well enough informed, never having dealt directly with an Ebola epidemic before. Nevertheless, I was very concerned.

Over the next few weeks I heard that cases had now been reported in Liberia. This was also significant – no Ebola epidemic had ever spread across a border into another nation before. Still WHO stated that the epidemic would run its course. Next, a couple of cases were reported in Monrovia, the Liberian capital. These were from people who had travelled there from Guinea. So in the space of about a month the Ebola epidemic in Guinea had crossed an international border, reached two capital cities – whose airports had international flights that connected across the world – and the international community remained unconcerned. At this time there were also cases in the eastern part of Sierra Leone, but this information was not yet publicly available.

At the beginning of April, after cases of Ebola had occurred in the north of Liberia, Samaritan's Purse started considering a medical response. Once again I received an email enquiring about my availability to respond, and without hesitation I replied that I would be willing to go.

However, at this time the number of cases in both Liberia and Guinea seemed to have subsided and, for a period of a few weeks, no new cases were reported. Perhaps WHO had been correct – maybe the epidemic was indeed burning itself out?

Sadly that was not the case. Ebola was smouldering in rural areas where surveillance was lacking. In addition, these cases eluded detection for some time, simply because people were afraid to admit that they might be sick with the symptoms of Ebola, so they didn't initially seek medical attention.

By May cases had surged again in Guinea and northern Liberia and there was now another cluster of cases in Monrovia. These people had become infected while attending a funeral in Sierra Leone, where it was now clear there were also cases.

Initially, Samaritan's Purse decided against sending a full medical team, since the case numbers were down, but they supported three doctors at the mission hospital – Dr Debbie Eisenhut and Dr John Fankhauser, working with SIM, and Dr Kent Brantly, working with Samaritan's Purse World Medical Mission – in opening a small Ebola treatment facility in the grounds of the Eternal Love Winning Africa (ELWA) mission hospital, just outside Monrovia.[6] At the time there was no other treatment facility in Monrovia as the Ministry of Health had decided to close the treatment

---

6   SIM used to refer to Sudan Inland Mission when it originally started over 100 years ago. It now has a much wider remit and is referred to as Serving in Mission.

facility based at the John F. Kennedy Medical Center when the case numbers fell.

Acutely aware that if a case presented to the emergency room at ELWA there was nowhere to send patients to isolate them from other patients, as well as protecting the healthcare professionals looking after them, Dr Debbie Eisenhut obtained permission from the ELWA medical director, Dr Jerry Brown, to convert the chapel at the mission hospital into an Ebola treatment facility, which in time became known as ELWA1.

I continued to follow the epidemic online as best I could during this time. In April, when I had received the original email, I had spoken with my clinical director and raised the possibility that I might be asked to go at some point. After that I didn't hear much more until the beginning of July, when I was invited to travel to Monrovia to work at ELWA1.

I didn't hesitate to volunteer and sought approval from work. I knew it was where God wanted me to be and though this may sound crazy to many, for me it was simple: if I didn't volunteer, along with the many others who already had and would in coming months, then this epidemic was going to be completely out of control before the world woke up to it. I couldn't sit there knowing what was developing, and the level of suffering involved, and not act. It was also an opportunity to work with a disease that most doctors only get to read about in their careers.

Eleven days later, on 14 July 2014, I was on a flight to Monrovia. I knew the risk that I was taking – that if I contracted Ebola I would die a painful, lonely death in Liberia. Plus, I had no actual experience of managing the disease, or of using personal protective equipment. I would learn on the ground, trained by Dr Kent Brantly, Dr John Fankhauser and Dr Debbie Eisenhut, who had been working in Liberia long before Ebola ever arrived. They had set up ELWA1 and now Ebola was on their doorstep. Despite all the risks involved, however, I knew this was what God had planned for me all along. Let me explain…

THE HOT ZONE

I had known for a long time that fighting Ebola was what I was meant to do. God had spoken to me at various times about my life, and, in essence, I'd known since I was fourteen that one day I would work to combat this deadly virus. I realize that might sound strange – especially since I wasn't a Christian when I was a teenager – and what teenager has heard of such a rare disease?

It began when I was twelve and my brother Ben bought a book called *The Hot Zone* by Richard Preston. We were both avid readers at the time, so I was interested.

"What's that you're reading?'

"Oh, it's about the outbreak of a disease called Ebola," Ben said.

I looked at the cover, which carried the subtitle: The Chilling True Story of an Ebola Outbreak. A back cover quote from the author Stephen King said, "The first chapter of *The Hot Zone* is one of the most horrifying things I've read in my whole life – and then it gets worse."

"Can I read it after you?" I asked.

"Sure."

When Ben finished reading the book, I grabbed it and read some of it. I didn't finish the whole book, because it was pretty heavy going for a twelve-year old, but I read enough to learn about this horrific disease that would intermittently spring up in rural Africa, causing people to bleed to death. I was both fascinated and horrified that there was a disease that could do this.

This was around the same time that I heard my mother talking about changing the world. From that time onwards I started to consider spending my life doing some kind of humanitarian work, though at that point I had no idea what that might look like, or in what capacity I would do it. Having read *The Hot Zone*, however, I couldn't get out of my mind the thought that one day I would come across the Ebola virus and be challenged to do something about it.

A year or so later the film *Outbreak* was released, starring Dustin Hoffman as an investigative virologist. The film was loosely based on *The Hot Zone* and was about a disease similar to Ebola – although in the movie it was called something else and the virus was airborne; Ebola is not transmitted in this manner. The feeling hit me again: one day I am going to work with a disease like this. It was odd, because all of this was before I decided that I definitely wanted to study medicine. But that was irrelevant – in the mind of a teenager all things are possible.

Looking back, I also believe that God was at work in me. Despite the fact that I had not yet acknowledged his presence in my life, he was sowing seeds in my young mind regarding his future plans for me. I didn't give Ebola much more thought after this, but the information was filed away in the back of my mind and it was an issue that held a fascination for me whenever it cropped up. By the age of fourteen I had decided I definitely wanted to be involved in medicine, since this would be one of the best, most sustainable ways in which I could help deliver humanitarian aid. I then became focused on making that happen.

Once I started medical school I had the opportunity to learn more about viruses like Ebola, but we didn't study them during our early years. Ebola and the family of viruses it comes from do not occur in the UK. Occasionally there were imported cases of other similar viruses in travellers infected overseas, but there had only been one case of Ebola treated in the UK prior to this epidemic, that of a laboratory worker who accidentally infected themselves in a lab setting over three decades ago. As I learned about physiology though, I became more fascinated: what was it that viruses like Ebola did that caused people to haemorrhage? Why did these viruses have such high mortality rates? It didn't make sense to me. Surely the goal of a virus is to spread so it can replicate itself and "live"? It can't do this without an animal or human host, so why would it want to kill its host so quickly? Wasn't that counterproductive to its own survival? Thoughts like these whirred around my mind and my curiosity never abated.

After I had given my life to Jesus, especially during the first few months of being a Christian, I talked to God a lot about his purposes for me, and whether I was following his plan for my life. Once I knew for sure that God wanted me to continue with medical school, my discussions with him turned to the issue of humanitarian aid, and again he confirmed that this was the right path for me to take. One day, as I was sitting praying, he made it specific.

"Nathalie, one day you will work with the Ebola virus."

It was the confirmation of all the thoughts, feelings and gut instincts I'd held on to for a long time. I still had no idea in what capacity it might be, or how it could come about, but now I knew for sure.

The average UK-trained physician will not generally get the opportunity to work with a disease such as Ebola. The outbreaks that occur in rural Africa tend to be dealt with by people specially trained to handle such situations. Even working with such diseases in a laboratory or research setting is difficult for two main reasons. First, rigorous and sophisticated safety facilities and procedures have to be in place to prevent research workers from becoming infected – and only a handful of such laboratories exist around the world. But, second, viruses like Ebola are considered to be potential biowarfare or bioterrorism pathogens, and as such are classified in different ways by different countries in order to prevent easy access for research purposes. Based on this, when I heard God telling me that one day I would work with the Ebola virus, in my limited understanding I assumed it would happen some time towards the end of my career, perhaps as a senior researcher in a lab setting. Never for a moment did I imagine I'd find myself at the forefront of the fight against the biggest Ebola epidemic in history. But then, God does have a sense of humour.

Zechariah 4:10 (NIV) says, "Who dares despise the day of small things?" This is the word brought by the prophet Zechariah to the Israelites taken captive by Babylon. It was an encouragement to them, particularly to Zerubbabel, to lead the rebuilding of the temple in Jerusalem. God has a plan for all our lives and that plan has been in existence since we were created. Even though we may not know God, he already knows us and the plan he has for us. That plan doesn't necessarily start when we become a Christian; we just become aware of it then, and it takes on new meaning. We should not "despise the day of small things" because it is in those beginnings that God sows his seed and waters it in our lives; this is when his plan becomes our heart's desire.

These are the days when he prepares us for what is ahead, even when our view may be obstructed and our vision limited. He always reveals what we need to know at the right time. If I had known what lay ahead of me in Liberia, and in the years that followed, when I boarded that plane to Liberia on 14 July, I would have been overwhelmed. Not only that, I'm not sure I would have believed I was capable of doing all that God was asking me to do. So instead, God sowed the seed, watered it, and grew me into the person I needed to be in order to follow his plan and cope with it. He grew the desire in my heart, then opened the door for me at the right time. He remained by my side constantly through the storm, holding me up when I was certain I couldn't take any more. The truth is, he is a good, good father and we can trust him to guide our lives.

CHAPTER 13

TWO WEEKS OF HELL AND HOPE

As I boarded my flight on 14 July the reality of what I was doing finally hit me and I had to push aside a huge sense of apprehension. I spent the flight distracting myself with films and games, but intermittently wondered what it would be like to manage patients with Ebola.

I arrived late that night and the following morning I went to the small Ebola treatment unit known as ELWA1 – a unit developed in the small chapel belonging to the mission hospital with five beds and a cot space, and the only location where it was possible to create a proper isolation area. I met Dr Kent Brantly on the way and he showed me around the treatment facility and introduced me to the team. Then he had to dash off to a meeting with Dr Lance Plyler, our disaster response team leader.

The previous night had been busy. Two patients had been there for a few days, and there had been two new admissions overnight. One was a woman in her sixties whose husband had died of Ebola in the last couple of weeks, the other a woman my age who was eight months pregnant. Both had very recently died by the time I reached the facility that morning. Another patient, also a lady, died about an hour later. I observed the horrifying scene. One of the patients was surrounded by her own excrement, having collapsed in an awkward position on her bed.

I learned the personal protective equipment (PPE) and decontamination procedures that morning, and by the afternoon I was putting on PPE for the first time and entering the treatment unit with three colleagues. We had one purpose – to decontaminate three dead bodies and carry them to the morgue, then clean their bed spaces in preparation for more patients.

This was how my time working with Ebola in Liberia began. I would like to report that things got better, but they didn't. During these first two weeks almost every day was more difficult than the one before. *How could things possibly get any worse?* I constantly asked myself, and then they did. At times I thought that this must be what hell is like.

It is difficult to explain what was happening in Monrovia at that time, but it was a unique situation. Tension and fear hung over the city like a suffocating cloud. As the cases increased rapidly during those weeks, outright panic ensued. The population was divided: a large proportion didn't believe that Ebola was real. Rumours circulated that it was a government scam to gain aid money or a way for westerners to steal the organs of Liberians and sell them to other countries. The conspiracy theories were so numerous they could fill a book of their own. The other section of the population believed Ebola was real, but clear information about the disease had not reached many people, so there was little understanding. There was enough, though, for people to be very afraid of this disease that seemed to kill almost everyone who was infected with it.

Local people didn't want an Ebola treatment facility on their doorstep in Paynesville, the community that ELWA was based in. They were afraid it would help spread the infection there. As cases increased and we outgrew the ELWA1 treatment facility, Samaritan's Purse, alongside our SIM colleagues, rapidly constructed ELWA2. This treatment facility was based in the first completed building of what was to be the brand new ELWA mission hospital. The only part that was finished at the time was the laundry and kitchen facility, so that became the ELWA2 Ebola treatment unit.

About four days before we moved into ELWA2 the Ministry of Health asked if Samaritan's Purse would take over caring for all Ebola patients throughout the whole country. We were already operating a second treatment facility in Foya in the north of Liberia, near the border with Guinea, which we had taken over from Médecins Sans Frontières to enable them to focus their efforts on Sierra Leone and Guinea. We agreed to the request, but only because we were aware that at the time there was no one else willing or available to do it. We knew we didn't necessarily have the capacity, but there was no other choice and time was not on our side. The government had reopened the treatment facility at the John F. Kennedy (JFK) hospital a few weeks prior to this, when cases started to increase in Monrovia again, and they asked us to operate this facility as well as ELWA2. Concerns regarding its management led to a decision to close the JFK facility and amalgamate all patients in ELWA2 when it opened. That meant that when ELWA2 became operational, it was almost immediately over capacity.

Due to the ever-increasing numbers of patients Samaritan's Purse looked at building what later became ELWA3. We wanted to build this about 500 metres away from ELWA2, but the community would not give approval. Each day during that second week they would riot outside the ELWA compound, protesting against an Ebola treatment facility in their community. Somehow they hadn't fully realized that ELWA2 was already there. I believe this was God's protection to us at that time, enabling us to continue to work in the face of this ongoing unrest.

Kendell Kauffeldt, Samaritan's Purse Liberia Country Director, attempted to negotiate with the community and they allowed us to start preparing the land, but then the rioting recommenced and we had to stop. It was making the building of a larger facility almost impossible, unless there was military intervention to protect the construction. Tensions were increasing greatly. On the Wednesday of the second week a relative of a patient who had died of Ebola set the Ministry of Health on fire as he was angry at the government's handling of the situation. All the while, more and more cases were appearing and more and more areas were becoming infected. We seemed to be surrounded by chaos, both outside the compound and inside the treatment facility. While we were somewhat protected from the disruptions outside, and distracted from it by trying to manage a facility beginning to burst at the seams, it constantly played on my mind.

What if at some point they attack ELWA2... and us?

You have to understand the background to this situation. Liberia is a country still recovering from a horrific civil war (1999–2003), which vastly damaged its infrastructure and left people hurt and untrusting. A large proportion of the now young adult population were forcibly recruited either to the Liberian army or to militias as child soldiers. While they are now at peace, and doing normal jobs, they are shaped by their previous experience of how to deal with confrontation or disagreement. Discussion, compromise, and mediation are not tolerated for long; escalation to violence is frequent.

On Sunday 20 July we moved into the newly-completed ELWA2 facility and relocated the remaining patients from JFK there on Sunday and Monday. Two of these patients were a young man called Johnson, who was 21, and his older sister, Lorpu. They had become infected through their mother, who was a nurse. She contracted the disease whilst treating a patient in Lofa County, unaware that the patient had had contact with Ebola and might be infected. Unfortunately, this led to several more healthcare worker infections at a hospital in a different county where she presented herself for treatment. Many of those healthcare workers were now being treated in ELWA2, so there was some animosity – particularly towards Lorpu.

I never got to know Johnson very well, as he was admitted from the JFK treatment unit on the Monday afternoon and began haemorrhaging during the evening. He died in the early hours of Tuesday morning. My team informed me of his death as I arrived on site that morning. His body had not yet been moved, and I was concerned that his sister, Lorpu, might pass his cubicle on the way to the toilet and discover his body. So after our team meeting, one of our local nurses, Eleanor, and I put on PPE and entered the high risk zone. We checked on a few patients before going to Lorpu; I would have to break the news to her.

As I crouched in front of her in my protective suit, which not only muffles your voice but also hides your facial expressions, I wondered what the best way might be to tell her the news and how she would take it. I tried to convey as much emotion as I could through my eyes, the only part of me she could see.

"Lorpu, I'd like to talk to you about your brother, Johnson," I said.

"Yes," she replied.

"You know that Johnson was sick with Ebola? I am really sorry but he passed away last night."

Lorpu just stared at me with a rather puzzled expression and I didn't think she had heard me. After a pause she asked,

"What was my test result?"

My heart sank as the truth of the situation dawned on me. None of the patients from the JFK treatment unit had been told of their diagnosis. We had been informed that they had tested positive, but the patients themselves didn't know. In Liberia people believe that you shouldn't tell someone their diagnosis, because if it's bad they will be more likely to die, since they will become dispirited and give up fighting the illness. Whilst I knew this, I didn't realize it had been applied as a blanket rule to all the patients at JFK, and no one had told us about it.

I now had to break a double amount of bad news to Lorpu. I had to tell her that she too had Ebola.

"I'm really sorry Lorpu, but your test result shows that you have Ebola. Your brother, Johnson, also had Ebola and I am sorry but he died early this morning."

Lorpu's eyes widened and she begged me to tell her differently.

"No, please no! Please help me! No, no!"

There was nothing I could say, other than,

"I promise we will care for you as best we can. I promise you now that we will not leave you."

There was a belief at the time that if you were diagnosed with Ebola, no one would care for you any more – you would be abandoned and left to die. It was important Lorpu understood that we were there for her and we weren't going to leave her.

"Can I pray for you, Lorpu?" I asked.

"Yes, please do."

I asked Eleanor to pray as my Liberian English wasn't that good and sometimes people found my English hard to understand. Eleanor prayed for peace and also healing. During the coming week almost all of our patients died, but Lorpu did not. I discovered after I had left Liberia that she was one of the few patients who survived that July at ELWA2. While her survival is a testimony to God's healing power, it was bittersweet as she lost almost all of her family to Ebola.

This was an awful situation to deal with and it affected me a lot, but I didn't have time to dwell on it or process it, because there was so much to do. This became the pattern for the rest of the week, moving from one horrendous situation to the next without the time to digest what was happening. There were so many moments when I wondered what on earth was going on, as if some kind of insanity had descended. We went from admitting patients to decontaminating dead bodies on a loop. The only reason we had just about enough beds was because so many patients were dying. It didn't seem to matter what we did – and we did our best with what we had. It just wasn't enough.

The patients were presenting very late, having often had symptoms for between five and seven days before coming to the treatment facility, which meant their disease was well advanced. Several died in the suspect ward within 24 hours of admission, before we'd even had a positive test result. Some even died on arrival at triage. I would welcome patients at triage and tell them all the same thing, just like Lorpu:

"We will do our best for you. We're going to treat you and care for you. And I promise we will not leave you. But I need you to fight too, because you can beat this disease."

Even as I repeated these words, time and again, I knew that in five to seven days we would be likely to be carrying this person back out in a body bag, as if we were in some never-ending horror film – a nightmare from which we couldn't wake up. Each night, as I closed my eyes for just a few hours' sleep, I would hope for relief but instead be plagued by weird dreams. Waking early the next day, for a split second I would think this was all a bad dream, then I would realize that it wasn't and wonder what horror awaited me that day.

On 22 July, Kent, who was serving as the medical director of ELWA2, asked if I would become team leader for the remainder of my time in Liberia so that he could be freed up to handle other administrative tasks. I agreed, although I'd only had one week's experience of managing patients with Ebola and had little knowledge of how to run an Ebola treatment facility. I took comfort from the fact that Kent would still be around if I had questions or emergencies – or so I thought at the time.

A TESTING DAY

One morning I needed to enter the suspect zone to remove two patients who had tested negative. I needed the help of two of my team. Eleanor was available, but the only other person available to assist me was Paul Mungai, who was newly arrived from Kenya and had not been in before. He was working as a hygienist, cleaning up spills with chlorine and decontaminating dead bodies. I had no choice but to utilize Paul and teach him what to do as we went. We needed to be very careful, so I explained to them both that we would remove the first patient, assist her with decontaminating and escort her to the exit from the suspect ward, then repeat the process over again.

We entered the high risk zone in our PPE, carrying buckets of chlorine and soap and water. Then we got clean clothes and a towel for the first patient. We walked past the cubicle of a young man called George on our way and I looked in on him. George was sitting on his bed staring forward. He noticed me and looked up, his eyes bright red. He looked very afraid. I noticed that his gums were bleeding. He leaned over and spit blood into a bucket at the side of his bed.

"Are you OK, George?" I asked.

He nodded slightly. I couldn't go near him as I needed to remain clean and these symptoms of haemorrhage suggested it was very likely he had Ebola.

Eleanor and I got the first patient and walked her outside,

took her into a shower cubicle and washed her down, first with chlorine, then with soap and water. Then we dried her off, dressed her, and took her to the exit from the suspect ward where we handed her over to colleagues who were waiting for her on the other side. Then we needed to prepare new buckets of chlorine and soap and water and repeat the process with the next patient.

As we went back through I looked in on George again. He was still spitting blood into his bucket, but blood was now running down his chin. This time he looked confused and disoriented, his eyes glazed over. He stared at me, but when I spoke he didn't respond.

We reached the second patient's cubicle and tried not to rouse him as he was very unwell with another condition, and quite confused. As we moved him he became agitated. I gave him a dose of diazepam to stop him from becoming more aggressive, so we could get him out safely. We moved him on to a stretcher and began to manoeuvre it out of the cubicle. But there wasn't much room and this took longer than I would have liked in our sweltering suits. I felt increasingly out of breath.

We finally got the stretcher out and put it down for a brief rest. Eleanor looked at me and spoke, her voice muffled by her suit.

"Nathalie, I'm sorry, I have to leave. I'm exhausted with the heat."

This complicated things, but I asked her to carry a spray can of chlorine out while Paul and I carried the stretcher between us. We had just picked up the stretcher and begun walking when George accidentally kicked over his bucket, sending a large pool of blood and diarrhoea skidding across our path – the only route to the only exit. Eleanor and Paul looked at me.

"What do we do now?" Paul asked.

How should I know? There is no instruction manual for this! was my first thought.

I considered the options and figured we had two choices. Neither was good. If we stopped to clean up the mess we would have to put the patient down, and risk contaminating him. The alternative was to walk through a pool of infectious blood and diarrhoea and try not to touch anything else or allow anything to make contact with the patient. I was also aware that the longer we took to decide, the more chance there was that George, disoriented as he was, could come stumbling out of his cubicle and accidentally make contact with the patient.

I shouted loudly for some help to the team in the low risk zone and told Paul that we would walk through the contaminated mess. I told Eleanor that she would need to use the chlorine spray to decontaminate our feet when we reached the other side, and then we would also walk through the chlorine footbath we normally used.

George was very confused and agitated by this point. He had begun bleeding profusely from his mouth and nose. We made it past him, but he was now extremely frightened and began roaming around the suspect ward. Eleanor left to decontaminate and exit the high risk zone and I remained outside the suspect ward to wash down the patient we were trying to remove whilst he was still on his stretcher. He was trying to fight me off. Even though the diazepam had weakened him, it was still a struggle and I became increasingly hot and dizzy in my suit. After about ten minutes of this I stood back and went to squat down against a wall, desperately trying to catch my breath.

An amazing physician's assistant from the US, Allison Rolston, arrived to help and took the situation in hand, as by this time I couldn't speak. I gasped for oxygen that felt like it would never come. Eventually, through gasps, I told Allison and Paul to get the stretcher to the door which led to triage, so that other colleagues could take over, and I followed behind them. As we approached, it seemed as if Allison intended to enter the triage area, and I tried to shout, "No, stop!" to prevent her. It came out as a barely audible rasp. It was too late; Alison entered triage, contaminating the area. She and Paul had known no different, so they logically opted for the easiest method to transfer the patient. I realized later that I should have had a back-up plan in the event of a team member having to leave, like Eleanor, and being replaced by someone who didn't know the drill. I had also not accounted for how breathless and dizzy I would be from the physical exertion, limiting my ability to communicate adequately.

Once the cavalry arrived and my colleague Bev Kauffeldt – along with Médecins Sans Frontières staff Cokie van der Velde (a hygienist supporting Bev) and Dr Sarah

Temmerman – joined Allison to help her with George, I staggered to the decontamination area. I could barely stand up as I was sprayed down and I removed my suit. I was drenched with sweat and it took me a long time to recover. As I came out of decontamination, Kent arrived. Knowing nothing of the trauma I'd just endured he smiled as he greeted me.

"Hi Nathalie, how has your day been?"

I looked at him in disbelief before finally gasping,

"There are some things that women shouldn't have to do!"

Kent took me to one side and we sat underneath a tree. He got me to tell him everything that had just happened. We discussed George and decided that, even though we did not yet have a definitive diagnosis of Ebola, we would have to move him for fear of him contaminating other unconfirmed patients. Kent joined Sarah in the high risk zone and helped move George to the confirmed ward, but sadly George died the next day.

ANOTHER INCIDENT

Hardly a day passed without some sort of crisis. One day, Bev and I were standing outside the decontamination area discussing something when we heard shouting. Looking around, we saw our security guards waving and pointing to the rear exit of ELWA2, where bodies were removed from the morgue and placed in the burial trucks. Bev and I glanced at each other and dashed to see what was happening.

Bev was in front as we came around the corner, with me just behind, and she came face to face with Cecelia, a patient from the high risk zone. She was wandering around and was about to exit the zone. Both her eyes were bright red from blood under the conjunctiva and looking as if they were starting to openly bleed. I grabbed Bev's shoulder and hauled her back. Neither of us was wearing PPE.

Bev began to freak out, so I placed myself between her and Cecelia. I didn't know quite what to do, so in a slight panic I shouted at her,

"Go back inside!"

Bev was shaken by this incident. I held her shoulders and looked her in the eyes.

Cecelia looked confused, but stopped momentarily. She was right at the exit of the high risk zone. Then she began to tell me that her husband had come to pick her up to take her home to her children, who needed her.

"Cecelia, I'm sorry, but your husband isn't coming for you," I tried to explain. She looked more perplexed.

"But I must go home because my children need me and there is no one to look after them," she said.

"Your children are OK," I told her. "They are safe, but you can't leave. If you do, your children may become sick. To protect them you must stay here."

Cecelia still looked perplexed but began to back away. At that moment, Dr Sarah arrived in PPE and was able to console her, escort her back inside, and sedate her.

"It's OK. You're OK!"

She seemed to snap out of her state of shock and went to wash her face with chlorine in the decontamination area.

It was a near miss. Again I wondered if this was some kind of horror film, but it wasn't; it was real. Once again I was grateful for God's protection.

UNWELCOME NEWS

George's situation taught me a great deal. Above all I learned that often, in the midst of an extremely challenging situation, there really is no good solution – just one that is perhaps marginally better than another. It helped me to understand that people in positions of leadership sometimes have to make decisions that they don't like; they just know that the option they are choosing is slightly better than the alternatives. There is not always a straightforward solution to every problem, much as we would like there to be. Fortunately, we serve a King who does have solutions – we just need to make sure we are listening to them.

Shortly after the morning team meeting on the morning of Wednesday 23 July, Bev, who was managing the hygienists at ELWA2, received a phone call from Lance. Discreetly, she shared with me the contents of that phone call to prevent the rest of our team from hearing. Kent had developed a fever in the early hours of the morning. He had isolated himself in his house, but we now needed to go and test him for Ebola.

This was a moment we had all been dreading: hearing that one of our team had a fever. We didn't believe at the time that he could be infected. No international healthcare worker working at a treatment facility with proper protective equipment had ever been infected with Ebola before. We thought that with the correct equipment and safety protocols for putting on and removing protective equipment, we should be safe. Many local health workers had been infected during epidemics, but this was always thought to be due to their lack of access to the right protective equipment. Also, this tended to occur in health centres, but not actual Ebola treatment units, where patients were always at least suspected, if not diagnosed, with Ebola. There was no history of contact that we knew of for Kent and we were not aware of any breach of protocols, so initially we felt it unlikely that he had Ebola. Something else must be causing his fever, but we still took the appropriate precautions by isolating him and treating him in protective equipment.

Despite all this, it was news we didn't want to hear and it made me feel queasy. Testing my colleague and friend for Ebola was an odd moment. That first test returned negative on the Thursday afternoon, but we would need to repeat it at 72 hours into his symptoms, which would be Saturday morning. After that first test result I turned to Bev as we drove to Kent's house again.

"I am so relieved that result came back negative. Right

now I am holding everything together, but if Kent tests positive for Ebola I think that will be what breaks me."

The week progressed and each day brought more and more challenges – situations I had never faced before, where it was hard to know what the best course of action was to take. Each day we dealt with one chaotic event after another, on the back of decreasing sleep and increasing exhaustion. During the first week at ELWA1, missionaries from ELWA had kindly brought us lunch each day and we had eaten adequately in the evenings, but as we moved to ELWA2 the food was provided by a local cook for patients and staff. Often there was hardly any time to eat, but the fact that our food was being cooked off site and brought in made me uneasy. The last thing any of us needed was a fever with a diarrhoeal illness that could mimic the early signs of Ebola. So I avoided the local food. Soon after, a cook was hired to prepare our evening meals in the guesthouse kitchen. The food was good, but the increasing exhaustion and emotion meant that I simply ate less and less. At the end of the first week I had been eating a normal amount, but as the second week progressed, even though I was taking the same amount of food, I would only eat three-quarters of it, then a half, then a quarter, and by the Saturday night I barely ate a few mouthfuls.

The suits we wore were very physically demanding in the heat. We could not wear them for longer than one and a half hours as they became too hot. At one point later on in Guinea, one of the MSF doctors put a thermometer in his suit while he worked, and when he took his suit off it read 45°C. It was estimated that people lost two to three litres of sweat each time they wore a suit for that period of time. During that second week I was not drinking enough to replenish the losses, because there simply wasn't time, and, due to the patient-to-staff ratio, the frequency with which we had to go in meant we were suited up as often as three times per day, sometimes more. When I decontaminated and removed my suit, I usually looked as if I'd stepped out of a shower fully clothed. As I sweated in my suit my face mask would fill with sweat, making it increasingly difficult to breathe. Then the goggles would fog up or the sweat would run down the inside, making it hard to see and stinging my eyes. The work was often physical, carrying heavy patients on stretchers, and washing immobile patients, and once out of breath it was difficult to catch it again.

Even though Kent's first test was negative he continued to deteriorate during that week, despite us treating him for malaria. On the Friday morning I received a phone call from my colleague John Fankhauser to say that Kent was not doing well, and asking if I would be able to go with him to Kent's house to treat him. I smuggled all the equipment we needed out of the treatment unit in a bin sack, so that the rest of the team wouldn't notice, and Bev and I drove to Kent's house. Bev would help John and I to decontaminate afterwards. By this point, even though we were trying not to raise awareness of the situation, we put on our protective equipment outside the house as we felt the risk of putting it on in the hallway was too high. Unfortunately, this meant the security guards would observe what we were doing. It was a risk we were going to have to take.

Kent was looking weak, but he was putting on a brave face. I sited an intravenous line and we gave him fluid and antibiotics. We spent about an hour treating him, bringing some food items from the kitchen, and trying to encourage him. I realized shortly after siting the intravenous line that I had not brought a special sharps box for the needles. I found a polystyrene container and made a mental note to bring a sharps box the following day. John and I then decontaminated and removed our protective suits as we exited the house.

As we left, Kent's neighbour, also a missionary from the US, opened the door to talk with us. She was aware of the situation. She spoke briefly with John and Bev and then offered all of us a freshly baked cappuccino muffin that was still hot. Right then, it was the best muffin I had ever tasted! It was moments of kindness like this that brought glimmers of light through the heavy darkness.

CHAPTER 14

FROM CRISIS TO CRISIS

At around the same time as Kent, it was devastating to learn that one of my other colleagues and friends, Nancy Writebol, had also developed a fever. She worked with us at the treatment unit helping people to decontaminate as they removed their suits. She never went into the high risk zone though, so from our perspective it was unlikely that she had Ebola. She had also had a positive malaria test, so we assumed this was the cause of her fever. After a few days of being treated for malaria, however, her fever persisted, so we decided to test her for Ebola.

I was going to test Kent again on Saturday morning, so we arranged for me to test Nancy around the same time. The night before, I prepared all the equipment we would need and again smuggled it out of the treatment facility in a black bin sack. We stored everything in the boot of Bev's car overnight. That night I toyed with the idea of whether I would actually wear protective equipment to test Nancy. We really didn't believe she could have Ebola, since there was no history of contact. Kent, on the other hand, had been working at the mission hospital, so there was a small risk he had been infected by a patient there. I didn't want to scare Nancy by wearing a suit, but then if I was testing her for Ebola I had to believe there was at least a small chance she could be infected. I couldn't rationalize doing the test without protective equipment.

The following morning I woke up at around 4.30 a.m., having had less than four hours' sleep. Bev collected me and we went to Nancy's house first. As I stood in her doorway putting on my protective suit, I chatted with her. She appeared so well at that time, I felt like an idiot for putting on the suit and I apologized if it was causing her to be afraid. I did her test, decontaminated and removed my suit, then Bev and I drove to Kent's house. Nancy later told me that when I put on my suit in front of her she thought, "Oh, they must really think I have Ebola!" Prior to this she had just considered the test a matter of course.

John was already there when we arrived at Kent's and I put my suit on and joined him. Kent was looking less and less well, and my ability to deny to myself that he might have Ebola was diminishing. Again John and I treated Kent and I took his second blood test for Ebola. I had forgotten to bring the sharps box again for disposing of the needle, so I used the same polystyrene container from the day before, being careful as it contained several contaminated needles now. As I completed the blood test and went to put the contaminated needle in the box, the fan suddenly caught the lid of the box, flipping it upside down and scattering the needles on the bed. I stared in horror.

John carefully started to pick the needles up and I went to help him, but he stopped me.

"No," he said. "Only one of us should do this, just in case. We don't need two of us with a needle stick."

I was grateful to him for protecting me, but I also felt sick at the thought of this test coming back positive.

I left soon after as I needed to be at ELWA2 for the morning handover meeting. John stayed a while longer. That is the last time I saw Kent. I didn't get the chance to say goodbye to him before I left Liberia the following Sunday evening. The rest of that Saturday and Sunday were such chaos that I did not return to treat him since John was staying with him.

A DARK DAY

On the Friday evening I had fielded a referral call for a patient from Bomi County who had been confirmed as infected. This was significant – it meant that a new county had been affected which had previously remained untouched by the disease. In other words, many more new cases would follow. The phone rang again and I was asked to go to collect a suspect patient at the entrance. I donned my PPE and set off. As I walked by the low risk zone I saw Jerry, one of our hygienists, sitting in the visitor's booth. I realized in that moment that *he* was the suspect patient. I looked at him and my heart sank. I could see that one of his eyes was bright red, while the other was normal.

I walked Jerry over to our triage area. As I questioned him about his symptoms he didn't quite fit the case definition. His symptoms were vague and he said he hadn't had a fever at all. As I spoke with him his eye appeared to improve by itself and no longer appeared red. I took his temperature – it was normal. My gut told me that I shouldn't trust what Jerry was telling me, but my head said, *he doesn't meet the case definition*. Admitting him would have implications as it meant I had potentially identified a contact for Kent and Nancy, so I hesitated. I rationalized that he'd had no history of contact, working purely as a decontamination sprayer. He'd never entered the high risk zone and denied any contact in the community. I discussed his case with Dr Sarah Temmerman and she agreed that he didn't fit the case definition. We agreed to let him go, as long as he came back the following day to be checked.

Jerry left and I walked away from triage still holding in my gloved hand the thermometer I'd handed to him, that he had put in his mouth. I washed my gloved hands with chlorine and put my apron in a "burn" bin, still holding the thermometer. Then I removed my goggles and face mask and dropped the face mask in the bin too. I was about to put the thermometer down on a table in the staff area of the low risk zone, so I could remove my gloves, thinking Jerry didn't have Ebola so I could clean it with chlorine and reuse it since we were almost running out of them, when a voice cut through the chaos in my head and spoke clearly.

"It's *not* worth it."

The voice was so compelling it brought me to my senses and I froze. I looked at the thermometer in my hand and then turned and dropped it into the burn bin. I then walked over to our decontamination area to clean my goggles and boots and discard my gloves. I didn't think much more about it at the time, as several further situations arose that required my attention.

The following day on the Saturday, a few hours after I had tested both Kent and Nancy, Jerry returned to the treatment unit as promised to be checked out.

"I'm feeling a bit better," he told me. But I noticed he had an IV line in his arm, which was strange.

"Where did you get the IV line?" I asked.

"Oh, I went to my local health centre because I was feeling weak," he said.

"But why didn't you just come straight to us?" I wanted to know.

He shrugged his shoulders. I took his temperature again – normal. Even though he still didn't fit the case definition, and claimed to have even fewer symptoms than the day before, I no longer trusted that he was telling me the truth. This time I decided to admit him to our suspect ward and test him for Ebola. Later that same evening Jerry began haemorrhaging profusely. He died the following day, less than 24 hours after he was admitted – from Ebola.

That same day we lost four patients in the space of two hours, one a prominent physician in Liberia. His death triggered increasing unrest among our healthcare workers and the Ministry of Health, and due to his seniority the President of Liberia needed to be notified of his death. At the same time we were knocking through into the old outpatient department of the ELWA hospital to expand our treatment facility, as we had been informed on the Friday night that six relatives of the patient from Bomi had tested positive and would arrive the following day. At that stage we only had one confirmed bed space left, three patients confirmed in our suspect ward who needed to be moved, and then these six new admissions from Bomi. We were fortunate to have the support of Eric Buller, who had played a key role in the development of ELWA2, Richard Kyle who was supervising the construction of the new hospital, Lance, and John Freyler (our staff chaplain), who undertook this work while we tried to continue caring for patients. Throughout the two weeks it had felt like we were sitting on a time bomb waiting to explode. Finally we seemed to have reached the point of explosion, and we did not have the bed space or staff capacity to care for the number of patients that would shortly be coming our way.

MORE BAD NEWS

All the chaos, constant stress, minimal sleep, and tragic cases like Jerry's took their toll on me. Keeping the secret of Kent's and Nancy's tests from our team, and wondering what their results would be, added stress upon stress. Then, on Saturday night, things took a turn for the worse.

The entire team was called to gather for a briefing in our guesthouse living room. This was not only the Ebola disaster response team, but all the international staff working for Samaritan's Purse in Liberia. Kendell began by informing everyone that Kent had been unwell since Wednesday morning and that only a few of us had known. As he said those words, I knew what was coming next:

"I'm sorry to have to tell you that Kent has tested positive for Ebola."

There was a stunned silence in the room. Kendell went on to give us a few further administrative details before leaving. Hushed conversations went around the room and some began to cry. I was devastated, but the tears wouldn't come at that moment. Thoughts cascaded through my mind, so many I thought my head might explode, and I couldn't properly focus on any of them. I heard Bev speak:

"We should pray."

I agreed, but right then I had no words. It was now that I truly understood the words of Romans 8:26: "In the same way, the Spirit helps us in our weakness. We do not know what we ought to pray for, but the Spirit himself intercedes for us through wordless groans" (NIV). I couldn't speak, but I felt the Holy Spirit crying out to the Father on my behalf – for all of us.

Bev came over and gave me a hug. We had a "no physical

contact" rule designed to protect us from Ebola, but at that moment it felt right to break it. You can't receive devastating news and keep your distance while people are breaking down. As Bev hugged me I broke and the tears flowed. I spent the remainder of that night crying intermittently. I barely slept. What was occupying my mind now was Nancy's test result. I picked up the phone and tried to call our laboratory technician, Darlington, but he wasn't answering his phone.

I got up the following morning to go up to the treatment facility. My eyes were red, puffy, and dry from crying all night and I felt sick to the bottom of my stomach. I went into the kitchen to get a cup of coffee and my colleague Linda Mobula was there, talking to Lance. Linda had not long arrived in Liberia; she would be replacing me when I left to go home that night. I poured my coffee and looked at the breakfast food, but knew I couldn't eat anything. I told them that I had been calling our lab technician all night, trying to get Nancy's test result. Linda looked at me with sadness in her eyes.

"I am really sorry, but Nancy tested positive too."

The news hit me like a ton of bricks and I erupted into tears again. Lance hugged me and repeatedly said he was so sorry. At that moment all I could gasp through my sobs was,

"I nearly didn't wear a protective suit."

Lance looked at me.

"Well, I am really glad you did."

John Freyler, our chaplain, offered to drive us all up to the treatment unit for our team meeting. At that point I was in no fit state to go anywhere, and through sobs I said I would join them all shortly. I just needed time to compose myself. I went to my room and sat there and wept. I chatted briefly with Dorothy McEachern, my roommate and a nurse who had been a great support to me at ELWA2, as I tried to calm down. About ten minutes later Lance called me from the kitchen saying that I was really needed at ELWA2 as we had barely any staff.

I tried to pull myself together. I washed my face and had a few more sips of coffee, then I started to walk up to ELWA2, a ten-minute walk from our guesthouse. I felt so sick that I thought I might vomit at any minute and my legs were shaking uncontrollably. I wasn't sure they were going to hold me up. I had to focus just to put one foot in front of the other; my legs felt like lead. With each step I kept telling myself, "One more step, one more step."

After the terrible news of the last 24 hours a fear had descended upon our team. No one knew how Kent and Nancy had become infected. At the time I thought that Jerry could have been the link. Sadly, he had not been truthful about his condition. Maybe there could have been some contact? He had been working alongside us all whilst symptomatic with Ebola for close to a week. It was the uncertainty as much as anything that bred the fear. Suppressed anxiety swelled to the surface as people questioned whether our safety protocols and equipment were, in fact, sufficient to protect us. Were our local colleagues safe to be around? Who else felt ill but wasn't telling us? So many questions coursed through my mind. Meanwhile, I prayed for Kent and Nancy and believed for a miracle. At that time, the harsh reality was that 95 per cent of our patients who had Ebola died from it.

DIGGING DEEP

When I arrived at ELWA2 I found about two-thirds of our usual staff numbers. Some international staff were no longer prepared to work at the treatment facility, a decision which I fully understood and respected. Many of our local staff had not turned up that day either. The night before a well-respected local physician's assistant had died of Ebola in the emergency room at JFK. For some this was the final straw.

Linda and I gathered the small team together and she broke the news that Kent had Ebola. They were shocked, but by this time had seen so much that they were numb. No one said anything.

Just then, our meeting was interrupted by a representative from the Ministry of Health, who had arrived to collect the day's blood samples. She was early and none had yet been taken. Darlington, our lab technician, normally did this, so I called him to see where he was and he told me it was his day off. I was in no fit state to be taking blood – I was still trembling and light-headed and thought I might vomit at any moment. I looked at my team.

"Anyone feel like taking blood today?"

I was met with sullen looks and the shaking of heads. I turned to the lady from the ministry and said, "Sorry, there won't be any samples today. Come back tomorrow."

She shot me a dirty look, but turned around and left.

That morning I was supposed to train Linda and Christine McCubbing, a nurse who had just arrived from Canada, in how to get into and out of the PPE, and how to safely care for patients. I turned to Linda and told her, "I'm not sure I can go in there today."

"OK," she replied calmly, but looked at me slightly dubiously.

First of all, I wasn't sure my body could take the physical demands of suiting up. But secondly, I was terrified – afraid that I, or another member of the team, would become infected. Even as I said the words to Linda, I knew that that wasn't who I was or who I wanted to be. I looked around at my team and thought, *how can I ask them to go in, if I, as their leader, am not prepared to?* Then my thoughts turned to my patients – the people the world had abandoned. It really felt as if their lives did not matter to anyone outside our team, but they did matter to me. I wasn't going to abandon them. Even if I couldn't save them, I wanted at least to bring them some comfort and relief.

I stepped into the room where we put our suits on and gave myself a brutal pep talk, telling myself to snap out of it and put aside my fear. All that week, each time something awful had happened – which was several times a day – I'd told myself, "Get over it and get on with it."

It was the only way to keep functioning, and at that point in time functioning was all that mattered.

"Pull yourself together, Nathalie," I said under my breath. "Get your suit on and get your butt in there."

It was enough to cut through the chaos in my mind. I helped Linda and Christine get into their PPE and we entered the high risk zone together.

Going into the treatment facility that day cost me a lot; I feel like I lost a part of myself. What I gained, though, was so much greater. It was one of those moments that defines you as a person – when everything within you is screaming *enough is enough*, and yet you somehow keep going. All I can say is that God continued to sustain me. His work in my life over many years helped me to make that decision, because ultimately I trusted him. I could have given into my fear and no one would have judged me for it. But I would have judged myself.

I recalled the time at Lake Frederick when I made the decision that I would rather die than know that someone else had died as a result of my actions. In this time of extreme fear and confusion I came back to that decision. Giving into fear, at the cost of my patients' lives, was not who I was. I know that God had been preparing me for this situation back then. I also know that there will be times in the future when that decision will help me make the right choice again.

The fact that I decided to carry on that day, I believe, empowered my team, particularly the local staff. That was essential for the months that lay ahead, when I would return home and they would be left to care for patients on their own.

Given the circumstances and situation we were in, I know it will sound strange when I say that, despite everything we faced, God was incredibly good to our team. He broke through whenever we needed him. Despite the chaos, he made himself heard. When we had nothing left, he was there holding us up. He also protected us. That probably sounds ironic, given that two of my colleagues became infected with Ebola, but I know that his sovereign hand was over that situation and over us throughout this time. There were numerous times during decontamination when something would splash me in the eye and I would think, *was that just chlorine or something else?* Twice, while inside the high risk zone, I was smacked in the face across my goggles – once by the flailing arm of a very sick patient and another time accidentally by a colleague whose hands were contaminated. On neither occasion did my goggles move the slightest amount to cause me to be exposed. It was certainly painful and disconcerting, but those flimsy goggles, like the ones you would wear in science class, somehow stayed in place.

When it comes to Kent and Nancy being infected, I know that wasn't God. But what the enemy intended for harm, God used for good. In Romans 8:28 Paul writes,

"And we know that in all things God works for the good of those who love him, who have been called according to his purpose" (NIV).

God took Kent and Nancy's situation and used it to wake

up the world to what was happening in West Africa. When they became unwell, news of their evacuation reached the highest echelons of US politics and alerted President Obama to the urgency of the situation. For this reason, finally, the world started to listen to what Médecins Sans Frontières, and later Samaritan's Purse, had been saying for months. The US committed troops and money to Liberia and WHO declared the situation a "public health emergency of international concern". Then the British government committed to support Sierra Leone in this fight. Soon after, many other nations committed finance, personnel, and equipment to help battle this epidemic.

God took the worst situation we could possibly imagine and used it to galvanize an international aid response, which eventually helped to bring the epidemic under control.

CHAPTER 15

ISOLATION

I left ELWA2 on the Sunday afternoon and set off back to the guesthouse to shower and pack my things. I had handed over to Linda, although this was done hastily and was a little disorganized, given all that was going on. As I walked back, a wave of mixed emotions swept over me. I felt so exhausted that I could barely connect with any thought for more than a second or two. I still felt weak and sick. I was less shaky than I had been, but I thought that having eaten and drunk very little for many days was catching up with me.

I felt relieved at the prospect of finally being able to get some decent sleep. At the same time, I was full of questions.

What will happen to my patients once I've gone? Who will be caring for them? What will happen with this epidemic?

Monrovia was exploding with new cases and the rest of the world still didn't seem to care. Deep inside I had a feeling of utter despair that the situation had been allowed to get this bad and still no one was listening. The feeling overwhelmed me and part of me wanted to run away, while another part desperately wanted to stay and fight. But I didn't know if I could give any more; I felt as if I was being torn in two. I worried about Kent and Nancy. *Would they survive?* The odds were not in their favour, and yet we serve a miracle-working God for whom nothing is impossible.

I got back to my room and began to pack. I threw away several items as everything stank of bleach. Packing didn't take long and then I showered, trying to get the chlorine and sweat out of my hair. Afterwards I checked my email. I saw one message from Samaritan's Purse UK, requesting that I be checked by a physician before flying home. I couldn't really see how that was possible, given how stretched everyone was. But John Fankhauser arrived at the guesthouse at that point, so I discussed it with him.

"Do you have any symptoms?" he asked.

"No, none."

"Do you have, or have you had, a fever?"

"No."

"It's a shame that all the thermometers are at ELWA2, as it would be good to verify that," he told me.

I hesitated and then said, "Oh, I've got a thermometer in my bag, but it's OK because I don't have a fever."

John looked at me strangely.

"Would you go and get the thermometer so I can check?"

I have never been so reluctant to do something in my life. Even though I knew full well that I did not have a fever, I was terrified of what the thermometer might reveal and the implications of it. I put the thermometer in my mouth and tried to hide my apprehension. After what felt like an age it beeped and I handed it to John.

"37.1 °C," John said. "Normal. I'm happy with that."

John signed me off to go home and we said our goodbyes.

I decided that I should try to eat and drink something before heading to the airport. I made two slices of toast and peanut butter and poured a glass of weak, watered-down juice. I forced down a few mouthfuls, but couldn't manage the second slice of toast. As I was waiting for the car to take me to the airport, my phone rang. It was John Freyler. He put me on a conference call with Kendell and several members of the US Centers for Disease Control and Prevention (CDC). They interviewed me for close to an hour about how Kent and Nancy may have become infected and we talked a lot about Jerry. At the end of the call a member of the CDC told me,

"We're really relieved to hear that you had at least modified PPE on when you triaged Jerry. We thought you might also have been a contact, but we're pleased to hear that you aren't. Have a safe flight."

My car had been waiting outside for some time, so I put my bag in the trunk and we set off. En route we picked up another colleague, John Akudago, who would be travelling on the same flight as me. On the way to the airport we drove by ELWA2 and I called Linda. She brought out some gloves and masks for me and John, for our flight home. After recently hearing about Patrick Sawyer, who had been heavily symptomatic on a flight to Nigeria a week before, I was not taking any chances that someone sitting near me or John may be unwell.

I was so jumpy now that I didn't touch any part of the vehicle we were sitting in, wondering who may have sat in it before, and I constantly applied alcohol gel to my hands to cleanse them. John wanted to chat in the car, but I apologized:

"I'm sorry John, all I want to do is sleep."

My head was pounding and I longed to be able to give in to the exhaustion. I woke up as we reached the airport. Inside things were quiet, which was extraordinary, all things considered. No screening was taking place there at this time. I still didn't want to touch anything and I tried to give every person a wide berth. Eventually, as we left passport control and sat in the departure lounge, I was impatient to board the plane. I had an overwhelming desire to be somewhere where it was safe to touch things; somewhere I could feel safe enough to sleep.

In due course we boarded and I was relieved to see our flight was far from full. We could spread out and not be close to other people. As the plane began to taxi down the runway, my exhausted body let go and I was consumed by sleep – but it wasn't peaceful. I dreamed of being back in Monrovia and testing positive for Ebola.

ANOTHER SHOCK

I stirred as our plane landed in Brussels and I came round groggily. I felt as if the whole experience had been some kind of nightmare, but then reality kicked in – I really had just lived this horror story. However, though I didn't know it yet, the real uncertainty had yet to begin.

At Brussels Airport John and I got coffee while we waited for our connecting flights. It was 5.30 a.m.. I felt exhausted and numb, and it was hard to see "normality" going on all around me. I checked my email and discovered two messages from Samaritan's Purse UK. The first read:

"We are so sorry to hear that you have been quarantined in West Africa for the next twenty-one days."

I was bemused. *That's odd, because I'm in Brussels. Did I miss something?*

I opened the second email, sent fifteen minutes after the first. It read:

"We heard that you didn't get the previous message before you boarded your flight… "

As I read on, my phone began buzzing in my pocket. It was Alan from Samaritan's Purse UK. It was 4.45 a.m. UK time. We discussed the situation at length and while ultimately Alan advised me to continue as usual, he said that when I reached the UK I should drive home and avoid large gatherings for the next twenty-one days; we'd talk further when I arrived home.

"What about work?" I asked.

"I don't think you should go back to work," he said, "but that's your bosses' decision and you'll have to discuss it with them."

He mentioned that Samaritan's Purse in the US had put out a press release about Kent and Nancy and it made me wonder whether the UK media knew about me. Would I be ambushed by the media at Heathrow Airport?

I told John about what had happened and he tried to contact Samaritan's Purse US himself while I went to the bathroom. I was still nervous about touching anything, given the number of flights coming into Brussels from West Africa, but there was some sterilizer in the toilets, so I cleaned the seat thoroughly. Apprehensively, I took my temperature again and to my relief it was normal. Shortly after, John and I parted ways and went to catch our respective flights. I was glad to be boarding a flight to the UK and looking forward to being back home. At the same time I fought feelings of guilt. *How will ELWA2 survive and who will care for Kent and Nancy? Who will be the glue that holds our increasingly fragile team together?* I felt guilty for wanting to be somewhere else, somewhere safe.

I slept briefly on the flight to London, but wondered what awaited me at Heathrow. Would the media have worked out that I was somehow connected to Kent and Nancy? Before going to passport control I took my temperature again. Normal. In due course I walked through the glass doors to exit customs, my eyes darting around, but there was no one waiting. No media or paparazzi. I let out a huge sigh of relief and felt suddenly light-headed. I realized I'd eaten almost nothing in 48 hours, so I bought a sandwich, most of which I was able to eat.

I went to collect my car. Although it had been just two weeks since I'd parked it at the airport, it felt like a lifetime ago. I sat in the driving seat and checked my temperature again. Still normal. Then I set off for the drive to Cardiff. Another stop and another temperature check on the way showed that nothing had changed.

Arriving home felt very strange. Once again the disconcerting quietness hit me. I dumped my bags and sat on my bed staring at the wall, trying to process what I'd just been through. I thought I'd only sat there for about ten minutes, but then I looked at my watch and saw that two hours had gone by. Eventually I called into work and spoke to my clinical director to explain what had happened and to ask if I should come in. He told me to call the occupational health department. I spoke with a nurse who told me she would need to discuss the matter with Public Health Wales, who would then be likely to contact me.

Meanwhile I called my friend Gabs and told her everything that had happened over the previous two weeks. She cried with me on the phone. I asked her to let our church elders know, as they were away attending our annual church Bible week. After hanging up, a call came through from Dr Jorg Hoffmann at Public Health Wales. We talked for about an hour and a half about my time in Liberia, discussing what had happened with Kent and Nancy and the risk of exposure.

"I need to go and discuss this with my colleagues," Jorg told me, "but it looks like we will probably ask you to remain in your apartment for the next twenty-one days. I'll call you back after I've spoken to my boss."

His parting shot was to ask me to monitor and record my temperature at least twice per day from now on.

I sat in a daze for a while, but then communications began popping up from everywhere. Samaritan's Purse US contacted me to arrange a debrief phone call. Then the Centre for Disease Control and Prevention in Liberia contacted me via Linda. They wanted to talk to me again about Kent and Nancy's infections, so we arranged a call for the following day. Then I received a message from Roger, my church leader, saying that the BBC had been in touch wanting to speak to me. I messaged back to say that I couldn't talk to them and later called Roger to explain the whole situation, emphasizing how important it was that the church keep everything quiet, diffusing the media attention for now. Then I spoke to Alan from Samaritan's Purse UK to give him an update.

Sometime later, Jorg called back and confirmed that I must remain in my apartment for the next twenty-one days – the full incubation period for Ebola. He said that since I had no symptoms it was OK for me to go out and buy food that evening, but thereafter I shouldn't leave home, other than for an occasional walk on my own, keeping a safe distance from others, and I must take my temperature four times each day.

ISOLATION BEGINS

Finally, I felt that I'd better let my family know what was going on. I texted my brother, Ben, to arrange a Skype chat and told him what had happened. Then I called my dad. I discovered that my mum was abroad, visiting Kruger National Park in South Africa, with limited phone signal and no Internet access so I texted her and simply said:

"Hi Mum, I am home safe and sound. Please don't worry if you see anything on the news. If the media contact you please say 'no comment'."

Finally, around 10.00 p.m. I forced myself to get up and shop for food at the supermarket near my apartment, when it would be relatively empty. I went around feeling dazed, only picking up items that didn't make my stomach churn when I thought about eating them. Back at home I had some tea and toast and went to bed.

That night the nightmares about Ebola continued and I woke feeling groggy and disoriented. So began many days, all blurring into one, filled with endless calls and emails to either give or receive updates.

I spoke with my Samaritan's Purse contacts again in the US and UK, then to the CDC in Liberia again. We spoke at length about Kent, Nancy and Jerry. They seemed surprised that I was in quarantine. Then Jorg called to check my temperature and said that his colleague, Dr Brendan Healy, an infectious diseases consultant at the University Hospital of Wales, would be in touch. Meanwhile, I did my laundry.

Everything smelled of chlorine. Later Brendan called and we talked through what would happen in the event of me becoming ill. I had to send him pictures of my apartment in case they needed to come in and retrieve me at some point. Later that day I spoke to Alan again from Samaritan's Purse UK and he updated me on what was happening in Liberia. Due to the sensitivity of the situation a sudden ban had been imposed on information coming out of Liberia, so thereafter I was only able to get second-hand information. One thing I did hear, however, was that Kent was deteriorating.

I felt exhausted the next day and spent a lot of time either staring at the wall or the TV, but not really watching it. I took long naps. Even though I was allowed out for walks I didn't feel up to it. The day after this I woke up exhausted again. My temperature was normal. Through the unofficial grapevine I learned that Kent had begun haemorrhaging and I began to sob. I prayed and pleaded with God to spare his life. I didn't know what else to do. Later that day Brendan called to tell me about the plans in place to manage me if I became unwell. That evening he and his colleague, Dr Harriet Hughes, came to my apartment and spoke to me from below my balcony.

The next day I decided that I would go for a walk around Roath Park Lake, about 1.3 miles in circumference. I felt apprehensive about going, but knew it would be good for me to get a break from the solitude of my apartment. I waited until around 8.00 p.m., when I figured most children would be at home, and when I was less likely to bump into someone I knew. Just before I left I received news to say that Kent was stable. Well, at least he was no worse.

Outside, my main concern was: *What will happen if I feel unwell whilst I'm out? What will I do then?* I told myself that I had been fine all day, with a normal temperature. It was nice being outside with the breeze on my face, but I kept a good distance between myself and other people in the park. I saw someone walking a chocolate Labrador puppy and suddenly realized how crushing the lack of physical contact had become. I longed to just go up and pat the puppy, but of course I couldn't. I returned home about an hour later and felt nonetheless refreshed.

The next day I learned that Kent was being evacuated and would travel back to the US. I was ecstatic about this news, but also worried, and prayed that he would survive the long flight. Meanwhile, Gabs stopped by my apartment and left a tub of Ben & Jerry's ice cream outside the door, which was very kind, before chatting to me from my balcony.

Almost a week had now passed and the next day was the first that I felt I had more energy than the previous day, instead of less. That afternoon I saw the international news cover Kent's arrival at Emory University Hospital in Atlanta. I was amazed to see him actually walking into the hospital; I almost couldn't believe it. For the first time I thought that he would probably pull through and tears of joy streamed down my cheeks.

The following day some good friends, Cez and Lester, were due to get married at our church. Of course, I couldn't attend. Instead, I arranged to FaceTime into the wedding, so that I could see and experience the ceremony. I watched the wedding and spoke with several friends who were there, including the bride. It was a lovely experience, but afterwards I felt drained and lay on my sofa. That evening Gabs and I had planned to go for a walk together, whilst maintaining a respectable distance. It was great to get out, walk with her (keeping about two metres apart), and just chat.

When I got home that evening I thought about making myself some food, but I had no appetite. I forced myself to eat something, but half an hour later was hit by a wave of nausea. I sat by my toilet for half an hour, sweating and heaving, but nothing came. My temperate was borderline, marginally below what would be considered a fever. I was concerned, but generally I felt OK. Maybe I was just getting the flu?

The next day I learned that Nancy would also arrive at Emory Hospital later that day and I was relieved to hear it. Later, when Jorg called to check on me, I told him that the previous day I'd felt unwell. He said he would call me twice a day from now on. That evening I saw Nancy's arrival in Atlanta on the news. She looked to be in a much worse state than Kent and was taken in on a stretcher with oxygen. I prayed that God would heal her.

That afternoon a friend dropped some cheesecake round for me and we chatted from my balcony. Later she called to say that she'd had coffee with a friend from The Western Mail who would like to interview me. I panicked. I told her I couldn't speak to anyone and wondered what she'd said. My friend reassured me that all she had said was that she had a friend who had just returned from West Africa. My heart sank, but I put it to the back of my mind.

HEADLINE NEWS

The following day Jorg called as normal, but in half an hour he was back on the phone, which was odd. He told me that their media office had been contacted by a journalist claiming to know about someone who was quarantined in their apartment because they had been exposed to Ebola.

"I have no idea where the leak came from," he told me, perturbed. I had to tell him about my friend and the chat she'd had.

"I don't think anything has been released that would identify me, though," I told him.

"Well, we tried to prevent the journalist from releasing the story," he told me, "but she insisted it was in the public interest and was going to publish it anyway."

To try to limit the damage, Public Health Wales issued a general statement. It didn't identify my gender, where I was, or say that I was a healthcare worker. We braced ourselves for the worst and discussed what might happen if my identity were revealed. Thereafter I was constantly looking out of my window to see if reporters were lurking in the street.

Jorg had already asked me to curtail my walks for the time

being due to my not feeling very well, but later he phoned me and said,

"The BBC have just called and asked if the person in our press release is Nathalie MacDermott. We told them that we could neither confirm nor deny that information and asked them please not to release it. They agreed not to."

That evening I watched TV and I made headlines news on all the channels, albeit anonymously. They all spoke of a person who had returned from West Africa and was in quarantine. It was surreal, listening to this and knowing it was me. A well-meaning friend put up a link to one of the reports on Facebook and tagged me in it. I had to urgently get her to take it down, which fortunately she did immediately.

TESTED

I continued to feel exhausted and aching, nauseous, with no appetite, and my temperature remained borderline. I relayed all this to Jorg and then Brendan started to contact me to check how I was feeling. As I did not start to feel better, in due course it was arranged that Brendan and Harriet would come to my apartment to test me for both Ebola and malaria. That evening he called to explain how it would happen.

I felt numb; I didn't really think I had Ebola, but at the same time I couldn't really talk about being tested. I didn't tell anyone about it apart from one trusted American friend, Kelly Sites, who knew what was going on. She had been working as a nurse at ELWA1 prior to my arrival in Liberia. Samaritan's Purse had enough to worry about with Kent and Nancy, without needing to think about me. I avoided a call from my brother and spoke briefly with my mum to tell her I was fine. I couldn't cope with the thought of them worrying about me.

Brendan and Harriet arrived at 6.30 p.m. that evening. They put on protective suits outside my apartment door. They prepared everything in the hallway before coming into the living room. Brendan appeared first, with Harriet hanging back to hand him the items he needed. It was strange to have the tables turned on me.

Hang on, I'm supposed to be the one in PPE aren't I? Why are people in suits talking to me? This isn't supposed to happen!

As Brendan prepared to take my blood he said to me,

"Are you glad we're testing you?"

I found this an odd question, but then I supposed he meant that it would put my mind at ease – if the test came back negative!

"I don't know how I feel," was all I could manage in response.

With samples collected, Brendan told me that the first result would be available at around 3.00 a.m..

"Would you like me to call you when I have the result?" he asked.

"Not at 3.00 a.m.," I said. I didn't know what I would do with the result at that time, all by myself in my apartment. I also knew that I wouldn't be able to go to sleep if I was waiting to hear the result at that time. I figured if I expected it in the morning then I might at least be able to sleep.

Harriet interjected and said that, should the test prove positive, they would need to arrange transport to get me to the Royal Free Hospital in London immediately, so in fact they may have to call me at 3.00 a.m.. I just shrugged. We agreed that Brendan would simply text me as soon as he had the result and we'd take things from there.

That night I tried very hard to distract myself and keep my mind occupied, but at one point had extreme muscle spasms in my arms shortly before Brendan called to check I was OK and tell me that I had tested negative for malaria. He was still waiting for the Ebola result.

When I woke up the next morning I leaned over and picked up my mobile from the bedside table. There was a text from Brendan. I'd slept through it. Reading anxiously, I saw that the Ebola test had come back negative. That morning Brendan called to say they wouldn't do another test unless the situation changed in any way.

After I got off the phone I ate some breakfast. A little later I began to feel hot and shivery. My temperature was 37.8°C, so now above normal. Feeling apprehensive I called Brendan to let him know. He told me that he'd thought this might happen, and he was very glad that I'd informed him as he had worried that I might not. After a discussion with his team they decided to test me again the next morning, which was Friday. I felt sick at the thought. We had avoided them being seen by my neighbours putting on suits the first time, which was a miracle given that I lived in a block of twenty-three apartments, but what if someone noticed them this time?

The next morning Brendan and Harriet returned, this time suiting up just inside my front door for fear of being seen and spreading panic. Miraculously, no one saw them come or go. I was actually feeling better that morning, but we repeated the procedure again. Later that afternoon Brendan phoned again with the news that the test had come back negative.

Over the following days I began to feel better and was allowed to resume my walks around the park. My appetite slowly began to return and I had more energy. I was, however, getting cabin fever and even gave my oven a thorough clean – twice.

Eventually, thankfully, the twenty-one days had passed and I was signed off. Normal life could start again. I decided to travel to Switzerland to see my family, so early on day twenty-two I found myself back at Heathrow Airport. I realized that it is virtually impossible to get around such a busy place and not touch a soul, even when you are being careful. Although I'd been given the all-clear, the habit of being careful not to make contact clung on for longer. Later that day, when I arrived in Zurich, my mum was the first person I touched properly in five weeks. I hugged her for a long time.

Looking back, people have often asked me if I was afraid during this time of isolation, and particularly if I was afraid about being tested for Ebola and getting the result. The truth is, I can't really say how I felt. Perhaps it was because the traumatic events of Liberia had seemed to anaesthetize my emotions, or perhaps because I couldn't rationalize the tension between not really thinking I had Ebola and contemplating a positive result. In any case, I was overwhelmed by how much the situation had deteriorated in Liberia, and I was very concerned about Kent and Nancy's health – so my capacity to worry about myself was virtually non-existent.

Thoughts about being tested for Ebola played at the back of my mind, but I couldn't imagine that I really had it. The mitigating factor was that I did feel ill. Whenever a "what if?" thought surfaced I would push it aside and distract myself with something else.

What I couldn't do, however, was tell anyone. It was as if there was a barrier to speaking about this out loud. I also couldn't bear the idea of anyone else worrying about me at that point. I had enough on my mind without worrying about the stress it would cause my family.

I spent much of my time in isolation sleeping, praying for my colleagues and trying to get updates about the situation in Liberia. While I did spend time with God, I didn't ask him why everything had happened in the way it had. I wasn't sure I would hear him correctly and to be honest, it didn't matter. Throughout my time in isolation I felt surrounded by God's peace and held tight by his loving arms. I never doubted that I served a loving, gracious, merciful God. He cares more for us than we can ever comprehend.

I know that God is good, and that is the foundation of my life. One day, in the light of eternity, I will know the answers to things I cannot presently understand. When that happens, I am sure I will also see the many times that God intervened and protected me when I had no idea I was in danger. Right now, I am content in knowing that I am walking in his purposes. I remain extremely grateful to God for saving Kent and Nancy's lives.

One thing I believe this situation highlights is how we tend to prioritize the lives of those more familiar to us. Why did it take two white Americans to contract Ebola before the world woke up? Was it because they were flown back home, so Ebola landed on America's doorstep? Or was it because suddenly people could identify with it: *that could have been me*. Why didn't the world take notice when Sierra Leone's lead physician for haemorrhagic fevers, Dr Sheik Umar Khan, died of the virus? We need to ask ourselves some difficult questions. It highlights to me even more, though, that God knew exactly what it would take for the world to wake up and respond, so he took an awful situation and used it for the good of the people of West Africa. In the process he preserved the lives of my colleagues, stood firm with us as we endured the battle, and carried us through to victory.

Throughout this experience I clung to God as never before and he proved himself faithful. Especially during my time in isolation I had numerous messages from friends, all quoting Psalm 91:1–7:

Those who live in the shelter of the Most High will find rest in the shadow of the Almighty… he will rescue you from every trap and protect you from deadly disease. He will cover you with his feathers. He will shelter you with his wings… Do not dread the disease that stalks in darkness … these evils will not touch you.

(NLT)

Nahum 1:7 also sums it up perfectly:

*"The L*ORD *is good, a strong refuge when trouble comes. He is close to those who trust in him."*
(NLT)

CHAPTER 16

COMING TO TERMS WITH TRAUMA

My stomach churned and I felt a flush of adrenaline. I was feeling jumpy and my heart was pounding. Yet I had no real need to feel this way – I wasn't in the middle of a crisis. What was happening to me? Was I having a panic attack?

*   *   *

Returning home from Liberia brought challenges of its own. The reality was – not just for me but for all of us who worked to fight it – that the Ebola epidemic had changed life as we knew it. Nothing would ever be the same again.

The BBC persisted in trying to get an interview with me and, after my time in isolation was over, I eventually agreed. The epidemic in West Africa, as bad as it was, was still barely grabbing the world's attention, so I felt that giving an interview would serve to highlight the situation. The more media attention it got, the more the world would wake up to what we had all been shouting from the rooftops for months.

Little did I realize, however, that doing this interview would open the floodgates. I found myself on every evening news channel again, only this time my anonymity was gone. Although on camera I appeared to be calm and composed, being filmed made me uncomfortable, at least initially, so each time I appeared on TV was quite stressful.

My face was splashed across the front page of the South Wales Echo and people started to give me odd looks in the supermarket. I wasn't sure if it was because they vaguely recognized me and couldn't place me, or whether people did recognize me and were edging away, lest I somehow infect them with the terrible disease I didn't have.

When I returned to the UK from Liberia I knew that what I'd experienced was an abnormal and traumatic event. I was realistic that it would take time to come to terms with that. I also felt that my response to the trauma was normal. Who wouldn't have nightmares? The emotional and physical cost had been huge. I had seen things that would haunt me forever. I can still see the faces of all my patients. I remember their names. I recall the circumstances of their death. No person should have to die in the way these people died.

After my isolation period, as I returned to work I was extremely distracted. At that time the epidemic was still exploding, as we knew it would. The television was full of images of people dying in the streets of Liberia, Sierra Leone and Guinea. People were dying outside treatment centres because there weren't enough beds inside. Stray dogs were eating dead bodies, because the teams assigned to bury people couldn't keep up with the numbers.

Knowing that I could do something about this, and feeling frustrated at how slowly the world was moving, didn't help my agitation. When I discovered that my current training programme would allow me time out to return to Liberia, I felt a sudden reprieve. I knew then that I would be able to go back and felt at peace about the decision.

It is hard to imagine that, after the living hell I had just been through, I would really go back and put myself through it all again. As masochistic as it sounds, my answer had to be yes. Why? Because I knew it was what God had called me to do. As difficult and challenging as it would be, it was part of his purpose for my life. I also couldn't sit still and watch people die horrific deaths, knowing I could at least do something to help.

Peter Piot, who discovered Ebola in the 1970s, said, "Ebola changed my life." I think Ebola changes the life of anyone who comes into contact with it. God allowed it to invade mine, and life would never look the same again. Although I knew this was all part of God's purpose for me, I couldn't see a clear plan ahead. I didn't know exactly where all of this was going to take me – I just knew that I had to keep fighting the battle, along with countless others, to bring this epidemic under control. No doubt some people will think I was crazy to contemplate returning to Liberia after such a close shave with the disease, but I felt a responsibility because God had given me the skills to assist. Yes, it would be a huge risk, but I felt it was one worth taking for those who were suffering, and for the good of our world.

On 10 October I boarded a flight to Monrovia with a mixture of determination, purpose and apprehension. Despite all I have said, returning to Liberia was not an easy thing to do. There would be plenty of reminders of what happened the last time – the need to remain in a constant state of hypervigilance; being sure not to touch anybody or anything; the constant washing of hands; having our temperatures monitored every time we entered a building. Then there was the constant smell of bleach. Bleach used to remind me of cholera after my time working in Haiti; now it reminds me of Ebola. I think I preferred the former.

BACK IN THE CRUCIBLE

As I arrived back at the ELWA compound in Monrovia, our car drove past the newly established ELWA3, operated by Médecins Sans Frontières. It was the largest Ebola treatment unit ever built and at maximum capacity could hold 450 patients. Then we passed the house where Nancy Writebol had lived. It was still cordoned off with "caution" tape. When I got to the house where I would be staying, I walked into the kitchen and saw a white board with dates from August scribbled on it. Next to "August 1" was a large arrow pointing to the words "Kent's Evacuation!" A sudden wave of emotion hit me in the stomach and I felt nauseous.

Over the coming weeks and months, the stress of my previous trip to Monrovia impacted me in different ways. Much of the time I wasn't consciously aware that something was concerning me, but I often had butterflies in my stomach and felt jumpy. Whenever I felt like this, I would stop and ask myself why. Eventually the root cause dawned on me.

It was the beginning of November 2014 and I was walking around a treatment facility with colleagues prior to its opening. It had been built especially for healthcare workers who might become infected with Ebola. As we walked round, I suddenly became aware again of butterflies in my stomach. I felt like I was about to sit the worst exam of my life. I felt sick to the bottom of my stomach and my heart was racing. It took me a few minutes to work out why I felt like this, since my head was quite calm and I was interested to learn about the facility. Then I realized. *I just cannot deal with another of my colleagues getting Ebola. I can't!*

The problem was, this time around I was the team physician for Samaritan's Purse and the only clinician in the country for our organization – so if any of our team did get sick, it was *my* responsibility.

I realized that these emotions were a response to my previous experience with Kent and Nancy, but I still believed to some extent that this was a normal reaction to an abnormal situation. It would just take me some time to come to terms with everything. These moments were not uncommon during the months I remained in Liberia, but

I became accustomed to feeling that way. I accepted the constant uncertainty that surrounded our staff working in the treatment facilities, fighting the progression of the epidemic. At times I was quite controlling, wanting to do my utmost to ensure my staff were safe, but eventually I had to realize that I couldn't possibly control everything. All I could do was my best to ensure that we had excellent protocols in place and that all staff were well trained. The rest I would have to leave in God's hands, and if someone became infected at least now there was a protocol and we would cross that bridge when we came to it. Fortunately, none of our staff became infected, despite a few concerning moments.

Putting in place effective protocols to deal with situations was vital, but I found it difficult at times. When I became a doctor I took an oath to make the care of my patients my first concern. But when it comes to Ebola, my first concern had to be the safety of my staff, otherwise the whole initiative could collapse. My staff had to feel safe and confident in the work they were doing. If they didn't, then there was no way the patients would receive the care they needed. At best they would get poor standards of care; at worst, none at all.

One day I found myself writing the protocol for the decontamination of dead bodies and stopped to ask myself,

"How did I end up here doing this?"

Medical school doesn't teach you how to deal with situations like this. It doesn't teach you how to make a decision when there is no good option. This was never more true than the day I had to sit down and write the protocol for the management of pregnant women in labour who were Ebola suspects. I started to wonder if I had lost all compassion. Which was safest – to admit the woman to our rural, resource-limited treatment facilities and put our staff at risk? Or not to admit her and take the risk that she would contaminate her entire family – or another healthcare facility that didn't have adequate PPE? I thought about it, prayed about it, and wrestled with it. In the end I decided that admission was the only truly ethical option.

But then, after admitting the woman, I had to decide whether a staff member should assist with delivering the baby – probably the riskiest situation I could put them in – or whether we should just aim to keep the woman comfortable and leave her to deliver the baby by herself. What a difficult choice to have to call! In truth, I couldn't call it, because it meant asking someone to risk their life, and only they could make that decision. I sat on the fence. My advice was that staff should not assist with the delivery of the baby to protect themselves, but if they wanted to intervene and were competent to do so, the decision was theirs.

In most of these situations the baby was stillborn, but also highly viraemic – a huge risk to anyone coming into contact with them. The next part of the protocol had to address the issue of where to place the stillborn baby. The only safe solution was in a bucket, subsequently filled with chlorine. Again I wondered: *How did I ever come to this?*

* * *

By the time I returned to the UK in March 2015 the Ebola epidemic was waning in all three countries and Liberia was close to being declared Ebola-free. Finally I could relax after nearly nine months of intense stress. Yet the life I had known before was very different to the life I returned to. I had now moved from Cardiff to London and changed jobs. I had begun doing a PhD in Ebola and was frequently contacted by the media. I realized that I was in a privileged position, having an opportunity to study this disease. If I had been asked five years before what I wanted to study for a PhD, I would have said Ebola, without a doubt, even though the opportunity to do such research would not then have been available to me. I couldn't get over God's goodness to me, but at the same time, that goodness was linked to having seen so many people die. *Why was I benefitting from such an awful situation?* On the other hand, much of the work I would be doing would hopefully further the medical community's understanding of this horrific disease and prevent us from facing such epidemics in the future. Despite this, however, it still felt as if I had just been handed an incredible career off the back of a huge amount of suffering.

I felt uncomfortable too that the media had tried to portray me as some kind of hero in many news articles and interviews. I was also one of many healthcare professionals awarded a special medal by then-Prime Minister David Cameron. So who was I now? In my view I am not a hero, however one defines that. I am just me, the person who loves to watch *The Great British Bake Off* and *The Apprentice*, and the person who chose to get on a plane to Liberia before the full crisis had really unfolded.

I know my identity is in Christ and during this time that was the one thing I could cling to. I knew that when I went to Liberia to work with Ebola, I was completely in the centre of God's will. I also knew that when I returned from Liberia, the doors that began to open for me were his will too. I was grateful for this because it helped to hold me together through extremes of emotion. Knowing that you are walking in God's will brings a deep sense of peace and certainty about where you are, even if it doesn't remove the troubles and challenges. The Bible talks about our roots going down deep into Christ. In the years leading up to that Ebola epidemic I know that God was deepening my roots and making sure they were anchored in him. At times I was frustrated, feeling as if I was treading water and going nowhere, but now I know that during that time God was preparing me for events I could never have anticipated.

On my return it was hard to see life as normal. When I went out for a drink with colleagues I didn't know what to talk about. Conversations seemed mundane and pointless, but who would want to talk about the horror I had witnessed?

Friends would ask me about my experiences, so I developed a watered-down version for them. No one needs to hear some of the stories, and people don't need those images in their minds. But even when I shared my sanitized version, I would look up and see people staring at me, shocked. Then I'd think, *Uh oh, I've gone too far, said too much. I hope I haven't upset them.*

On other occasions, I would be asked by healthcare colleagues to talk about my work in the high risk zone of the Ebola treatment unit. I would recount a story and look up to see them gaping at me in similar fashion. These stories had become my normal. I had completely lost sight of how abnormal they were.

Sticking to my diluted version of events meant that I never really spoke about what I'd seen, because there were few people to talk to about it. Occasionally I would catch up with one of my Ebola colleagues and we would talk. It was only then that I would realize it wasn't all a concocted story in my head – that it really did happen. The craziness of that July in Liberia was a reality we had faced together.

COMING TO TERMS

I knew that I had been through a traumatic few months, but whenever I had returned from disaster situations before life had gone back to normal after a few weeks. It always took a couple of weeks to recover from such an intense situation and to stop thinking about the events that had unfolded. In due course memories would settle down and, when I looked back, I would mostly think fondly about the people I had worked with. Of course there were painful memories, but often these help to mould us into the people we become.

But it's safe to say that this time I had lost my perspective. I was still thinking about and working on Ebola all the time, whether I was writing articles or collating data from treatment facilities. It consumed me.

In July 2015 I flew out to Freetown, the capital of Sierra Leone, to set up the fieldwork aspect of my PhD. The day I flew was the anniversary of Kent and Nancy's diagnosis. It was always going to be a difficult day, and perhaps not the best day to choose to return to a country still combatting Ebola.

The anti-malaria medication I had to take for this trip made my nightmares more vivid. My sleep pattern had been disrupted during my time in Liberia, and my efforts to restore it had been weak and unsuccessful. During July and into August I had constant migraines. Even once I returned from Sierra Leone, the migraines continued. At the time work was very busy. I was applying for further funding for my PhD, gaining ethical approval, and trying to overcome the many challenges that accompany undertaking a PhD with fieldwork in a low-income nation, especially involving a highly dangerous pathogen.

I threw myself into my work, even though I knew I really needed a break. I hadn't taken a holiday in over a year. Even though there was "rest and recuperation" time built into my Samaritan's Purse schedule, I often used this brief time back in the UK to catch up on necessary tasks. Plus, having to be mindful of the twenty-one-day incubation period meant that I never felt completely free, and had to keep taking my temperature and reporting on it daily. I had intended to take a holiday but it simply didn't happen given everything else I was trying to organize. I started to wonder if life would ever slow down, but I also wasn't sure how I would feel if it did.

In October 2015 I finally managed to book a holiday and went away with my mother. Unfortunately, during this time Pauline Cafferkey – the Scottish nurse who contracted Ebola whilst working in Sierra Leone, who was featured in the media a great deal – was re-admitted to the Royal Free Hospital's isolation unit. This meant that, even while on holiday, I received frequent phone calls from media outlets. I wondered if my life would ever not revolve around Ebola.

Although work continued to be very busy, I was increasingly distracted. I didn't notice it at the time, as I was focused on meeting deadlines, but I was constantly thinking about what had happened during July 2014. Even whilst at work, I would stare into space for what I thought was just a few minutes but would often turn out to be much longer. I would remember the events inside our treatment unit and see the faces of my patients who had died. It was as if the whole experience had been burned into my mind.

I drew a schematic of the treatment facility to try to help myself to process everything. I found I could remember exactly which bed space each patient had been in, the date they were admitted and the date they died. I could also remember how they presented and conversations I had with their family members. This was a period of my life that defined me and I wasn't sure that I wanted to forget. In fact, I was afraid that I would forget the faces and memories of my patients. During that summer of 2014 the world had ignored what was happening in West Africa until it was too late. At the time it had felt as though the lives of my patients, many of whom were healthcare workers infected by doing their jobs and trying to help their own patients, had not mattered. I felt that they had not counted in the world's eyes, and that their lives would be forgotten by a world who had implied they didn't matter. I wanted to make sure that I didn't forget to honour the memory of those who died; I wanted to make sure that their lives had not counted for nothing.

I continued to have intermittent nightmares and distressing dreams. I had frequent migraines and flashbacks, often triggered by random words or normal everyday things. Even with medication the migraines wouldn't settle. In December 2015 things slowed down at work. I obtained funding from the Wellcome Trust to continue my PhD and passed my early stage assessment. Suddenly, there was some space to breathe, but with that came more time to dwell on things. Good friends had said to me for many months that I should talk to someone, but I wasn't sure I wanted to. Even though I was going back over events daily, I wasn't sure I wanted to relive or confront some of the issues. I felt reluctant to talk about the guilt I felt that nearly all of my patients had died, and that even as a doctor I had been unable to prevent that. Criticism over the actions of organizations working at the beginning of the epidemic had come from many angles, some from people who never even set foot in West Africa, yet for some reason felt able to comment on the quality of healthcare delivered in extremely challenging circumstances. All I can say is that we did the best we could with what we had available to us at the time, but it was hard not to take these criticisms on board.

I was having dinner one evening with Helen Fowles, a long-time friend from medical school, who gently but firmly told me I needed to talk about my experiences and do it properly. I was beginning to realize that the migraines were unlikely to settle if I didn't. I finally admitted that I needed some help. That conversation with Helen was the final push I needed and I was ready to admit that I couldn't do this on my own anymore.

It had been nine months since I had returned from my second trip to Liberia and, if anything, things were worse, not better. Picking up the phone to call the helpline was one of the hardest things I have ever done – particularly when they informed me that they couldn't help me as they didn't deal with trauma. That was the ultimate low point. It was the only way I'd known to approach the problem and I began to feel that perhaps no one would help me.

But I had been praying hard about what to do and I firmly felt that God had said he would provide the people I needed. The helpline advised me to go to my GP. I wasn't really sure how they might help, given how difficult it can be to access mental health services in the NHS. Fortunately, however, they were able to point me in the direction of the

Practitioner Health Programme – set up to give confidential support to doctors with mental health problems. Through them I was able to access specialist cognitive behavioural therapy and start the process of coming to terms with what I had lived through.

* * *

People ask if I have lost some of my faith through this process. The honest answer is I haven't. If anything, I have learned even more how good God is and how much he cares for his children. Through it all I know he has never left my side and I have felt him carry me through it with arms wrapped so tightly around me I knew he would never let go. He has placed exactly the right people in my path, first to prompt me to get help, then to give me that help. He has also blessed me with incredible friends and church family to support me through the process.

I know some people believe that Christians should be immune to problems such as these, but I wonder why the church has for so long struggled to come to terms with the idea that Christians may suffer from mental health problems. While I believe in a God who is good and who protects and heals us, he does not remove all the storms from our lives. When I read the New Testament I don't see people who assumed life would be easy now that they were followers of Christ. I see people who, when pursuing the call of God on their lives, were persecuted, imprisoned, tortured, and killed. I see a people who faced many trials and tribulations; who at times were sick and needed healing. Being a Christian does not make us immune from difficult situations, but it does mean we have a God who stands by our side and promises to bring us through them.

People may identify with my situation, given all that I experienced, but we need to recognize that there are many Christians within every church community who suffer with mental health problems. For too long the church has remained silent on this issue. It is time we spoke up. Having a mental health problem does not make people weak. It does not mean they lack faith. It simply means they need love and support, as with any illness. The world is waking up to this – it's time the church lifted its sleepy head too.

TIME TO ACT

"We are not to simply bandage the wounds of victims beneath the wheels of injustice, we are to drive a spoke into the wheel itself."

Dietrich Bonhoeffer

As I write, in Europe and throughout the Western hemisphere we are experiencing a shaking. There is a shifting of the balance of power and economic prosperity. This is particularly clear in the political parties that have recently gained a footing in many European nations. For Europe, some of this shaking has come from the refugee crisis. We have seen nations closing their borders and calls to revoke the Schengen Agreement that keeps those borders open within the European Union, which has itself been shaken by Britain's Brexit vote.

In September 2015 I responded with Samaritan's Purse to the evolving refugee crisis in Europe. At that time some borders were still open, but over the period of the next nine months they gradually closed as numbers of refugees surged. I was initially sent to Macedonia, where my colleague Ralph Springett and I helped to set up a backpack distribution scheme with local partners. After a couple of weeks I travelled to the Greek island of Lesvos to determine medical needs and to see whether there was an indication for providing a medical intervention.

On Lesvos we saw first-hand the desperation of people who had boarded over-full inflatable dinghies with their tiny infants. I cannot imagine any mother would take a risk like that, knowing that every week some of these boats sank and people drowned, unless they were desperate. At the same time we faced heavy criticism as an organization for assisting people perceived to be "Islamic fundamentalists". It took pictures of desperate children and their families before people started to realize the true reality of what was happening. Later, a short film called *The Rising Tide,* made by the Samaritan's Purse communications team and directed by Bryan Siceloff, received over 50 million views and the tide of popular opinion finally did start to turn. Despite this, animosity towards migrants has increased in line with the popularity of far-right parties announcing policies for controlling immigration.

As the church we can be at the forefront of those who speak up for our fellow man – who speak to our governments about such crises. As the ambassadors of Christ we must become advocates for those who are struggling or unable to speak up for themselves. In the story of the Good Samaritan in Luke 10:25-37, we see the religious leaders of the time ignoring a man in need of help. The Samaritan man, however, who belonged to a race despised by the Jews at this time, stopped to help and show compassion. Jesus' conclusion to this parable was to tell us to "Go and do likewise" (NKJV).

As God's people, then, we cannot look the other way as events such as the migrant crisis unfold. This is contrary to what God has told us to do. Instead we can be a source of support, if not the solution to such problems. Churches may not be able to go it alone, but as a united body we can be the answer for thousands of desperate people in need. We can demonstrate our faith in action by praying for people's circumstances, but also by reaching out to meet their practical needs, and perhaps even opening our homes to accommodate those who have been forced to flee their homeland.

BEING THE GOSPEL

I believe the Bible is very clear about the mandate we as Christians have to demonstrate Christ's love to the world. As Heidi Baker likes to say, "Love looks like something." Love is a verb – an action, not a theory. Jesus has called us to be his hands and feet to minister to a hurting and self-destructive world. This call is clear in the Bible for everyone who calls themselves a Christian. Where that calling takes us in terms of our individual path is down to God's call.

It will look different for you and me. But whatever we are called to, as an embodiment of the gospel, our lives should be testimonies to his grace.

In Matthew 16:18 Jesus says of the church: "...the gates of Hades shall not prevail against it" (NKJV). I don't see in Scripture a defensive church that is struggling to survive. Rather I see the picture of a church on the offensive – demolishing the works of the devil as he seeks to destroy God's creation. We dismantle and destroy the works of the enemy through Christ's love and grace, which will always be far more powerful than the weapons of hatred and anger.

Our world has many questions, but no real answers. As God's people, we are called to be filled with the wisdom of God and to have a "sound mind" (James 1:5-8) in contrast to the flawed thinking that pervades. When people have no answer, God has given us the solution. The church is called to be at the forefront of the world's problems – a body that world leaders can turn to when they no longer know what to do, because Jesus has provided the answer. But for that to happen, God's people must get involved in the world's problems and not be isolated in a spiritual bubble. Those who dare to trust will run into the fire, speaking to the Nebuchadnezzars of our time; choosing to forsake the comfortable lives we have created for ourselves. We must trust that as we step out our Father God goes with us. There is nowhere safer or more perfect than being in his will.

Whilst I believe that our God is a Father who provides for his people and meets our needs, I don't believe he has called us to live comfortable lives, insulated from trouble. Instead he desires that we go beyond our comfort zones to radically love the person in front of us – no matter what their background. We reach out because we are all sinners, saved by grace. The New Testament reveals an outward-focused church that is built through adversity and sacrifice – not an inward-focused one built for the comfort of its members.

The church, moving in unity and in accordance with God's will, would be a force to be reckoned with: the church in action. When Jesus commanded us to go and proclaim the gospel, that word "proclaim" meant to demonstrate it with action, as well as expressing it with words. We are therefore to "be" good news to others – the embodiment of the message we bring.

It is time for us to break down the denominational walls that have separated believers and revealed us as weak and conflicted. It is time to realize that we have more in common than we think – that our differences are minimal in the light of eternity.

That which divides us is far less than that which unites us.

The World Needs More Good Samaritans

Help impact a hurting world in Jesus' Name.

Samaritan's Purse®
INTERNATIONAL RELIEF

samaritans-purse.org.uk

FAREWELL FOUNTAIN STREET

Selçuk Altun was born in Artvin, Turkey, in 1950. A retired banking executive, bibliophile and book collector, Altun served as a chairman of a major publishing house until his retirement in 2004. He is the author of four essay collections and ten novels including *The Sultan of Byzantium*, which has been translated into more than fifteen languages. He writes a popular monthly column for the Turkish periodical *OT* called 'For the Love of Books'. He lives in Istanbul.

Mel Kenne is a translator, editor and author. He has translated works by Enis Batur, Latife Tekin and Birhan Keskin. His collection *South Wind* won the 1984 Austin Book Award and in 2010 he was a winner of the Nazim Hikmet Poetry Award. He lives in Turkey.

Nilgün Dungan is a lecturer and translator. She has translated the works of Haydar Ergülen, Gülten Akın and Behçet Necatigil, Müge İplikçi and Ahmet Büke. She lives in Izmir, Turkey.

SELÇUK ALTUN

Farewell Fountain Street

Translated from Turkish by
Mel Kenne and Nilgün Dungan

TELEGRAM

TELEGRAM
An imprint of Saqi Books
26 Westbourne Grove
London W2 5RH
www.telegrambooks.com
www.saqibooks.com

First published 2022 by Telegram

Published in Turkey as *Ayrılık Çeşmesi Sokağı* by Türkiye İş Bankası
Kültür Yayınları, 2020

A full CIP record for this book is available from the British Library.

ISBN 978 1 84659 216 4
eISBN 978 1 84659 217 1

Printed and bound in Great Britain by Clays Ltd, Elcograf S.p.A.

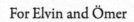

For Elvin and Ömer

'You find me. If I look for you, everyone will know.'
Gülce Başer

Artvin

'My name is Artvin, sir.'

'Art vin?'

I enjoyed people's surprise when they first heard my name, but lost all ownership of it if they subsequently inquired, as they often did, 'does it mean something?'

When I was old enough to ask the question myself, neither Mother Gülriz nor the internet were forthcoming with clues about the origin of my name. Uncle Cenk didn't know either, but declared that it was unique and poetic, so what did it matter? Then, in elementary school, I learned what 'art' meant, and that 'win' meant victory. 'Vin' also meant wine in French, confusingly. I picked all this up and wondered where in the world these cities of English and French existed.

I wondered how much of this the man sitting opposite me would consider relevant. He had asked me to tell him 'All about myself', no easy task. But, in the end, he did not ask me the question. He simply supplied the answer himself.

'A lack of information, particularly about oneself, is

inexcusable. Dvin was the medieval capital of Armenia, near the border with Turkey. Ard, in Armenian means "after". Hence Ardvin, your name, is a reference to where you are from, "after Dvin". Carry on, please.'

'I never knew my mother or father. Supposedly, my mother dropped me off at Doğancılar police station in Üsküdar when I was two days old and ran away. As the story goes, the deputy police chief who registered me at the orphanage added my name in the records as "Artvin Baby."'

'Did you ever speak to the police officer who found you?'

Strangely enough, I had kept up with the police officer. Only sporadically, and by post. When I learned how to write, I had sent him a postcard with a picture of the Maiden's Tower on it. I had addressed my letters to Uncle Niyaz, which was the name I knew him by. One day, while he was on his way to a distant town called Hakkâri on a reconnaissance mission, his vehicle plummeted down a cliff, and he was martyred. I had never had a chance to ask him why he'd registered me as 'Artvin'. The day he died, I graduated from elementary school, top of my class. When Mother Gülriz remarked that it was strange that the two events had taken place on the same day I felt sorry, as though I had caused the accident.

This seemed a strange way to conduct an interview. I wondered if my prospective employer really needed to know all this. He was looking at me curiously, then waved his hand. 'No matter, tell me what happened next.'

'Mother Gülriz, may she rest in peace, was a respectable teacher at Üsküdar Girls' High School. Because she taught literature, she considered herself superior to her colleagues. She was fifty years old when she retired and adopted me. I was ten months old. She had a kind of masculine beauty, with her short hair and horn-rimmed glasses. She was Thracian and her father was an imam. Teaching was her passion and I used to believe that she knew everything. She loved words and the meaning and power of them, regularly teaching me obscure etymology and word trivia. I was five years old when I learned that Gülriz in Persian meant "that which strews roses". We lived on Eşrefsaat Street in Üsküdar, and when I asked her its meaning, she was pleased; I was surprised to hear her whisper to me, as if she was revealing a secret, that it meant "the right time for something to improve".'

But she had never told me the meaning of my name. It had taken a perfect stranger to do that.

'You always knew that she wasn't your mother?'

'I hadn't yet started school when Mother Gülriz, over a white coffee and raisin cake, told me that I was adopted. She was an ideal guide and caretaker, but she never showed me any motherly affection. Her insistence that I call her "Mother Gülriz" adequately demonstrates that. After retiring from the Girls' High School, she occasionally tutored students who were preparing for private high school entrance exams. Sometimes, her former students would pay us a visit. If she hugged them, I would grow jealous, and aware of this she would come over to squeeze my nose and plant a dutiful kiss on my cheek.'

'Tell me more about Mother Gülriz.' The man was watching

me, carefully. I wondered where to begin.

'Her bedroom was lavender and dimly lit. A silver-framed photo stood on the bookshelf. It was a photograph of Mother Gülriz herself, on her first day of elementary school. In it, she is clutching the hands of two adult men and looking nervously at the camera. The sullen man to her right was her father Sahir, and the handsome man on her left was his close friend, the art teacher Baha Bey. Uncle Cenk claimed that Mother Gülriz later fell in love with Baha. He was a bachelor and died young of a heart attack. Mother Gülriz never married.'

The man opposite me nodded slowly, his eyes closed, and the tips of his fingers drawn together in a temple beneath his chin.

'As I was listening,' he said, 'I remembered a story about a famous author called Cevat Şakir, whose pen name was The Fisherman of Halicarnassus. He was a wise author, an Oxford scholar and a dissident sort. His father, Mehmet Şakir Pasha, was a distinguished diplomat, governor and experienced Ottoman minister. Over his father's objection, he married an Italian beauty called Agnesi, whom he'd met as a student at Oxford University. When, in 1914, in a twist of fate, Cevat Şakir found his wife and father in the same bed, he shot and killed Mehmet Şakir. It's said that his influential relatives saved him from the noose. The Italian Embassy's press attaché took Agnesi and her daughter to Italy. After some time, Agnesi married the attaché and parted ways with her daughter.

'In 2004, Agnesi's granddaughter Cinzia came to Turkey and found her relatives. In conversation with İsmet, Cevat

Şakir's daughter with his second wife, she revealed that her grandmother Agnesi had always kept at her bedside a photograph taken in Büyükada of her and her father-in-law Şakir Pasha cheek-to-cheek. I hope we'll have the opportunity to discuss the importance of that anecdote to me one day. Please carry on with your own story.'

I decided to talk more about Uncle Cenk, my 'father figure', if you like. 'Uncle Cenk was twelve years younger than his sister, and he feared her somewhat. Mother Gülriz would call him by his nickname, and when she said Mukhtar, she pronounced the second syllable in a way that showed she was being condescending. He left college in his penultimate year and became a sought-after carpet seller in the Grand Bazaar. He was able to communicate with tourists in five languages and thought they were impressed when he read Basho's haikus to them in English. I remember him working as an entertainer on the Southern coasts and as a guide at Topkapı Palace, too. He was a charming anarchist.

'Around the time I was brought home as an adopted child, he divorced his wife of eight months and moved into his sister's home. I must thank them for making the first twenty-four years of my life happy; not once did I feel sorry about having been parted from my birth parents.'

I paused. The man looked at me as though I had left off in the middle of something. The pause began to grow awkward. I continued.

'I loved the serenity of Üsküdar – experiencing yesterday and today, Ottoman and Anatolian, at once – and its modest people. Its history-laden houses, nameless shrines and bone-dry fountains defy time; its narrow, labyrinth-like streets mounting upwards in zigzags and worn out by the passing cars. After it rained, the scent given off by the fig trees grew stronger and the town was born again: the derelict mansions I stumbled upon when out walking astonished me in the sunlight, as if I were seeing them again for the very first time.'

I wondered if I was filibustering my own interview.

'Our home was on the middle floor of a three-storey apartment building on secluded Eşrefsaat. I was annoyed when my uncle referred to our street as "middle class", and I complained to Mother Gülriz when he compared our building to the carcass of a whale. I would rejoice at solving the virtual puzzles I created in the grey floor tiles out front, and, at other times, trying to count them made me sleepy. I liked the historical simit bakery down the street and imagined that the shrine across the way fed off the smell of sesame rising from it. Our street ended at Rum Mehmet Pasha Mosque; on the street behind it a professor had been killed, and I've always wondered if that professor had been guilty of anything worse than leaving a tender child in front of a police station.'

The man opposite was nodding along with me, encouragingly. 'I visited that small mosque more than fifty years ago', he said. 'I was curious about how the words "Greek", "Mehmet" and "Pasha" could join in a single place of worship. Mehmet Pasha was a mysterious Byzantine convert who rose to the position of grand vizier. The monument he had built, apparently to win the favour of Sultan Mehmet the

Conqueror, resembled a church more than a mosque. I don't know if it worked at the time, but he was eventually executed. I remember I bought some salep from a Greek pedlar I bumped into outside the mosque.'

I didn't know how to respond to that, so I continued. 'Doğancılar Avenue wound out the back of our home district. It was the picturesque artery of the neighbourhood, and I was always looking for an excuse to go there. Each time Mother Gülriz entered "101-Varieties Family Grocery Store", she would mention that its sign hadn't changed in thirty years. While quietly uttering the basmala, she would buy quarter-value National Lottery tickets and slip them inside her Quran. She used to rejoice when she won even the most trivial prizes. Beside the store was a three-storey wooden building. The fragrance of roasted chickpeas came from "Ödemiş Dried Fruits and Nuts" on the ground floor; from the second-floor window, the elderly Hatice Hanım and her cat kept a close watch on the street. When I saw them, I used to think that they were possibly the happiest couple on earth.

'Once a week, hand-in-hand, we would head down to Üsküdar Square, by way of Şemsi Pasha Avenue. That place seemed to me to have a system whereby the clocks ran faster. We usually ate lunch at the diner there called Kanaat, and I would be delighted beforehand that we were going there but would feel upset as my fried fritters dessert shrank with each fork stroke. After buying fish, desserts and pickles, we passed through the courtyard of Valide-i Cedid Mosque, where I would wait as Mother Gülriz spoke quietly of the Ottoman sultans' reverence for their mothers; then I, too, would lower my voice and say defiantly that I also revered my mother.

'What else? Oh, once every fortnight we would go to Süreyya Cinema, or to the municipal theatres, when a film appropriate for my age group was showing. I loved the name Süreyya; Süreyya, or the Pleiades, form the cluster of seven stars in the constellation of Taurus. If I ever have a son, I will consider this beautiful name for him.'

I paused. He nodded at me as though to continue. I fished around for something more to say. I wasn't used to talking about myself in such detail. 'Mother Gülriz read whenever she could. She was a fan of Anton Chekhov and Sait Faik Abasıyanık. I fancied becoming a writer more famous than Sait Faik, until I met the saxophone.' He smiled, encouragingly. I carried on, moving into a new phase of my life.

'For the private high school entrance exams, I studied with Mother Gülriz, alongside other courses. Her happiness was greater than mine when we learned that the prestigious Kadıköy Anatolian High School had accepted me. Sadly, the same news hurt my neighbourhood friends, as if by applying to Kadıköy, I'd shown them disrespect. Moda, where our school was located, was a popular neighbourhood on the Asian side, but I just couldn't warm to it; its high rises were unattractive, and its inhabitants were snobbish.

'One summer afternoon I was strolling down Doğancılar Avenue on my way home from school, reading the store signs backwards. After all the activity in Moda and on Bağdat Avenue, this quiet street filled me with peace. How honourable that the merchandise in the windows didn't follow current trends! Suddenly, in front of Ödemiş Dried Fruits and Nuts, I stopped. The window on the floor above Hatice Hanım was open and coming from it were the notes of an instrument that blended all life's joy and sadness. I was mesmerised. That's how I discovered the saxophone, whose name was beautiful too. If the player had come down from that window and on to the street like the Pied Piper, I would have been their first follower.'

I wondered if the man liked music. It was hard to tell. I went on. 'I immediately got my uncle to buy me a dozen saxophone CDs. I was permitted to listen to music for forty-five minutes a day, but if no one else was home I would watch hours of concerts on the television and online and lose all track of time. As you told me to summarise my life story sincerely, I'll tell you that whenever I whistled or farted, I would try to imitate the sound of a saxophone. Mother Gülriz once caught me doing a solo impression in front of a mirror.'

He laughed. I thought he'd appreciate a bit of honesty in the story and was pleased to be proved right.

'I fell in love with the famous alto saxophonist Candy Dulfer. I would focus on her playing as if I was watching a seductive striptease. I nagged my uncle to get a poster of her sent from the Netherlands. Performing a virtual duet with her as she played "Lily Was Here" was an orgasmic delight.

'It didn't take long to find out that the player on Doğancılar Avenue was Hatice Hanım's son, Safa. He was a friend of my uncle's and a relative of an idle Ottoman pasha who sold land or a building whenever the family ran out of money. Hatice Hanım and Safa, the only remaining members of the family, had no security besides their rental income from two dilapidated buildings. According to Safa, his alcoholic grandfather would tear loose the wooden rails on the staircase bannister and burn them to heat up their seaside residence in Kandilli.

'A graduate of the conservatory, Safa had played in a transatlantic band for three years before returning to Üsküdar to see his mother. Once his money ran out, he would set out to sea again. I felt something new inside when I saw the wind instruments on parade like noble knights in his living room; in my excitement I may have even peed a few drops in my pants. I gripped the Selmer-brand alto saxophone, and as its mysterious coldness slowly filled my insides, my body heat rose up to meet it. At that moment, I made my decision: I would be a saxophone player. Safa Abi said that to become a good musician I would have to attend a conservatory for at least four years. For a nominal fee, he would prepare me for the entrance exams.

'I was all set for Mother Gülriz to veto this adventure. Indeed, she brushed me off, saying, "Music might feed your soul, but studying will certainly feed your brain." She didn't expect me to go on hunger strike and refuse to go to school. When she gave her permission at last, on condition that I wouldn't skip classes or play when she was at home, I hugged her and kissed her cheeks again and again.

'First, I learned to respect my instrument; it was a part

of my body, a weapon and a shield. During the first lesson, Safa Abi showed me how to handle it correctly, explained to me how we would become one on stage, and said, "It's like a delicate woman. It must never be vexed." Three times a week I waited eagerly for my lesson to begin. My tutor had three other students, but when he said that he felt most hopeful about me, I was as proud as if I had won a prize.

'After I was accepted into the State Conservatory, which lay forgotten like a retired ferryboat moored at Kadıköy pier, Mother Gülriz lamented for days, and I'm sure she secretly wept, too, as if she'd heard that I had gone astray. Later, she consented, on provision that it would only be for four years and would not hinder my university education. With time she cheered up, as I succeeded at both of my schools. I was now an art major in wind and percussion instruments. Converted from an old market hall, that conservatory became my temple. I gained prestige at school, and while my neighbourhood friends assumed I was gay because I was in love with music, girls began to hit on me because I was a musician. The professionalism of the conservatory matured me early, and I was probably unable to enjoy my adolescent years as I should have.'

I could feel myself getting into my stride, remembering those heady, early days when I was discovering my instrument, my voice. 'I took up fusion jazz, which lets the artist interpret the work freely. I got interested in modern poetry at about the same time. My favourite poet was T. S. Eliot; I discovered him through *Four Quartets*, a book I only bought because of its title.'

I paused. 'A meaningful graduation diploma for me was seeing Mother Gülriz's eyes fill with tears as I played my saxophone to a Van Morrison piece called "Days Like This".

'During the summertime I grew bored accompanying outdated entertainers in resorts and missed Üsküdar. And when winter came and I worked at an auction hall, I couldn't warm up to the objects bought by wealthy but shallow customers. My horizons broadened with the concert given by our conservatory band in the legendary Albert Long Hall at Boğaziçi University. Lying hidden between Rumeli Castle and the Bosphorus, the campus surprised me. It could only inspire a musician with its tranquil atmosphere. According to Mother Gülriz, Boğaziçi University was the just the right place for a T. S. Eliot fan. When I got into the university's English Language and Literature Department, the celebrations lasted three days. Mother Gülriz had it that in time I would become a professor of literature and play the saxophone as a hobby. I was touted as being among the most outstanding students of the country; but the other students all appeared childish to me. I never missed a chance to join the musicians at Beyoğlu's Sax Bar. Some called it the "sex bar".'

Had I gone off topic? It was hard to know what the topic was. I glanced at the clock. The interview was only supposed to last forty-five minutes to an hour. The man opposite looked in no hurry to leave. I wondered how many other people he was interviewing for the position. I took a breath and continued. 'In April of the following year, when my mother died in her sleep, I remembered T. S. Eliot's line "April is the cruelest

12

month." That was my life's greatest pain. On Sundays, when I visited Karacaahmet Graveyard, I would take my Selmer with me.'

'Who's Selmer? Your girlfriend?'

I laughed. 'Selmer is the brand name of the saxophone Safa Abi gave me as a gift. Yes, Sir, I suppose you could call it my girlfriend.'

'You are a contrary man. I don't mean that to sound critical. What then?'

'Then I would play in concerts if a hall was short of a saxophonist, or if there was an improv evening, I would compose unpretentious songs. I had discovered Louise Glück – her depressing poems inspired me – and I watched films by the Coen Brothers. I had no high aspirations for my life, but dreamed of leading a simple life, full of music. I laughed at my mediocre friends who wanted to become famous musicians and make a lot of money. I didn't plan to leave Üsküdar; if I won the lottery, though, most likely I wouldn't have objected to a small apartment overlooking Topkapı Palace. For some reason, I had embraced those hazy, panoramic views, which wouldn't be out of place in *One Thousand and One Nights*. To make money, I planned to become an English teacher at language schools and translate.

'I was interested in my studies, although it seemed that our faculty's goal was to prove that William Shakespeare, who lived 500 years ago, was the best playwright of all time. I can't say that Shakespeare didn't help me mature. And at the insistence of Mother Gülriz, I had tried to learn French.

The teacher took every opportunity to whistle, so I was never bored.' I shrugged. It seemed the man still wanted more. I noticed that he smiled slightly at every reference to culture I made. I wondered if he knew the works of Shakespeare, the Coen Brothers, or T. S. Eliot intimately, or if he just didn't want to appear ignorant.

'Following my graduation, I passed my school's doctoral examination and felt a great sense of relief. This meant that for at least four years my musical life would remain unhindered by obligatory military service. That summer, Selim, a trumpet player who'd cheated by copying my papers in written exams at the conservatory, offered me a job. Like many middling musicians he was full of gusto, a highflier. His sights were set on Miles Davis's throne. He thought his name, which spelled "Miles" backwards, was a sign. He'd got a place in an orchestra that was hired to perform in Tarabya, at a nightclub called Eve's Evenings. The orchestra were looking for someone to replace their sax player who'd fallen ill. I had heard of the French bass player who led them, so I agreed to be interviewed. They asked me to play "The Ruby and the Pearl" by Branford Marsalis, and before I was even halfway through it, I was hired. Also included on the programme was a Ukrainian ballet group called The Slavic Swans, but as I don't like ballet and opera, I didn't hang around to watch them.

'Selim was dating Klara, the group's veteran ballerina. I didn't care for her affected ways, but the two of them did some matchmaking for me: Leysa, the star of the group, wanted to meet me. Selim said mockingly, "They're talking about how noble you appear on stage, how at one you are with your saxophone. And you know, of course, how curious women are about tall men." I watched the Slavic Swans for the first time that night; they were good. Leysa resembled the blonde saxophonist who sometimes accompanied Van Morrison, and I was intrigued by the colour of her eyes. We four met at a meyhane in Hisar. She was a conservatory graduate from Lviv and a year older than me. She was cultivated and had fluent English, and I had never dated a blue-eyed girl before. After she said, "You perform ballet with your saxophone", I kissed her for the first time. We seized on every chance to meet after that and listening to her talk so cheered me that I missed her, even the smell of her sweat, if a single day passed when I didn't see her. I felt happy and my self-confidence soared. When the summer programme ended, the band members scattered, and in October, I flew to Lviv, home of the poet Adam Zagajewski.

'I checked into the Astoria Hotel, whose interior, for some reason, I thought resembled a capsule. Leysa was due to return from her extended tour in a couple of days, so I set off to explore the city in the meantime. It was listed as a UNESCO World Heritage site, but I felt it was … carelessly lazy. Controlled by four different nations because of its strategic location, Lviv cannot shake off the fatigue of war. You can hear the moan of monumental buildings needing to be restored, of elderly people, and of outdated buses. When Charles de Gaulle visited the city, he declared poetically, "I have seen parks in a city before, but I am seeing a city in a park for the first time." Lychakiv Graveyard was more interesting than Rynok Square.

A café appeared at every step, and one lira equalled seven hryvnias. Lviv Opera House was more beautiful than the cathedrals. If my late mother could have seen the city spring to life at night, brimming with the vitality of young people, she would have found it ironic. If I had to summarise Lviv in two sentences, I'd quote these lines by Hilmi Yavuz: "Sorrow is that which most becomes us / Is perhaps what we best understand." Its atmosphere must nourish some latent inspiration; I could see myself spending six months each year there.

'I met a couple of obese American siblings, who had come to the city to trace their ancestral lineage. When Leysa returned and we embraced in the lobby, they embarrassed me by cheering from the bar, where they sat, swilling their vodka.

'I only remained in Lviv for a week. As Leysa and I were en route to visit her home on Stefanyka Avenue to meet her parents for the first time, I tried to suppress my excitement. Her chubby mother, who worked at the opera house, was surprised that I wasn't wearing earrings and that I had never heard "Norma" sung by the Turkish diva Leyla Gencer. I didn't care that her father, a retired officer, found an excuse to avoid meeting me – in Ukrainian, Leysa means "that which protects her man" and I didn't believe anything could part us.

'As Leysa and I walked the streets of Lviv holding hands, I remembered Marc Chagall's "Promenade". In the painting, two lovers are strolling hand-in-hand, and the girl is walking on air. I remember how on my return flight to Istanbul; I closed my left hand tightly to keep Leysa's warmth inside it.

'The following summer, the Slavic Swans were invited back

for the season at the same nightclub. However, because of their changing clientele, they hired a lightweight band that played arabesque music instead of jazz. I refused offers for out-of-town gigs and stayed with Leysa. When my twenty-fourth birthday arrived, I took her to Villa Bosphorus in Beylerbeyi for supper. Two years before I had taken my mother and my uncle there with the money from my first pay cheque. Mother Gülriz was fond of this fish restaurant. It had been an innocent Ottoman seaside residence until its owner, an author, rented it to the British Consulate General. As it happened, Kim Philby, the most infamous spy of the twentieth century, had lived there during the time he was working for the Russians. According to his memoirs, he would jump straight from his bedroom into the waters of the Bosphorus. What interested me about the place was that its elderly owners still lived above the restaurant.

'I felt strangely uneasy that evening but thought this was natural given that in four days my girlfriend would be returning to Lviv. However, my head began to throb, and as soon as we had eaten our fish we left. I planned to drop Leysa off at her hotel, take a painkiller, and go straight to bed. We headed up Yalıboyu Avenue and got into the only taxi waiting at the kerb. Immediately, the cab turned into a dark side street, a piece of cloth was forced over my face, and I lost consciousness.

'When I opened my eyes, I was in a hospital. A glance at my distraught uncle told me that something terrible had happened to us. I asked about Leysa first, but instead of answering, my

17

uncle stared at my left hand. I felt a strange pain there, as if something was missing. I couldn't see my index and middle fingers. They may as well have cut off my penis.

'I picked up the glass at my bedside and hurled it at the wall. A nurse swooped in, injecting me with a sedative that knocked me out again. When I came to, I was pinned to the bed with straps around my wrists and ankles. Bit by bit my uncle described what had happened that night. I'd been left at the hospital entrance, unconscious, with my hand badly damaged. The doctors at the hospital had subsequently had to amputate two of my fingers. Leysa had been sedated and her right arm broken in such a way that she could never dance again. She was left in front of the hotel. I was told that in the hours following the surgery I had moaned continuously and talked in my sleep. I couldn't believe that I'd been dead to the world for seventy-two hours. The Slavic Swans, who were departing Istanbul that morning, couldn't provide any useful information to the police, who were waiting for me to wake up and give my statement. I couldn't move past the question: had someone attacked me deliberately, or had this been a cruel mistake? Had my hand been injured deliberately or as collateral while I tried to defend myself and Leysa? Who would want me to suffer the pain of never again being able to play the saxophone?'

The man was listening silently. I wondered what shape the other candidate's stories had taken.

'As I lay shaking in bed, I gazed fixedly at a point on the ceiling and cursed Uncle Niyaz who hadn't left me for dead as a baby, my uncle who had introduced me to Safa Abi, and my mother who had let me take up the saxophone. I started blacking out. I cried silently at night. I couldn't get in touch with Leysa, who had been taken to a different hospital.' I had got to the climax of my small story now. I decided I'd better keep going – the man was looking at me intently.

'When the nightclub informed Selim about the incident, he came straight over. He had his own theory about who'd done it. He explained that a part owner of Eve's Evenings, Nemrut Beşir, had wanted Leysa for himself; Leysa had rejected him, and so he'd punished us both. A brutal man, credited with a number of other violent, sadistic incidents, he was also involved in drug trafficking and lived most of the time in Miami. If this was true, I wondered why Leysa hadn't mentioned anything about this man to me. I examined Beşir Kibaroğlu's pictures on the internet at length.'

The man opposite interrupted me.

'Could you repeat the name of that scumbag?' he asked.

'Beşir Kibaroğlu, Sir. An ugly, middle-aged man with a repulsive grin, from what I can remember from the photographs I found online. If I'd ever met him in person, I don't remember it. I didn't say his name in my statement to the police. On the night of the incident, he was in Miami, and my uncle said that, as there was no evidence, he wouldn't be arrested.

'Laz Cuma, my best friend from the neighbourhood, came to visit on the day I was discharged from the hospital. He was a secondary school graduate and worked at his father's bakery.

Taking hold of my arm, he said angrily in a heavy Laz dialect, "Why the hell did you have to go and become a saxophone player, man?" Following the psychiatrist's advice, my uncle gave me plenty of space. But everyone was looking out for me – whenever I went out on one of my long walks, Cuma would follow, secretly. I felt empty, cried desperately, and barely ate.'

'What about Leysa?'

'I tried to call her repeatedly at the hospital, but after I was discharged, I gave up. Her father opposed our relationship anyway. I think she had her telephone number cancelled. If she had wanted, she could have called me – but she never did. Honestly, during those days, my worst pain was that I would never again play the saxophone as I had. I didn't visit my mother's grave for months.

'I passed no nightmare-free nights. Cuma slept in the next room, and I figured that if I tried to do anything stupid, he and my uncle would stop me. I had some theatrical dreams. Once, I dreamed that I heard some off-key music as a saxophone moved towards me in the dark. As it got closer, I saw two severed fingers running amateurishly over its keys, and I woke up screaming. While my uncle wiped the sweat off my brow, Cuma pressed me to drink some water. As he recited the kalima shahadat in his Laz accent, I suddenly broke into laughter.

'Our street's wise women put out the word that I had only got what I deserved for going to private schools, attending universities, making weird music, and hooking up with infidel girls. Since I still hadn't pulled myself together when the academic year began, I took a year's leave of absence.

'By the time I visited the psychiatrist on the morning of 6 October, Istanbul's liberation day, my sleep problems had been resolved, I had regained my appetite, and I could watch TV, provided there was no music. However, I still felt empty and didn't want to see my musician friends. While reducing the dosage of my medication, the psychiatrist said, "Like Istanbul, you are now liberated", which I found tragicomical.

'After the psychiatrist advised a change of scenery, my uncle sent me to go and stay with his cousin in Melbourne.

'Uncle Izzy (Izzet) lived in a single-storey house in Dallas, one of Melbourne's suburbs. His first job there was as a waiter in an Italian restaurant, but by the time I went to stay, he'd been promoted to demi-chef. A widower, he passed a week of his annual leave in his hometown of Tekirdağ each year and the rest with his lover who lived in Genoa. He was one of the more charismatic residents in Dallas, home to many Turks, and his doorbell played janissary band music. His neighbour Jude was a rugged lesbian in her thirties who lived with her sick mother. In the evenings, Jude and I would go to the local pub to drink beer and get drunk. I told her that I hadn't lost my fingers in a traffic accident – which is what I'd told everyone since I'd arrived there. I cried. I found it hard to adjust to January as summertime in Australia. Jude sauntered about in low-cut T-shirts; her right shoulder bore the tattoo "The limits of my language" and the left "are the limits of my world." I took this as a personal message that I should get back to studying. For some reason I was afraid to ask her whose quote it was.'

'The last philosopher's – Ludwig Wittgenstein.'

I was surprised he knew that. Who was this man?

'You're doing fine,' he said. 'Don't stop.'

'Jude worked at the Melbourne Public Library, but I'd never seen a book in her house. I would go to her library branch often and fall asleep while reading the books that she recommended. I remembered Jack Kerouac was one of them. When I went on tourist trips with Uncle Izzy and Jude, I discovered on seeing Sydney that I missed Üsküdar. I found the kangaroos contrived, and the pissing contest of immigrants as odd. I felt relatively at ease working as a busboy at Uncle Izzy's restaurant on weekends and volunteered some evenings at the public library.'

Having got this far, I wanted to go on.

'I hope that you'll bear with me, Sir. We are almost here. You know how in a dream you can make love to a woman and wake up in the morning to find that you've come in your underwear? Well, it was one of those nights when I'd had four beers and passed out on my bed. In my dream I saw Nemrut Beşir; he'd been tortured and killed. A finger was stuck in each of his ears and nostrils, and six were in his mouth. I beg your forgiveness for saying this, but in the morning when I woke up, I noticed that I had come in my underwear. While I showered, I felt peace at having made a decision: I would kill this man who had made my life miserable, tormented dozens of others, and got thousands hooked on drugs. I would get my revenge. Deciding when and where, and planning how to do it without getting caught, seemed like an exciting project.'

Some of the things I was telling this man, whom I'd never met before, I hadn't planned to say before I'd begun talking.

'I have six months left to live,' the man said. 'Tell me anything you like; it seems probable I'll take it to the grave.'

'Your lawyer, who's a client of one of my uncles, told me you were ill. The job appealed to me. I thought we could support each other. Also I'm broke; a net monthly salary of 5,000 euros is far more than I'd be making as a translator.'

'I don't think you were quite finished with your story.'

'Uncle Izzy insisted I stay out there longer. He suggested that I could make a new start and continue to work on my doctorate in Australia. Hugging Jude, I said, "If I stay here three more months, I might fall in love with you, so I have to go away." In March I returned to Istanbul. I stopped by Karacaahmet Graveyard with two little unopened pouches of lavender I had found while rummaging through my mother's room. As I mixed in the lavender with the soil, I cried again, remembering the meaning of the name of our street. "Mother," I said, "were you meaning to insinuate something about our fate by living on Eşrefsaat Street?"'

I stopped. To my surprise, the man started to clap. Had he believed everything I had said? He looked moved.

'You can start working in April, which I don't believe is the cruellest month. As for your salary, it won't be 5 but 8,000 euros. It might be six months; it might be fewer.' As I kissed the hand he extended, a chill crept slowly up my body, just as it had when I had touched a saxophone for the first time.

2

Artvin

Professor of Philosophy Ziya M. Adlan, a Geneva resident for forty years, had returned to Istanbul to die. He was receiving chemotherapy, which would give him six more months, and during that time – as he told his lawyer – he had 'one final account to settle'. I visited Saim Bey, Ziya Adlan's lawyer, in his office in Kadıköy to sign the employment contract. Saim Bey must have worn the same suit every day for the last twenty years. I wondered what he hoped to convey by doing so but had no way of asking him; he wasn't a man for small talk while at work. His voice rose and fell sharply as he said, 'Ziya Bey is an important member of an Ottoman dynasty.' He appeared to be trying to impress me, to create an air of mystery (had I become more judgmental after losing my fingers or was I always this way?).

Saim Bey's wife, who was wandering about the office in her tracksuit, doubled as his secretary and sounded like a squeaking door. She introduced herself to me as Saniye Hanım. According to her, Ziya Adlan had an expert pair of carers already; I was to become his assistant. I was to keep him company during his final days with cancer, meaning that I would read to him, help him watch films, take him to places and people he wanted to visit, and, if he was in the mood, chat with him. As she listed off the tasks, I began to have second thoughts at the prospect of engaging in endless dialogue with an ailing Swiss-Ottoman philosopher for as long as his final months lasted. Saim Bey's office building had no lifts and as I went down after my briefing, I was struck by the smell of frying fish on the second floor. I felt a sudden urge to buzz the doorbell from where the smell was coming and then run away. Later, I discovered that the door I had passed was an apartment belonging to a rare books dealer.

When I heard Ziya Adlan lived on Farewell Fountain Street, my good hand shook as I took the spare set of keys from Saim Bey. It felt ominous to me. I had bid farewell to two loved ones at once, my girlfriend and the saxophone: was I being tested by fate yet again, or was I expected to find peace in that mystical address?

Like an old cowboy trying to draw his gun, Farewell Fountain Mansion stood diagonally opposite the cemetery and the fountain. Three-storeyed, with cut stone walls turning from pink to grey, it was in harmony with the street's sad mien. The makeshift perimeter wall, which didn't hide the mansion's symmetrical lines, gave more meaning to its stark construction. I rang the bell on the garden gate and waited in vain for the bark of an old wolf dog – this was the kind of house that surely had one, but no. The weary, middle-aged man who swung the gate open with a groan looked surprised to see me facing him. I might well have been the first guest in quite some time. Perhaps he thought the mansion would collapse before it had another visitor. Apart from a dry well and a scrawny silverberry bush, the garden was bare. I tried not to step back.

Inside the mansion, the furniture and appliances had clearly not been changed or replaced for the last twenty years. I wondered who had lived here before Ziya Bey and whether, at some point, I would get to learn the story of the previous owner. The mansion's only contemporary component was the second-floor hallway, which was larger than our entire apartment in Üsküdar. The newly installed, light blue wallpaper stretched out like a restrained ocean around a series of antique maps. Two round mirrors hung on the wall opposite a giant-screen television. If I caressed the tughra-embellished silver plate encircling the mirrors, would I see the noble and ignoble Ottoman figures that had been reflected there before me? This was a mansion for wonder.

As we toured the mansion, I began to get a feel for which rooms were for show and which were for living in. The living room itself had leather upholstery. On a glass coffee table there were boxes of medicine and cigars, bottles of cognac, a silver ashtray and foreign-language magazines. The bookshelf held works exclusively by or about Samuel Beckett. Two shelves were filled with old DVDs, and I felt embarrassed that I had never heard of any of the titles or their directors. At least I had a chance to do some research before Ziya Bey could discover my ignorance. In one corner of the living room stood two wheelchairs, and in another, a bed. Of special interest to me was an erotic Jean-Léon Gérôme figurine on a table by the bedside.

I was shown around the house by Ziya Bey's carers, an Uzbek couple, whom I can only describe as efficient. They introduced me to the only other residents in the house. Besides Ziya Bey and I, there was a Circassian couple, who I heard were Ziya Bey's servants in perpetuity. They lived on the first floor, didn't roam about much, and stayed quiet.

The third floor, covered with linoleum that released sighs when walked upon, was used for storage. The personal belongings of Ziya Bey had been dumped into two rooms; mostly books and folders that he told me he'd brought back with him from Geneva. Three spacious rooms were under Ottoman occupation; one was filled with uniforms, fezzes, enamelled badges, insignia, flags and weapons. When I opened the door for the first time, I would not have been surprised had I heard shouts of 'Allah, Allah' as charging men, playing at soldiers, braced against my invasion of the room. The second room contained framed calligraphy, certificates, tughras, coats of arms, plaques, engravings, maps of a palace, and what must have been thousands of books in Ottoman and French, stacked against the walls and in towers on the floor. It smelled like hay, like a time tunnel. The third room was full of furniture, vases, crystals, numerous silver objects wrapped in velvet, and bronze statues. As a former auctioneer, I had a hankering.

Finally, I was taken to the room that was to be mine, where I could leave the small bag of clothes and a few books – the only luggage I had brought with me. I liked it immediately, although there wasn't much to it. My room overlooked the Farewell Fountain and the shopping mall lying, as if in hiding, behind it. The small-screen TV, desk and bed were recent acquisitions, and the hanging of light pink wallpaper was fresh – I was told that it had been completed earlier, on the very day I was to move in. On the same floor, a few rooms down from mine, was another bedroom that overlooked a graveyard; this was occupied by Ziya Bey and I was forbidden to enter it.

On that first day, as I watched Ziya Bey wander through the mansion in his casual clothes, the style he radiated was impossible to miss. Even the way he clasped his hands behind his back as he slowly paced up and down the living room was classy. He had a handsome face: even, with an aquiline nose and large, expressive eyes. Away from the pressures of the interview environment and less focused on my own performance, I was able to observe him, and pick up on mannerisms I had not noticed the week before. He was a baritone and spoke Turkish perfectly. He was very knowledgeable and didn't shy away from sharing it, but when I once declared 'You know more than Google' he seemed embarrassed. He remained impressive even while he was listening to those around him. I imagined he must have been a favourite with students. He never spoke unnecessarily, and when he did speak, he would be brisk and support his statements with aphorisms and quotes from distinguished figures and thinkers.

I noticed in our first meeting that he did not welcome personal questions, and he was happy with the sensitivity I showed in not disturbing his privacy.

As I crawled into bed on my first night at the mansion, I shivered. I was lying in a desolate building abutted by a dry Ottoman fountain and a derelict graveyard; and it was ready to collapse once its final owner had passed on. But within a week I had grown used to the Farewell Fountain Mansion. Gradually, I embraced it and its proprietor and considered myself part and parcel of them.

Work began the day after I arrived. Ziya Bey introduced a timetable, and that was how we went on. We started off the day early with breakfast, just the two of us. Then, for two hours, I would read aloud works by Samuel Beckett in English. We began with *Watt*; his copy was number 830/1100 of the first limited edition. Published in 1953, the book had a nylon cover. These details were important to Ziya Bey, it pleased him when I observed them.

Before we started our daily reading, Ziya Bey would say to me, 'Understand what you're reading and don't rush.' If no cigar was in his mouth, he would sometimes smile as he listened with his eyes closed. He would ask weird questions whenever he felt the urge to do so, and then, seemingly pleased when I confessed that I didn't understand, go on to explain his own response. Bidding farewell to the world by listening to his favourite author's works one last time, like a lullaby before sleep, meant so much to Ziya Bey. I began to share his appreciation of poignant Beckett – Beckett hooks the reader in the opening paragraph, then sets up a mysterious feast of improvisation. I was particularly provoked in *Watt* when its protagonist, Mr. Hackett, feels uneasy at seeing another person occupying the park bench where he always sat.

Ziya Bey liked liquid foods for lunch, watched documentaries on television, took naps, on awaking would read, and would, in his own words, 'subject the internet to a test'. When the summer sun had descended and we took a cab to Çamlıca Hill, Fenerbahçe Park, or Çınaraltı Café in Kuzguncuk, he would swiftly scan the place and then lose himself in the horizon. Covered by a shawl, or something similar, sipping from his flask of cognac with a guilty smile, he truly became a Beckettian character. On Saturday evenings, he would dine out with Saim Bey and Saniye Hanım, whom I found tolerable when not in her tracksuit. I discovered that Saniye was Ziya Bey's cousin, and I think she was the only family he had left.

During those first few weeks, Ziya Bey also took me along to three farewell meetings with his remaining friends, and I felt proud to be introduced to them as his assistant. They, too, were characters. Fahrünissa Selvi Hanım Efendi's residence was a museum-house, and she was as elegant as a queen. I was happy to learn that she was acquainted with my favourite teacher, Professor Oya Başak and felt a little nostalgia for my own history, which I had been so quick to try to forget in Australia.

Ziya Bey was at ease with these friends – he called Tunç

Uluğ, a retired business executive and collector, 'abi'. Tunç's wife, Judith Uluğ, was an exquisite musician, and the stumps of my severed fingers ached when I saw her piano. They were interesting people, and I didn't feel at all bored in their company. One evening in June, we went to dine at a newly opened restaurant called Juno with poet and author Enis Batur and his wife Fatma Tülin. Enis Batur and Ziya Bey had been classmates at St Joseph French High School. I swiftly calculated that this must make Ziya Adlan sixty years old. As these two wise men talked in whispers, Enis Bey pretended that he wasn't upset at this farewell meeting. I told him how I had finished his novella *The Library* in two sittings. I would have put money on the fact that the central character was my boss, although I was too intimidated to ask Enis Bey directly. His wife, Fatma Tülin Hanim, an eminent painter, was, if anything, more intimidating than her husband. She was also knowledgeable and a good conversationalist; when the two friends went outside to smoke, she turned to me and said, 'I finally remember who you look like. You're a character straight out of a novel a friend of mine wrote.'

And so, time passed amiably enough. Ziya Bey did not speak to me often or at length, never matching the curiosity he had shown in me during our interview. I hoped that I was not a disappointment to him. I had Sundays off and used my first paycheque to treat my uncle and Cuma to a meyhane meal in Kadıköy. I shared my reservations with them. My uncle was of the opinion that Ziya Bey would open up to me 'when the time was right'. Cuma was a little less refined, proclaiming in his heavy Laz dialect, 'Watch it, I hope this guy's not some kind of pervert!'

However, over time Ziya Bey did go to great lengths to explain the history of the area to me, and between trips, or while Ziya Bey was napping, I had the opportunity to explore the area for myself.

Farewell Fountain Street was too short to accommodate a café or even a grocery store, and it was desolate. A derelict Ottoman cemetery lay across the way like a castle keep, shielding it from the evils of the city. When I first entered the street, I closed my eyes and waited for the welcoming of a sad hymn from the cemetery. The wooden building on the corner was the street's most senior occupant, and it proudly bore the 'Farewell Fountain' plaque. The stumpy two-storey buildings behind it had colourful façades. They were as quaint as a movie set, and had the same makeshift look, as though they could be moved away at a moment's notice. They were inhabited by reputable retirees, widows full of joie de vivre, artists and writers. I didn't mind the consultancy bureaus and quiet ateliers, which in any case, I didn't observe functioning. I would like to see how well the entire football team of Yeldeğirmenispor would fit into that little administration building. At the end of the street, a place vendors and cars were too lazy to enter, the Farewell Fountain shone like a lighthouse. It reminded me in many ways of my own neighbourhood, but the fountain here had recently gone through yet another restoration and was dry. Now it had a sad look, like a jilted bride.

The fountain had been revived twice in 300 years. It came to be called the Farewell Fountain because armies dispatched to the East, pilgrimage travellers and caravans were ceremoniously sent forth from its front. Mother Gülriz might have thought it ironic that a cemetery lay so close to this spot where armies were sent off on campaigns.

In the Byzantine period the place had been a pasture, famed for its therapeutic springs. The coming of the Ottomans saw summer cafés open under the sycamores. Whenever I read the line, 'Can you draw the picture of happiness, Abidin?', from a favourite poem of mine by Nazım Hikmet, I recalled engravings depicting Ottomans sprawled over divans, smoking hookahs, somewhere like here. In the sixteenth century, as an act of kindness, the chief Ottoman eunuch, Gazanfer, had first constructed the fountain. I would learn later those eunuchs were the highest-ranking officers after the grand vizier. Since I had lost two fingers, I identified myself as something like a eunuch and felt a warm kind of kinship for Gazanfer. He led an interesting life. Before being caught by the Ottomans he had been a Venetian sailor. He was eventually executed, of course.

Farewell Fountain Cemetery dominated the street. Cats strutted like pharaonic curios along the walls of the derelict graveyard, which resembled a looted nomad encampment. The very tombstones there, tilted and broken, appeared to be mourning. I found the design of all the epitaphs appealing. Some stones were fitted out with turbans to signify a pasha or a high-level bureaucrat, but most of the graves and their dried-up trees lay in a hasty sort of disarray, as if someone had quickly buried those martyred in the war before hurrying away. It was called the Arab Cemetery; no one knew why.

As I began to ask more questions and make observations about the local area, Ziya Bey began opening up more to me about his interest and place in Ottoman history. He told me about Nakşıdil Sultan, the mother of Mahmut II, an odalisque of French descent whose actual name was Aimée. It was said that she and Napoleon's wife Josephine were cousins. In 1790, at the age of fourteen, a ship Aimée was on board sunk and she was rescued by Algerian pirates. They sent her to Istanbul as a gift to the sultan, where she became Abdulhamid I's odalisque, married him, took the name Nakşıdil, and gave birth to Mahmut II. Ziya Bey's specialist period was the eighteenth and nineteenth centuries, and he was particularly aware of those whose place in history he felt had been overlooked.

Another time Ziya Bey told me about Mahmut II, who, because of the extraordinary conditions of his time, could be ranked, in terms of rulership, among the top five Ottoman sultans. Ziya Bey's exact words were, 'His neglect by history books is inexcusable; I empathise with emperors, statesmen, artists and authors who got a raw deal.' He went on to say, 'I like my last name because it starts with the first two letters of the Turkish word for justice, "adalet".' In the coming days, he went into a deep dive into Sultan Mahmut II. It began after I asked an apparently basic question, to which Ziya Bey responded, somewhat abruptly, 'I don't think you know Sultan Mahmut II well enough. Listen! He was born in 1785, and after Osman I (Gazi) and Sultan Ibrahim he's the third, and last, of the Ottoman ancestral patriarchs. Under the sharp eyes of his mother and his paternal uncle Selim III, he got a good education. During the one-year reign of his older brother Mustafa IV, he was put under house arrest and had to live with the fear of being assassinated at any moment. When in the care of the Grand Vizier Alemdar Mustafa Pasha he became sultan, the Ottoman Empire was passing through one of its most crucial periods. The war with Russia hadn't ended, the discredited Janissary army once more revolted, uprisings were a common occurrence in Anatolia and the Balkans, the plague reared its ugly head, the fires never ended, Europe was being hypocritical, Muslim-minority clashes broke out, and the Cavallan Mehmet Ali Pasha revolt had become the biggest threat of all.' How he remembered all this was beyond me.

'Despite having limited resources, Sultan Mahmut II solved problems by behaving much like a chess expert cum diplomat. When he stopped the Cavallan army headed for Istanbul with the help of the Russians, their arch-enemies, he said, "A man who falls overboard will clutch at a sea serpent", which in time became an aphorism. He was open to the European reform movements and sympathised particularly with the French. He reorganised the state with an emphasis on education. He opened modern schools, made elementary education compulsory and free, established respect for women's rights, issued the first official gazette, founded the postal administration, and initiated the issuance of passports. He abolished the Janissary corps and shattered the authority of religious orders. He banned the wearing by civil servants of turbans, shalwars and rawhide sandals, urging them to wear fezzes, pants and jackets instead. He introduced the idea of a merit system in the work force. He had his beard cut short, shaved each morning, and dinner would now be set out on a table. All this resulted in his being called an "Infidel Padishah". He had his portrait hung in public offices and instituted the practice of census-taking. In 1829 there were 359,089 people living in Istanbul. He supported social institutions and the arts, constructed the city's most elegant palaces and mosques, and restored ancient monuments, not forgetting to maintain the roads and bridges as well. Like his grandfather Ahmet III, he was an aesthete. He recognized the importance of justice and took steps to update laws and regulations. He wrote poems under the pseudonym "Adli" and was a calligrapher and composer as well as a player of the reed flute and tambour. He was modest and liked to chat with the public. Yet being a composed man and an opportunist, he could be ruthless when that's what was needed. In the process of abolishing the Janissary corps, he perpetrated a massacre, and when his ungrateful and inept brother tried to take back the throne, he had him killed.

'An unmitigated reformist, Sultan Mahmut II attempted to weigh out the positive aspects of the East and the West closely and adopt them. And with his eleven wives and nine mistresses, he had a full life. He wanted a large family, but of the thirty-five children he sired, only six survived. The aphorism, "the state to the ruler or the raven to the carcass", which means "to make or break", is attributed to him as well. He succumbed to tuberculosis in his sister's mansion on that hill in Çamlıca right across from us. It may be that out of respect for his memory three generations of us have also awaited death in this soulless mansion. I've listed here all I could think of at the moment about our sultan who could see 200 years in the future, and whose grandson I am proud to be. I can't hold you responsible for not knowing those details, since your history books tend only to record conquests and retreats.' I often made notes when Ziya Bey spoke at length about such things, and I think he liked that I did so. As for his being the grandson of the sultan – I was not surprised. I had already expected as much. But I found it interesting that he left that detail to last in his lecture.

At the beginning of July, we visited the Sultan Mahmut II shrine in Divanyolu. We stayed there for some time. As we were leaving, Ziya Bey reverently caressed the coffins of the sultan and his daughter, Atiye Sultan. I wondered if this was something he had always done on such visits, or if this was him paying a final farewell, but we had planned a full day and had to head off promptly to make our next stop. We were heading to the Atiye Sultan Estate, which now housed the Kâğıthane District Governorship. After the driver asked directions for the third time, Ziya Bey suddenly became irrationally irate. It was the first time I had seen him angry, and I felt that, despite his age and illness, only my grip on his arm kept him from beating the idiot with his cane. I was surprised; he never raised his voice at me and was always able to express his warnings humorously. Thankfully, he calmed down upon arrival, and while he paced leisurely in front of the estate, which had been recently restored, he told me that he belonged to the Atiye Sultan dynasty. I understood why he had been so angry at the taxi driver; he seemed to take the diminishing importance of the sultan personally. It was one thing to die, but it must have seemed to Ziya Bey in that moment that his whole family line would die out with him.

The following week, a middle-aged, well-dressed man with two big men at his sides paid an unannounced visit to the mansion. They were an odd trio. While Ziya Bey conversed with their boss, who I assumed to be an academic, the rest of the household were asked to wait in the yard with the bodyguards. As they understood the Uzbek carer who brought them a drink of water, I assumed the bodyguards were Russian. They had clearly come about something important – perhaps this was Ziya Bey's 'one final account to settle' before he passed away. On his way out, I noticed that Ziya Bey's acquaintance was holding an envelope, an innocent smile on his face. For some reason, I felt happy, too. I was curious about what had passed between them, but even though I had lived at the house for almost two months, I had grown no more intimate with Ziya Bey. I bit my tongue and asked no improper questions.

After chemotherapy caused Ziya Bey to lose his hair, he began to wear a Fenerbahçe football club cap, and with Band-Aids stuck to the sides of his forehead, he resembled a robot. He had a delicate build and needed five days to recover from each chemotherapy session. During this time, he slouched when he walked, swayed and groaned as he sat, vomited, and grew depressed. He also became somewhat smaller and slightly hunchbacked, but even while recovering, he wouldn't give up his silver-plated cane for a wheelchair. Once, after he'd fallen asleep while watching a DVD, I went over to cover him up with a blanket and he awoke screaming. As I said, I couldn't complain; he was smart, gentle, fair and punctual. And his mysterious air became him.

Ziya Bey's birthday was 20 July, and the two of us planned to have dinner at the Four Seasons Bosphorus Hotel. It was clear now that Ziya Bey's health was deteriorating, and this birthday was going to be his last. His carers got him dressed and we crossed over to Istanbul's European side in a chauffeured limousine. Getting out of the car was torture for him. We had a light dinner at Aqua with little conversation.

After we finished, I discovered that we were going to spend the night at the nearby boutique hotel that had formerly been an Ottoman mansion. Ziya Bey's suite was called 'Palace Roof'. And it was here, as I was helping him into bed, that he began to tell me all the memories I had expected him to share from the beginning. Not, as I had imagined, in small splinters here and there but all in one go, like a swollen river that has burst its banks and must exhaust itself before it can return to run its usual course.

3

Ziya Bey

Do you remember our visit to the Sultan Mahmut II shrine? Today marks the birthday of both Ziya Mahmut Adlan and the great Ottoman Sultan Mahmut II, who history books have ignored. His daughter, Atiye Sultan, died aged twenty-six. Some of the monuments my great-grandfather bequeathed to the city are the mosque in Karacaahmet and the grove in Üsküdar, which has now fallen off the map.

I was the only child of Asaf Hamit and Mesrure Adlan and I was born after several miscarriages. I was brought up like a crown prince but was never able to love my father. Two thousand years ago, the philosopher Epictetus said, 'A person's homeland is his childhood' and so, I'll have to begin with anecdotes from my homeland. My earliest memory is of a sweet little kitten, which had run out of the cemetery and taken shelter in our yard. But when I tried to pet it, it scratched my hand, so I took it over to the dry well and threw it in. My mother saw this and as soon as my father came home, told on me. Angrily dragging me outside, Asaf Bey gripped both my hands and dangled me into the well. When he shouted, 'Should I throw you down there with that cat?' my joyful response, 'Yes, yes,' stunned him. I was four at the time.

Like every other lazy bon vivant, Asaf Bey was very shrewd. At just the right time he put the plots he'd inherited to good use and ended up owning several blocks of apartment buildings on the affluent Bağdat Avenue. Every month he would purchase gold and allow a Jewish usurer to put some of his money to work. As a member of a dynasty, he had no doubts about being respected by others. His birthright allowed him to harass any young girl that caught his eye. The team of house servants included young girls, and when he was at home, he didn't hesitate to touch them when he had a mind to do so. His grinning and chatting with my mother as they danced at the Grand Club was an act. That's why I've always hated dancing and have never even watched ballet. My most pleasant memory from the club was of looking over the male dance partners, and asking myself, 'If I were my mother, who would I choose to have an affair with?'

My father was a burly man with the face of an innocent. When he climbed the stairs, he bent down low, a skill I felt sure he thought of as unique to himself. He worshipped anything Ottoman. On sighting a sultan's mosque, fountain, or even a monumental tree, he would walk over to caress it. He performed the Eid prayers at Nusretiye Mosque, which was built by Mahmut II, and always paid a visit to the shrine afterwards. The first time he took me there, I counted eighteen coffins. Lying side by side in its burial section were the tombs of princes, grand viziers, ministers, commanders, high-level bureaucrats, academicians, authors and poets. I imagined them waiting until eternity to appear before the sultan and walked on tiptoe so as not to disturb them.

If my father chose to perform the Friday prayer, he would go to Beylerbeyi Mosque because its founder was Abdülhamit I, the father of Mahmut II. On those days when we went there together and I waited for him in the courtyard beside the fountain built by Mahmut II, I couldn't help but reflect on what a terrible sultan my father would be. Once, when I asked him the name of the mosque's architect, he flicked my nose with his prayer beads and said, 'How the hell would I know!' Still, my father was devoted to his family and generous. If he decided to beat his veteran driver, whom he'd helped become a family man, he would ceremoniously spit in both of his palms.

My father never pressured me nor anyone else about religion, but I greeted Ramadan with joy because then I could finally have pitta bread with sesame seeds, drink lentil soup, and feast on pastırma. To show his respect for the month of Ramadan, my father would content himself by rubbing up against the young servants only. If I noticed this, he would carelessly start scratching around his crotch. On Fridays, a rich iftar feast was served in the mansion to a group of distinguished invitees. On those days, I too would fast; then, a moment after the nostalgic cannon shot, I would devour the lentil soup, happy to have passed a test. After dinner, we would all go through to the guest room, and during tea and coffee service my father would smoke a hookah. Straightening the bottom of his moustache, he would begin with 'You see,' and proudly discourse on the Ottoman dynasty. He had two favourite topics, and when the time came to broach them, he would add and omit numerous details. He wasn't a bad narrator, but after a while I would get bored and ask to be excused, saying I had to study.

My father's childhood home had been a wooden mansion in the Doğancılar neighbourhood of Üsküdar. It was a special place for him and regularly used to reflect on its importance. His lectures would always begin with, 'Our state register could never be moved from Üsküdar' and proceed to praise the neighbourhood's deep-rooted history. I remember the passage he used to relay from his own father about the streets, all lit by gas, being readied for the night shift. 'While praying, he used to wait at our mansion's bay window for the attendant who lit the streetlamps. The young man, the very picture of an oil wrestler, would arrive like a hero bearing a long stick on his shoulder; skilfully, he would ignite the lamp's burner with a greasy piece of cloth stuck on the end of the stick, and then exit the street singing an Anatolian folk song.' As he listed all the highborn viziers, scribes, ulama and poets who had lived on the street from the eighteenth century onward, he gave priority to those whose mansions had burned down, caught up in his nostalgia.

My father used to regularly visit the estate of Nail Bey from Enderun School and Nihalnaz Sultan from the harem. He would go on to narrate the story of their marriage as if he had witnessed it himself: 'One day, while Nail Bey was reading the Quran after his morning prayer, there came a knock on his door. It was an attendant from Sultan Reşad's Palace who has come to take him to Yıldız Palace. Nervously, Nail Bey boarded the steamboat, and when he arrived, Sultan Reşad told him, 'Until now, we haven't conceived with Nihalnaz Sultan. Last night, we prayed for the Supreme Being to send us a lucid dream for guidance. Those in the spiritual realm showed you to us. I will divorce Nihalnaz Sultan and marry her to you. Your marriage will be consummated at once, and tomorrow you will be sent off to Fizan to be its governor.' As was his style, he drowned this dubious anecdote in irrelevant but atmospheric details.

My father left Üsküdar after the family's mansion caught fire. While there wasn't too much damage, they thought the place was ill-fated now. That's when they bought the Farewell Fountain Mansion at the tip of Kadıköy. Purchased as a bargain from a bankrupt Greek merchant, it dates to Byzantine times and is rumoured to be cursed.

The story of how my father met my mother is a typical one. Her parents were friends with my father's parents as they were all members of the exclusive Grand Club. Of them all, I only got to know my maternal grandmother Sadakat Hanım. My grandfather Rauf Pasha graduated from St Joseph with honours and was then accepted by Sorbonne University in Paris. My father rarely spoke about his father, so he probably didn't get along well with him, either. He had two sisters, but the eldest died in childhood because of poor medical treatment. The other one eloped with a penniless Turkish-

Armenian musician, died of unknown causes, and nobody attended her funeral.

My mother, however, was beautiful and followed a traditional route and married as soon as she graduated from Üsküdar American Academy for Girls. Her father managed legal affairs in a foreign company. My maternal grandmother was a funny woman who lived on the bottom floor of one of our buildings in Caddebostan. When speaking her name, she drew out the second 'a' delightedly, and when my mother complained to her about my nose-picking, she said, 'Well, at least he's not picking anybody else's nose!' 'Mesrure' in Arabic means 'the thing that fulfilled her desire'. I was her mesrure.

Despite her love for me, my mother never stopped resenting her husband. Each morning as she tied his shoelaces, I wanted to strangle them both. While she could tolerate her boorish husband, she couldn't bear partings; even running out of shampoo upset her, and she would whine about having to throw away the bottle. She dressed stylishly but was an average cook at best. I fumed at her demand that her guests eat a second slice of the cake she'd made.

My early memories of Farewell Fountain Street are all sad ones. Once, I plucked all the delicate flowers from the garden, thinking that they would bloom again the next day. When my father asked me why I had done so, I replied, 'They were crying for me to pluck them', and he smiled at my answer but pummelled my ears with his amber prayer beads. Just now, retelling this, I can still feel the pain. I had very few peers in the neighbourhood, and I was not allowed to play with them.

However, I do remember a poor, unkempt homeless man who lived in the area. He used to say 'Sulhi, Sulhi' melodiously when someone asked his name, and then he would go quiet. Most of the time he carried a transistor radio as he walked and mimicked the sounds of static while using the radio's dial to conduct a safari between stations. Whenever I ran into him as he rested at the Farewell Fountain, I would give him 25 kurush and ask him to perform for me. I also used to chase the cemetery cats and watch the seagulls taking a break on the fountain when I was allowed out of the garden. I thought they were dressed in white capes and could disappear instantly at will. When asked what I wanted to be when I grew up, I used to say 'Seagull!' Once, on hearing this, my father angrily said to my mother, 'Mes, is this boy taking after your brother, I wonder?'

My father was referring to my Uncle Nüzhet, who'd drowned as a young man long before I was born. For that reason, I wasn't allowed to swim. There weren't many recreational activities that it was acceptable for me to do as a boy. I never had a bicycle because one of my father's relatives had been hit by a bus while biking. Asking for a guitar was out of the question, as they'd say such a thing was unbecoming for a pasha's grandson.

I was circumcised when I was eight and hated all the crazy celebrations that came with it. My only good memory of the act was being introduced to 'tincture of iodine'. Following my circumcision, I scheduled times to get scratches on my arm so that I could run to my mother and have iodine rubbed on it. As my arm burned, I would inhale that magical smell and maximise my pleasure, so to speak.

As a child I was curious, no matter that my parents scolded me for asking why chickens had wings but couldn't fly and why all the seawater didn't evaporate. School was something of a freedom for me as a boy – there, I had the freedom to learn. After I'd learned the alphabet, I remember feeling bitter towards my father for having a name that began with 'A' while mine began with 'Z'. The males in our family traditionally attend St Joseph, the French missionary high school and my acceptance into St Joseph pleased my father. He kissed my forehead, gave me his hand to kiss, and said, 'If you finish school with honours and get into a good European university, wish for anything you like, Ziya Mahmut!'

My feeling when I stepped through the school's main door was that of walking into a barren prison courtyard. I thought of my classmates who'd fully enjoyed their childhood as odd, and frequently took shelter in the dim-lit library. I had discovered Le Petit Larousse encyclopaedia, which was scorned by Anglo-Americans, and read five pages every day. I surprised even myself by screaming with joy when I saw the Larousse that had been brought from France for my fourteenth birthday. My father, pleased at having made his son happy, laughed brusquely as he twirled his prayer beads faster.

My closest schoolfriend was Enis Batur. We were close and opposites. When he called me 'Ziya Mahmut Bey', my brisk response was, 'Yes, Master Ahmet Enis.' I envied his courage when he found a way to get kicked out of St Joseph. He became an important man of letters and an aesthete.

Our composition teacher held that a love of poetry was important, and that Arthur Rimbaud was the last great poet. Two criteria governed his appraisal of prose: the topic had to provoke interest, and the writing had to be concise. For a composition in ten sentences, I responded to the question, 'If you could be a "thing", what would that thing be?' with 'potkal'. If you don't know what that means, it's a bottle with a message inside, thrown into the sea from a wrecked ship to alert those on land; in practice, it usually ends up at the wrong time or in the wrong place or in the wrong person's hands. When my teacher said, 'You're Samuel Beckett's perfect student', Beckett hadn't yet won the Nobel Prize for Literature.

Beckett ran in the family. My father held that our last name, 'Adlan', was a Beckettesque tragicomedy. When the surname law was legislated in 1934, the retired statesman Rauf Pasha applied at the civil registry office for the surname 'Hilat'. Suspicious of a name evoking the word 'hilafet', meaning 'caliphate', the clerk opened the dictionary at his side, baulked at the definition: 'caftan given by sultans to placate or reward someone during the Ottoman period,' and suggested its reversed form, 'Talih,' meaning 'fortune'. Rauf Pasha then requested 'Adli,' with respect to Sultan Mahmut II, who wrote poems and composed under that pseudonym. Knowingly or mistakenly, the clerk listed it in the registry as 'Adlan'. My grandfather didn't check it at the time and couldn't be bothered to change it later. I was entertained by the thought that our surname could so almost have been amalgamated into 'Hadilan', meaning 'Get the fuck out of here!'

My favourite subject was philosophy. My teacher once remarked, 'I could give you an A+ just for the questions you ask.' I spent as much time in the library reading philosophers' biographies as their theories and understood their contrariety as superiority: while René Descartes slept in a warm bakery to be able to concentrate, he found cross-eyed women attractive and impregnated his maid. Arthur Schopenhauer, who defined passion as the mother of all things evil, described in his essay '38 Ways to Win an Argument', thirty-eight different ways to beat a person up. Immanuel Kant, who thought asexuality a virtue, never left Königsberg, where he was born. Baruch Spinoza, the proprietor of an optical shop, refused to believe that he'd ever been a child.

The summer before my senior year in high school I decided to become an academic in the field of philosophy. One weekend, Pertev, the class playboy, and I visited Caddebostan Beach with our girlfriends, who were twins. Pertev was browsing my answers to the questions written two years before in his diary. To the question, 'What animal would you like to be?' my answer had been 'a vegetarian seagull that had swallowed a message bottle'. I patted myself on the back as the others laughed at my answers. I used to take girlfriends home if any of them asked to see our mansion, but I would pick days when my father was out of town.

One evening when my parents were away at Yalova Thermal Springs, my grandmother and I had dinner at the Grand Club. For the first time, I saw her tired and thoughtful. The agonising live music notwithstanding, she shared a family secret with me that had even been kept from my father: my mother's younger sibling, the boy-genius Nüzhet, had committed suicide. He had been in love with Nükhet, a girl from a wealthy family. He and Nükhet, who was in the sculpture department in the Fine Arts Academy, had been high-school classmates. They were such a perfect match and looked so good together that people referred to them as two peas in a pod. Nüzhet was a sharp and high-spirited student of civil engineering at Istanbul Technical University. Upon graduating, Nüzhet launched into his doctoral studies in hydraulics and water resources engineering while Nükhet moved to New York for two years to get her master's degree. They planned to get married when she returned. The next summer his beloved married a ballet dancer there, and Nüzhet fell into depression. He stopped eating and became sullen. One September afternoon he entered the sea from Caddebostan Beach, and his lifeless body was retrieved later. The note he'd left in the kitchen read, 'Please forgive me. I can't take it anymore.'

Later that night, my grandmother wanted me to go through the belongings Nüzhet had left in his groom's chest, to see if I'd find anything to take as a keepsake. She told me, 'I liken you to your uncle, but you're not so fragile; you can be defiant when you have to be.' From his belongings, I chose the edition of *Watt*, which you are reading to me now. That book has fired up my passion for Beckett. The second book I took was *Aganta Burina Burinata* by The Fisherman of Halicarnassus, which was autographed to my uncle. If you haven't read it, it's about a love of the sea, the murderer of my uncle.

When we walked home from the Grand Club that evening, Sadakat Hanım took my arm. With each step, I felt her moving slowly away from my arm. On New Year's Eve, we lost her; she'd kept her cancer hidden from us all.

4

Ziya Bey

My professors recommended Ligne d'Horizon University in Geneva. This boutique school only had faculties of philosophy, mathematics, art history and sociology and 2,000 students at most. It had been founded by a billionaire executive with a passion for philosophy and getting accepted as a student wasn't easy. Having a professorship at that school or a degree from it were said to rank high in importance. Application required grade reports of the last three years, two references, and completion of a special three-hour exam. My father did not meddle with my decision and only said, 'As long as you become a professor, I don't care what field it's in.' For him, becoming a professor at a European university was no less important than becoming a pasha in the Ottoman administration. This was how he would outclass his father.

During the fifty-minute entrance exam we had to write an essay, and the topic for that year was 'history's most underrated philosopher'. My choice was Empedocles, who lived in the fifth century BCE. He was a wealthy physicist, doctor, cleric and rhetorician. Empedocles suggested that the four essential substances of all matter (fire, air, water and earth) conjoined and separated through the forces of love and strife. Being a proponent of democracy, he rejected the offer to become the King of Sicily. Two stories explain his death: he either flung himself into the crater atop volcanically active Mount Etna to show his followers that the phenomenon of coming into or going out of existence had no basis, or he was killed during the confusion in the Peloponnese, where he was sentenced to exile for his ideas. That brave man was living as an academician beyond his time, and overlooked was his attestation to the concept of 'element', the foundation of natural science. I came second in the philosophy faculty exam and my essay was later published in the faculty's journal.

On 3 November 1970, the day the socialist leader Salvador Allende became President of Chile, I was booked to fly to Geneva. My father had signed over to me a six-storey building on Bağdat Avenue, with a bank branch and a boutique pharmacy on the ground floor. When he said, sounding petty, 'Now, don't forget that your monthly income is more than that of the President of Switzerland', I couldn't respond, 'At the start of the day everyone has twenty-four hours', since I'd forgotten whose adage it was.

To my mind Geneva is like the mechanism of a clock that gets wound every morning. City-dwellers form its hour and minute hands. The clock may look robotic, but it can still break down. The city is grey. If you hear a hearty laugh, its source is most likely an alcoholic or a homeless man. The trees lining avenues and streets are lonely, too. Every time my plane descended to the city's airport, I missed Istanbul, but I couldn't break away from Geneva for fear of disturbing the clock setting of the last forty years.

Once, one of Geneva's accomplished Turkish doctors asked me why I jumped at every chance to go to Istanbul. 'Because,' I began, 'I'll never pass up an opportunity to visit a city where people drive straight at a friend as a joke; answer the question "Who is it?" with, "It's me"; fight with someone to pay the bill at a restaurant but never give an inch to that same person in traffic; show their son's penis to guests; play it safe by buying extra loaves of bread when it snows; quickly clean the house before the maid comes; consider stepping on their friend's brand new shoes a hilarious joke; take pleasure in watching heavy construction equipment work; wait until the very last day to pay a bill; mess up newly-laid cement with scribbles; don't rush when caught in the rain without an umbrella; who will, during a power outage in their building, check other buildings too; are excited to fire shots in the air at weddings and soccer games; buy mobile phones worth three times their salary; offer gifts of fake gold coins at weddings; replenish the shampoo bottle by adding water to it; repair an appliance by beating it first; find more pleasure in reading another person's newspaper than the owner did; who, when they hear, "There's none" ask, "None at all?"; first wipe their hands with a wet towel and then their shoes; at a funeral want first of all to know the age of the deceased; write "wash me" in the dirt caked on a car's windows; embellish their most sincere gratitude with profanity; use swear words as semicolons; fill the ashtray with water to keep ashes from flying away in windy weather; eat potatoes first at a meal, peas next, and meat last; add salt to their food before they taste it; wedge a piece of paper under a wobbly table leg; choose the oldest and most worn-out bills when paying for things; continue to chat at the door after they've said their goodbyes; choose the urinal nearest the wall; harass even the snowmen; check a gas leak with a lighter; blow their horn to salute friends; brush their teeth – for the first time in years – before they go to a dentist; put a doily on top of everything in the house; shroud the remote control in nylon; count the number of seats at a concert and estimate how much the organiser is making; scream out directions to tourists; think they'll get good results by speaking in a scolding tone when they themselves ask for directions; include in one of their cheerful songs the line, "since there's fire, we tend the fire"; feel of two minds towards terrorists who arrive late for the ambush soldiers have set up, wondering what may have gone wrong; sing out as an innocent oath the swear words, "let my mother be my wife". There, in that city,' I said, 'lies a hidden world that Beckett would envy.'

The apartment building in Geneva where I lived for forty years lacked charm. A Jewish acquaintance from Istanbul had found the apartment at Place du Bourg-de-Four for me. Facing it were the Palace of Justice, which resembled a church, with a wine house beneath it called Palace of Justice Cellar. I think I was too lazy to move away, and I liked the Turkish name of the place, 'Adalet Sarayı' – Turkish for 'Justice Palace' – which was so like my last name, Adlan.

Ligne d'Horizon University was hidden away in the coppice forest covering a desolate hill in the city's Cologny suburb. Ambitious postgraduate students came there with their colourful personalities from Beirut, Montreal and various French cities. My first date was with Sofia from Lugano, an art history major who was a year older than me and who planned to write her dissertation on our Hagia Sophia Museum. She taught me to ski and helped me get my driving licence.

I frequently visited Refia Hanım, who lived in Geneva and was descended with no certainty from whichever sultan, to convey my father's respects. She lived alone in a rented apartment in a middle-class neighbourhood. She appeared to be about sixty and looked sad. Her Turkish accent must have come from the palace, but I couldn't inquire about that. An elegant, introverted lady, she had nothing in her home that spoke of her past. Not daring to question her for fear of offending her or of saying something about myself that might offend her, I was nevertheless drawn to visit her once a month. If we dined out, she would wear a thick, thirty-year-old outfit smelling of mothballs, and I would find myself in an Ottoman imperial caïque, advancing slowly through a time tunnel. According to my father, she and her relatives co-owned a small office block in Istanbul, and she got by on the rental income. I never once heard her complain.

There were other old members of the Ottoman aristocracy living nearby. A law had passed in 1924, decreeing those men who belonged to the Ottoman dynasty must move abroad with seventy-two hours' notice, and the women within ten days. The exiles scattered in a panic to Cairo, Beirut, Damascus, Amman, Alexandria, Tunis, Hyderabad, Paris, Nice, London, Buenos Aires, Sofia and San Remo. They soon went broke and led unhappy lives. It wasn't until 1974 that those who survived were allowed to return to their country. You must have heard, I assume, that in the 1980s, the head of the Ottoman dynasty was a man called Mehmed Orhan Efendi, a retired cemetery guard living in a one-bedroom apartment in Nice. I went there once to attend a dynasty meeting. It was a simple event, the attendees brought with them both sorrow and great joy. I heard stories that did not impress me, such as the story of an exiled prince who, before being granted a return permit, missed his country so much that he cried as he gazed at Izmir and Istanbul from the deck of a ship cruising the Mediterranean region. The previous dynasty head Ali Vasıb Efendi said, 'We die, we Ottomans in exile, and are reborn each spring. All our youth and our most beautiful memories are adorned by Istanbul's spring.' My genealogy was questioned by an academician; to her mind, the end of the Ottoman reign was brought about by separatist pashas. While the dynasty was sent abroad without a penny, the pashas took bribes from arms dealers, stole from soldiers' rations, and set about pillaging the palace even before the exiling began. All these ancestral frictions! I decided not to remain in contact with any dynasty 'victims' other than Refia Hanım.

And then I met Zoe Mistral. She had gained the highest

score in the departmental entrance exam. She had a seductive voice and didn't indulge in needless talking or gossip. If she beat someone in an argument, she would conclude her case with an apology of some kind. Her coiffure was reminiscent of the French singer Mireille Mathieu. Of all our girls, she was the most petite. She was quite chic; whenever I saw her, I felt embarrassed about my clothing. But the moment her classes finished, she would disappear, and I thought she probably didn't have any friends. She would walk away slowly, holding a cane in her left hand. I noticed how carefully she tapped that black stick before her. Raphael from Lyon, who saw himself as the class philosopher, thought the cane made her look noble. She lived off-campus, and nobody knew where the private minibus took her after class. I waited for a chance to tell her I liked her.

It happened during our first year there, in the winter when the walks were slippery. Returning from the cafeteria, Raphael and I saw a girl lying on the ground. Zoe lay there in agony and started to cry when she saw us. She had fallen and was unable to get back up; she had to go to the infirmary at once. Raphael said that I was bigger and so I lifted her on to my back. She was lighter than I'd thought. Shivering on my back, she apologised again and again. She started laughing when I said, 'If you apologise one more time, I'll throw you into the first puddle we see.' She'd suffered a sprained right ankle.

After Zoe was better, she took me and Raphael to a restaurant in Cologny called Le Lion d'Or, and my girlfriend Sofia, out of curiosity, came with us. Under the spell of the wine, Zoe's tongue almost broke loose. She lived with her family in Basel who had an antiquarian books business there. David Mistral Antiquariat, managed by her father of French descent, dealt in rare, signed books, manuscripts and engravings. During term time, she stayed in Cologny in a rental property with her carer. She limited herself to mentioning that her left leg had been bothering her for a while. Interestingly, she, like you, was a fan of Louise Glück. I wish you two could have met. When she spoke, it was as if she was reading poetry. I felt embarrassed to see Raphael watching me with a grin as I admired her. When I found out that Zoe had chosen Ligne d'Horizon because of its proximity to the Martin Bodmer Library, I said to her, 'Did you have to enter the department as its top student for that, though?', and made her laugh. That night as we were leaving, Sofia punched my left leg in a kind but firm way and said, 'It won't be long until this lame duck falls in love with you.'

Zoe and I started going out to dinner once a week and took turns paying the bill. I tried to keep us from being seen together at school; as the tallest and the shortest ones in our class, we might be thought a funny pair. Gradually, she became my confidante and guide. If I missed seeing her for two days, I would worry. We started going to the cinema and theatre, and she stopped returning to Basel on weekends. I discovered the savour of Bergman, Rohmer and Bresson movies and learned how to make sense of Samuel Beckett's plays. The furnishings of Zoe's lakefront student accommodation spoke of her father's success as a wealthy bibliopole. The first time I visited the house, Ines, her gigantic Portuguese carer, displayed a scowl like a warning. When I told her, 'Draw the curtains, Zoe and I are about to make love', she ran away screaming, but later we made our peace.

Our relationship was quite one-sided. Most likely, Zoe didn't think I was worthy to be ranked as a confidant, as she hardly ever talked about her health or family. She always wore trousers, and I was curious about the legs hidden under her stylish clothes. I told her she was a good and valued friend, but Raphael figured that a woman so young might be unable to control her feelings towards a man who showed an interest in her. I was careful while hugging her, but for some reason I didn't try to date her. Sofia and I had long since stopped dating, but I began seeing Yulia, an immigrant from Sevastopol and a retired ballerina, whom I met in a nightclub frequented by the Turks. She was a stripper and thirteen years my senior. Don't ask me why, but she saw a resemblance in me to Nicholas II, the last tsar. She was amusing and wore her heart on her sleeve. Once a month I had to visit her at home and eat her tasteless pastries.

One spring evening, Zoe's father arrived in Geneva. I didn't think he was on a business trip; his business was to meet the Turkish student who had come into his daughter's life. All at once, Zoe enlightened me about her family. Her mother, who was seventeen years younger than her husband, had been his secretary and was now his second wife. Her grandfather, David, who was in his nineties, was the real boss of the business. She had no brothers or sisters. We went to a French restaurant with her father. Paul must have been around sixty-five and he looked more like a retired Nazi officer than a high-ranking bibliopole. He embarrassed Zoe by seizing the first chance to reveal his kinship with Frédéric Mistral, the 1904 winner of the Nobel Prize in Literature. Without changing gears and with all the excitement of a live broadcast, he launched into a discourse on Mistral as a type of cold wind that blew from France towards the Mediterranean, and I understood why his ninety-year-old father had not turned the business over to him. As a warning, Zoe said, 'Father, the most well-informed person in our class is sitting just across from you.' That was the first compliment I had heard from her, indirect though it was, and it pleased me. Being young and rash, I couldn't keep from replying, 'We know that wind from the Aegean Sea, but we call it "Karayel". Nevertheless, Mistral is such a lovely name that I might choose it for my daughter when that time comes,' which messed things up some, I'm afraid. As this polite duel of words continued, and so did the wine, I told him that my own family's ancestry reached all the way back to Sultan Mahmut II, and that his mother Aimée and Napoleon's wife, Josephine, were cousins. However I may have expressed it, the whole table fell silent. I felt uneasy when it occurred to me that I hadn't told Zoe any of this before. At the end of our dinner, Paul Mistral buttoned up his jacket and invited me to Basel for the weekend.

On Friday afternoon, we took off in the minibus being driven by Tomas, Ines's nephew. Tomas followed Turkish football better than I did, and I had to caution him to drop the subject. Zoe was anxious throughout the three-hour-trip.

I started to wonder if something I saw in her home would embarrass her. The Rhine growled as it flowed through cosmopolitan Basel, which had four different names. Hearing Turkish and Kurdish reproaches and expletives on its streets helped ease my homesickness.

The Mistral family lived in a four-storey historical building on quiet Münsterberg Avenue. Entrance into David Mistral Antiquariat, which took up the first two floors, was by appointment only. The third floor belonged to the grandfather David Mistral and also functioned as archive and storage space. The fourth floor was home to Paul, his wife Lea and Zoe. The makeshift lift located beside the fourth-floor entrance could only indicate that Zoe was not expected to get better. This made me feel bad, and when I saw her mother Lea, I realized the source of Zoe's anxiety. I have to say that at first sight her beauty would shake up any man. Zoe's face resembled her mother's, but the rest of her body could not. Over the next month, I dreamed twice of making love to Lea.

Before dinner, Tomas took me on a tour of the historical Münsterberg. Bicycles were the only vehicles small enough to enter the narrow, labyrinthine side streets. The whole town seemed to have gone away to attend some event. I couldn't imagine any murder scenes taking place behind the few windows with light filtering through them; Switzerland was a mystery-impaired country. The small fountains I stumbled on at unpredictable corners reminded me of Üsküdar. I came to the fabulous conclusion that when I came there again, they would be fully grown clock towers. On our way back Tomas said, 'If you like Zoe, you'll like her grandfather too', and I picked up my pace.

David Mistral didn't look a day over seventy and had piercing eyes. He treated me like an esteemed guest. While speaking, he would turn from David into Goliath, and held listeners under his spell like a magician. The decor of the house was an extension of his antiquarian taste, with silver forks and knives that had to be at least 200 years old. We sat in rows around the dinner table like Éric Rohmer characters, making brief speeches, but without taking turns. David Mistral directed the current of dinner; Paul and Lea quietly answering questions. Zoe watched me from the corner of her eye, as if something might happen to me. The servant was Ines's cousin and was named Ines, too. When David asked me about my favourite author, without hesitating I said Stendhal and received a pleasant nod. When he asserted that Oscar Wilde's *The Picture of Dorian Gray* was the world's last classic, it was clear that anyone who objected would be exiled from the table. As if in answer to a riddle he revealed that his birth year was the same as Atatürk's, and he took great pleasure in relating his reason for coming to Istanbul and lodging in Pera Palas for four days in the 1940s. At an old mansion in Kuzguncuk he'd bought two rare manuscripts from the daughters of a late pasha. The books had been owned by the Hungarian king Matthias Corvinus, the world's first serious book collector, and when Hungary became an Ottoman possession, as spoils, they were destined to be kept in Topkapı Palace. I didn't know what to make of it all.

After dinner, Zoe retreated to her room with a visiting female friend, and David Mistral led me on a tour of his Antiquariat. I felt nervous about getting too close to the ornate bookshelves. While he was showing me Comedies, Histories and Tragedies by William Shakespeare and the first editions of books by Victor Hugo, he spoke as if he were praying. As we left the place, he presented me with a copy of Yaşar Kemal's *The Wind from the Plain*. It was signed by Yaşar, with a dedication from Yaşar and Thilda Kemal to William Saroyan, '... from one Anatolian to Another'. I have never forgotten that David then said, 'Once the author of a book has given you a signed copy, they'll be reading their work to you themselves.'

On my second night, the last night of my stay, when Zoe turned in early, David Mistral and I descended to his store again, and I paid him my compliments for the signed books and engravings he'd acquired the week before. On this occasion I heard the story of a loan-shark family, the Kamondos, who had gained a great deal of wealth from the Ottomans. The family, all of whom perished during World War II, donated hundreds of valuable paintings they had purchased in Paris to the Louvre and d'Orsay Museums. He also did not forget to laugh as he relayed the indirect contribution of the Ottomans to those museums. However, he himself took two historical manuscripts destined for Topkapı Palace back to his store, and by doing so harmed the Ottomans. But I preferred to keep quiet, as I had warmed to this man who was so full of joie de vivre. On the condition that it stayed between us, he told me about a malignant tumour on Zoe's left hip. I learned then that metastasis referred to the spreading of the tumour to other organs and tissues. As you know, medicine and treatment methods in the 1970s were more limited, and her doctors gave Zoe at most one more year to live.

My relationship with Zoe continued as before, and I tried not to treat her with more sensitivity that could be mistaken for pity. A tenacious girl, she never stopped laughing at my jokes. After promising to take her to Istanbul in the future, I returned to Farewell Fountain Street for the holidays. But, at the beginning of our second year, Zoe was admitted to a private hospital in Basel. I went there every weekend and sat beside her for as long as the doctors allowed. After visiting hours were over, I would go up to my hotel room, drink until I passed out, and sometimes cry. It seemed that Zoe had to be in a sickbed for me to understand that I was in love with her.

In the third month, Zoe began to deteriorate quickly. When she said, 'Please don't come here anymore', I let myself go, and turning my back, started crying. And when I bent down to her ear and said, 'I love you', her face seemed to brighten as she tried to say, 'Thank you, Ziya.' On the day the 12 March Military Memorandum was issued in Turkey, we lost her. I thought I was prepared for it, but for two weeks I walked around like a ghost, trying to live off antidepressants.

Lea came to Geneva the following month to pack up her daughter's things. Zoe had left an envelope addressed to me before she died. When I arrived in Geneva to pick it up, I was stricken with a headache. I looked beseechingly at the ceiling of the living room as if some vestige of Zoe's voice might be trapped there, and drew in the air deeply, with the hope of catching some trace of her scent. Her possessions were packed in boxes, ready to be loaded on to the pickup truck that was due to come the next hour. No one else was there. Lea clutched my hands as she awkwardly thanked me for adding a dash of colour to her daughter's last year and a half. I couldn't free myself, and her hands seemed to caress mine. Was this woman Zoe? I lost control, hugging her and our lips locked together. Before I could ask myself what in the world I was doing, Lea embraced me tightly, too. We made love on the carpet, and for several minutes after, I kept my eyes closed and held her. Had I finally reached Zoe? Could this be her daughter's final request? Did any film or novel contain such a scene? I stopped thinking, got dressed quickly, picked up the envelope, and left without saying a word. I never even thought of opening the letter. Sometime later I did and found three original Edgar Allan Poe poems inside. I suspected that David Mistral would have liked to present them to me, but assuming that I wouldn't accept them, he'd made them a gift to me on Zoe's behalf. Had I opened the envelope back then, I would have returned the manuscripts, which, after all, were offered as an expression of gratitude for my friendship with Zoe.

The year I graduated; I ran into Paul Mistral in Rue de Rive. His father had passed away, and he'd sold the store to one of his rivals and divorced his wife. He was happy and standing beside him was a girl young enough to be his granddaughter.

Much like men in search of the women of their lives, I

started a search for the aphorism of my life. If I couldn't find any of Zoe's traits in the women I met, I shunned them, and as I strolled down the streets, I would cast glances at middle-aged women with the hope of seeing Zoe's mother among them. During those years, I started to like my own mother more, and I took her to the capital cities of Europe every summer, as the sight of her childish joy pleased me. As she happily packed her suitcase, my father would say, 'Is there a better place than Istanbul?' while secretly savouring the prospect of being left alone.

After I graduated in 1974, I was accepted in the doctoral programme. Raphael entered the Sorbonne, and I was the only student from my class remaining on campus. My proposed PhD title, 'Samuel Beckett: The Mysterious Philosopher of Tragicomedy' wasn't approved because Beckett was still alive and might have objected to my ideas. I decided to wait until Beckett died to write my dissertation as a book. In 1989 he did, but I couldn't even conjure the first sentence.

I finished my PhD when I was twenty-eight years old and my feet weren't planted any more firmly on the ground. I suppose I found an aphorism for that period: Elias Canetti, 'an evening of sorrow and spices; in front of the window an egret'.

Raphael thought I was a masochist for not entering the Sorbonne with him and that I would die of boredom in Geneva. Yet the city was an ideal dervish isolation chamber for an up-and-coming philosopher, with European metropolises nearby. I got into an associate professorship programme that exempted me from having to move and adapt to a new environment for at least five more years.

I liked my students and making them laugh. Cheerful types were my favourite, even, unfortunately, those who were frauds – I must tell you about Suavi the Kancık. There was a restaurant near the train station in Geneva called Chez Anadolu, which served as a meeting place for Turks. Every time I saw it, I would recall the waiters serving shopkeepers in Istanbul and feel warm inside. On Saturdays, it was my habit to go to Chez Anadolu for their pinto beans and rice. I was genuinely revered there and felt proud to hear them call me Ziya Hocam. In that sincere form of address, hocam, I had always felt respected by Anatolian people who hadn't had a chance to be sufficiently educated. I had treated most of the young folks there to dinner, chatted with them, and loaned money to a few.

The sweet curse of that naive environment was Suavi, whose last name no one knew. The first time he showed up at Chez Anadolu, he announced with pride his nickname: 'Kancık'. It's a kind of slang for 'untrustworthy', although in a coincidence worthy of Beckett, his name in Arabic means 'a person who helps everyone'. He was a short, bowlegged, curly-haired, fidgety and theatrical man. One of his large, restless eyes seemed to exude wit, and the other, dishonesty. No one had any idea where he stayed or what he did. His face was beardless, and he appeared to be in his twenties. He was charming and funny, a smooth talker who added colour wherever he went. Entering the restaurant with two different shoes, he would shout out, 'I stole these from the mosque by mistake, so sorry!' or dance while loudly singing folk songs. He had a fine voice, knew what was happening in the world, and was a good judge of character. He called everyone in the restaurant 'abi', but I was 'the abi-est one of all.' He was always broke, but his inability to pay previous debts kept him from asking anyone for a loan. Knowing how to make himself be missed, he would disappear, then at the most unexpected time, reappear. He was a carefree, contrary character who seized the moment. I liked having him around me.

When he'd begged to do my housework or be my driver, people had warned, 'Hocam, don't you dare entrust your home or car keys to this crook.' But after my house cleaner Zaliha got pregnant, I gave him a chance. He surprised me by being hardworking and practical when he had to be, and I learned from him how to make soup, how to cook scrambled eggs with tomatoes and green peppers, and how to make pasta. He took me to out-of-the-way eateries, and his companionship never bored me. We started going together to the cinema and exhibitions, and on shopping trips, and he got a generous daily allowance for the time he spent with me. He became a member of the household. He dressed in my old clothes and did my grocery shopping, but he wasn't allowed to stay overnight. He admitted that he'd worked as a gigolo when he was broke and slept with men. A prodigal, thoughtless man, he played the horses constantly, purchased lottery tickets, and never tired of telling me what he would do if he hit the jackpot one day. He was mesmerised by gold watches and vowed that he'd wear a different brand every day: Patek Philippe on Mondays, Schwarz Etienne on Tuesdays, Chopard on Wednesdays, Parmigiani on Thursdays, Cartier on Fridays, and Corum and Panerai on Saturdays and Sundays. When I reminded him of the 1-in-140 million odds he faced, he said, 'The bottom line is this: somebody always wins it, and everyone has an equal chance.' If we were sitting in a café and the woman at the next table was wearing a Patek Philippe, he would begin his line of flattery by praising her watch choice and within five minutes would be invited to her table. If a young couple was sitting three tables away, he would fabulate the stages of their lovemaking from foreplay to orgasm, unable to hide his inquisitive look as he awaited my reaction.

His sense of humour was unique: at a restaurant he might ask to be refunded for the uneaten portion of his meal or request a 50 per cent discount when we left the cinema during the interval. Once, when a pair of Italian shoes I'd admired in a store struck him as being overpriced, he made the female salesclerk laugh by asking her if that price was for only one shoe or for the pair. Five minutes later he asked her out and she accepted. He later charged me for the expenses of their date, saying that I was responsible for it.

Once, as we stepped out of a café, I caught him taking the tip I'd left and when we were outside slapped the back of his neck. As a greatly exaggerated response, he threw himself on to the ground, provoking an eighty-year-old couple passing by to shower me with abuse. Finally, on a visit to my house,

I caught him pinching the silver cigar ashtray sitting in a corner and kicked him out. The next morning, I found him sleeping at my front door. Swearing, he threw himself at my feet. His weeping eased my rage. Despite everything, he could be considered my only confidant in the city. I told him about my pasha grandfathers and that I was a descendant of Sultan Mahmut II. When I saw that he wasn't aware of the importance of this sultan, I didn't hesitate to explain his reforms. We were both a bit tipsy, and on hearing me out as he swayed, he asked, 'Why don't you put together a book about our Mahmut, Abi, instead of writing a thesis about some guy from another nation?' One weekend we visited Zoe's grave. He washed off her tombstone with a can of water he'd carried with him, prayed, and got me feeling all emotional by saying, 'Abi, I hope you can find another woman to love as much you loved Zoe yenge.' You couldn't do with Suavi or without him.

On the professor of my department's seventy-fifth birthday, I decided to throw a party for my colleague in the school's small conference hall. I delegated the task of providing food and drinks to Suavi. When I caught sight of the uniformed girl working the drink stand, I couldn't tear my eyes away. A gorgeous apparition of Nastassja Kinski seemed to have stopped by to look over the party. Bewildered, I edged closer to her. She stood stock still, as if she were posing for a statue of Aphrodite, and my heartbeat quickened. I mustered the courage to ask her for a vodka. While she was asking if I wanted ice or lemon, her soft accent told me that she was an immigrant. In two sips I finished the vodka, and calling

Suavi over, told him that if he set me up with the barmaid for dinner, I'd erase half his debt. He stopped beside her as if he had known her forever, laid his hand on her shoulder, and started talking. When all at once he pointed towards me, I felt sweaty in my embarrassment and turned away. Suavi returned triumphantly, and when he said to me, 'The girl's name is Alina Ivanova. She's a culinary student and has always dreamed of having dinner at Brasserie Lipp. I'll make a reservation for two Saturday at 8 pm', I hugged him for the first time. 'What's more,' he said, 'for 500 francs I'll be your driver that evening.'

Alina was a senior in culinary school, but when she held a menu, she was as tense as if she were holding an exam paper filled with questions she couldn't answer. It transpired that, after Alina's brother had been killed in a street fight, her family emigrated from Odessa to Copenhagen. When Alina was thirteen, her mother had deserted Alina and her father, running away with a Mexican tourist. Her father had sent Alina to live with his sister who worked at a Chinese restaurant in Geneva. Alina showed herself to be the most beautiful and the worst-dressed woman of the evening. Her dress didn't harmonise with the environment and her shoes were old and tacky. To me, this only emphasised her beauty, sending the message, 'Your norms mean nothing to me.' She might as well have only arrived from a mountain village near Odessa a week before.

The following day, we took a trip by car to the surrounding cities. She was easy-going and well-intentioned. On our second date I had already decided to become the lover and guide of this Alina, who was unable even to have a proper orgasm. I, like George Bernard Shaw's famous Professor Henry Higgins, could create my own Eliza Doolittle. I had a knack for such matters as clothing, make-up, hairstyle, perfume and women's magazines and was patient about other things. Her habit of running up to hug me tightly whenever we met pleased me, and I liked to watch other women eye her as we walked arm in arm. I was nine years older than she was, but like a well-brought-up child listening to her father, she never hurt my feelings and always recognised my good intentions. I thought I might marry Alina, but whenever I pondered the idea, I couldn't keep from remembering The Fisherman of Halicarnassus and his father Şakir Pasha and felt uneasy at the thought of having to protect my future wife from my father.

A couple of months after meeting Alina, I returned for a three-week holiday to Istanbul. At the start of the vacation I was cheerful. I even bantered with my father and took my parents out to dinner three times. The way I slid down in a lounge chair in the garden and whistled even surprised the servants. The talk launched by my mother on the last evening was, I believe, pre-planned. Now that I was thirty-three, my marriage to someone suitable for our family was overdue, she said, casting a look at my father who sat awaiting his turn, slowly twirling his prayer beads. When I told them that I loved a Ukrainian lady and might marry her the next year, my father rose to his feet and loudly announced that he did not want a Christian and communist daughter-in-law as a part of the family. I tried reminding him that Mahmut II's mother was

Christian and Suleiman the Magnificent's wife was Ukrainian – but to no avail. As our talk became an argument, my mother started to cry, and when I raised my voice, my father hurled his prayer beads at my head, yelled insults at me, and threw me out the house. On my way out, I was stopped by the sound of radio coming from a side room. Naile, a young housekeeper who had held a live-in position for the last couple of years, was sitting there, knitting and listening to the radio. I knew Asaf Bey molested her. Boiling with resentment at being unable to react properly to my father, I stormed into the room with the intention of raping Naile. She was sitting there in a T-shirt and shorts. Her legs looked like lily-white columns, and in my perverted state of mind I thought getting at her would hurt my father. I lunged towards Naile, but to my surprise she responded positively. I came to my senses, froze, apologised. I was afraid of myself and confused by the way Naile had responded to my advances, which I had thought unwanted, but despite my hesitation we did not stop and with an intense sense of urgency, made love wildly. I had once wished for an excuse to stay at the historical Pera Palas Hotel, and on that night I saw my wish realized. The following morning I departed Istanbul as if in retreat. I have no idea what became of Naile, and I never saw my parents again, either. I made a vain attempt to settle accounts with my mother, but when I called her, she told me, in tears, that my father had forced her to swear never to see me again.

A bitter surprise awaited me on my return to Geneva. In my mailbox was a farewell letter dated two days earlier: Alina

Ivanova had left me. She said that our relationship lacked a foundation; that I treated her as though I were 'training a monkey', that after her beauty faded or I had grown tired of her, I would simply dump her; that we were not at all alike; and she thanked me for taking an interest in her. After reading the short letter twice through, I broke into a strange laugh. Those sentences were Suavi's doings.

When Alina called the next day she was crying. Suavi had informed her that I was a hypocritical pervert, an aristocrat who'd strung her along as he listed in detail the kind of future torments I had in mind for her. He'd convinced her that they'd make a fortune by selling the objects I'd given her, and then he disappeared with the jewellery box. She apologised and wondered if we could take a holiday together. I hung up without answering.

A couple of years later, I came upon Alina at Boulangerie Eric Emery. She, her husband, and the little son lying asleep in her arms made a charming family. We greeted each other and chatted. Her husband was the manager of the restaurant where she had worked. As she introduced us, she said, 'I hope that when Max grows up he looks like Mr Adlan.'

I assumed I would never see Suavi again, but I did. Years after, I went to visit my friend Raphael, once he had started teaching at Bordeaux University. One day, while wandering around the Saint Michel district, I went into a Turkish restaurant. As I asked for white beans and rice, I heard 'Ziya Hocam!' Emin, cousin of Hâzım, who owned Chez Anadolu, had opened up a Turkish restaurant in Bordeaux. As we hugged and kissed, he served me rice pudding himself and sat down at the table and shared some surprising news with me. Suavi, who had been spotted now and then in Bordeaux, had been left a paraplegic by a traffic accident and was now begging on a wheeled sleigh in Saint-Émilion, a winemaking town near the city. Having no social security, he was in debt for hospital expenses. His friends in Bordeaux had twice collected money for him. This news left me neither happy nor sad, but curious. I felt like seeing him at once. Emin found out where he begged and handed me a piece of paper covered by bad handwriting filled with spelling mistakes. The next morning, I headed to Saint-Émilion.

You can imagine the town. It is frequented by rich tourists who think of themselves as oenophiles and has a population of 3,000. The whole journey from the station to the town was lined with vineyards. People wobbled about half drunk in winding streets smelling of wine and spices, and every nine out of ten stores boasted a wine-related business; I probably didn't come across any cafés because drinking tea or coffee was seen as unethical. The town's monolithic church clings to the edge of a cliff and looks as if it might tumble down at any moment. It was surrounded by uninviting restaurants, but then, there! Might that bearded and bespectacled man, sitting inside a makeshift wooden box on wheels on a shady corner, be Suavi? Approaching from the rear, I began watching him as he swayed back and forth in pain, holding out his hand to passing tourists and whimpering as he begged. As I waited, I seemed to soften some. Right there in front of me was a bizarre swindler who had paid, tit for tat, for the things he had done. No longer able to stand it, I got closer, and whispered, 'Su-a-vi.' Looking back at me, he cried, 'Abi, is that you?' He wept as he shivered and, breathing rapidly, told me everything. He would never be able to walk again and he had vision problems. While he was driving drunk, his car had crashed into barriers and flipped over. At fault and without health insurance, he had found himself paralysed and in debt for his hospital expenses. 'I guess my ingratitude and all the bad things I had done destined me to pay my dues this way, Abi,' he said. An Algerian family that had taken over caring for him seized three-quarters of his daily earnings. He was also indebted to a gambling friend who had paid his hospital bill. Weeping once more, he said, 'Since I'm no longer strong enough to stand all this, I quit taking my pills and going to the hospital. And God has also denied me the power to commit suicide. I can't ask you for another dime, but let's have one last meal together. You're a noble fellow, so please give me your blessing.' We ordered two sirloin steaks and wine from a restaurant nearby and ate in silence on a sheet of cardboard. My head ached with sadness each time I heard him groan or sniffle. Before leaving, I insisted on paying off his debt to his friend. After stuffing the cash I gave him into the pocket of his dirty T-shirt, he said, 'Since you want to perform a good deed that does you proud, send me 10,000 francs to keep him quiet for a good long while.' Later on, he did send me his friend's account details. As we drank another glass of red wine, I said, 'I actually owe you thanks for saving me from a naive girl I'd fallen in love with at first sight.'

After turning thirty-five I became an associate professor. A week later, when Saim Bey, who acted as the liaison between my father and me, relayed the news of my mother's death, I didn't care enough to cry. The lawyer didn't miss a beat as he transferred the rent money from the property to my name. For a while I expected my father to be a bad sport about it and was surprised that he wasn't. No cause was given for my mother's death, and I didn't ask. She wasn't all that old, but then again, I'm not all that old, either.

5

Ziya Bey

Samuel Beckett was eighty-three years old when he died of emphysema in 1989. T. S. Eliot, your favourite poet, succumbed to the same disease. Could those two intelligent men, who didn't refuse to become smokers, be considered suicides? That same year, the old professor of my department entered a nursing home, and I was promoted and settled into his office. Having read all of Beckett's works at least twice and taken all the necessary notes for my book project, I piled together all the research, letters, interviews about his biography, along with every book and catalogue that analysed his works. I guess I had just been waiting for him to die so that I could work freely. After telling myself that I could at last sit at my desk in peace, I stopped by Chez Anadolu and was thrown into a mad rage by what I heard there.

That scumbag Suavi was bartending at a hotel in Lyon! So once more the crook had made fools of us all. I tried to laugh it off but couldn't. I couldn't banish from my mind this ingrate, who had made me appear naiver than Alina. And so

I could not get started on my Beckett project. He mocked me in my dreams, and with a start I would awaken, feeling embarrassed. The only solution I could think of was to meet him one last time and punish him, then the last laugh would be mine. By getting rid of that vagrant scumbag, I would be serving humanity. I couldn't force myself to forget the idea. My mother believed that I had inherited this vindictive streak from my father, and I remembered throwing the little kitten into the dry well when I was a kid. I could never write the book or progress with my academic career until I got news that Suavi had got what he deserved. No philosopher could dissuade me, and I kept returning to that anonymous aphorism dear to writers and artists: 'No good deed goes unpunished.'

Revenge was in the family. Sultan Mahmut II had ordered his brother – who intended to do evil to him – to be strangled. Other sultans had condemned sixty-one people in the family to death, and forty-one Ottoman grand viziers had lost their heads. In another time, Suavi could have been my grand vizier.

In truth, Suavi was an artist in his own chosen field and an antihero worthy of any novel.

The gossip in Chez Anadolu had it that Suavi was working in the bar of a luxurious hotel in Quai du Dr Gailleton by the Saône River. Coming up with a hitman presented no problem, as I had a solid candidate.

Actually, I had two. The first was a Russian man with a Cambridge accent, who had turned up at my office one day unannounced. He had heard – who knows how, or from where – that I had three original poems by Poe. He wanted to buy them, and after starting at $300,000 he went up to 900,000 before I told him that I already had $900,000. Before leaving, he left me his card 'in case you need to change your mind one day', and said, if necessary, he would do anything to get the manuscripts of the three Edgar Allan Poe poems. I believed him, but I did not like him and I did not want to have anything to do with him. The second candidate was more promising. Some time ago, I had met a poor Kosovan named Mahmut. I called him 'Namesake' and he called me 'Hocam'. He was a burly, quiet Albanian who spoke Turkish. I must have been destined to meet him in Chez Anadolu, too. He poured ketchup on to his double serving of rice, and while eating it with pickled hot peppers had a minor heart attack. As I relive the moment when I administered first aid before rushing him by ambulance to Dr İzak Roditi, I can't forget how after his escape from death he kissed my hand and said, 'Hocam I owe you a life.' He had a reassuring, upright kind of posture, and every time I saw him I remembered Bromden, the Indian chief in *One Flew over the Cuckoo's Nest* that everyone thought was deaf. After he'd gained Dr Roditi's sympathy, he was hired as a security guard in the hospital. If he and Suavi happened to be in the same room, his look told Suavi that he would like to tear him to pieces. So, I chose Mahmut to do the job, and we met in the park beside the hospital, where I laid out the situation for him. I finished by saying, 'As long as Suavi feels like he's got away with it, I'll have no peace of mind in this world.' After I'd appealed to him for help without saying a word about him owing me his life, and he started scratching his forehead,

I grew suspicious. However, when I added, 'If you like you can forget that I brought this up', he scowled, smiled, and held out his hand. As we were discussing this, I'd wondered if Suavi had done anything to annoy him. I had heard that, on Mahmut's second visit to Chez Anadolu, Suavi had sat down at his table, got him to take the money out of his pocket – even though he'd declared that he was unemployed and broke – and snatched 40 of his 78 francs. When Mahmut asked for his money back a month later, Suavi had scolded him, then tried to take his trousers off to give them to Mahmut before other customers in the restaurant stopped him.

It was the second half of August, blazing hot, and Europeans unable to go to the beach sulked like unwilling sentinels. During my journey from Paris to Lyon I read Nazım Hikmet's *Life's Good, Brother* on the train. I felt as if I'd arrived in Batumi as it was depicted in that novel. Lyon was as desolate as a single-street cowboy town, and I couldn't believe how the chirping of birds overwhelmed the noise made by vehicles and people. The rivers Rhône and Saône, with their names as powerful as gladiators, were sound asleep, too. Staying calm, I entered the hotel neighbouring Suavi's on tiptoe.

On my first night, I visited a Michelin-starred restaurant. I tried to convey to the headwaiter, through my facial expression, my opinion that they were using salad and dessert as cover for the fiasco of their main course. For two nights I waited behind the tree outside Suavi's hotel for him to come out. He worked the night shift, and I fended off boredom by watching the flow of people passing through the door. Suavi would walk to Antonin Poncet Square then suddenly disappear. I had to catch him before he left that desolate place, and during the process of my rehearsal, I felt like stepping out and throttling him there and then. The square had one clock tower, which was named after a doctor who had identified a rare type of disease that manifested in patients with tuberculosis. Two hundred years ago, as it was being built, a condition was established granting mothers who were unable to care for their infants the right to entrust them to the tower attendant. This gave legitimacy to those seeking justice in this place.

I studied Suavi's routine, then I summoned Mahmut from Geneva and explained my plan to him. We rehearsed once together and set out to complete the operation the next night. As Suavi walked along towards Antonin Poncet Square, I hastened after him, sipping from my hip flask of cognac. As we neared the square, I shouted, 'You, Prick!' causing the last two people in the square to scurry away from my echoing voice. This startled Suavi, who stopped dead in his tracks. I expected him to start his pleading with, 'Abi, it's a miracle of medicine ...' Unable to escape from his position as he watched Mahmut approaching him, he turned around and knelt in front of me, and said, 'Abi, you're a noble member of a dynasty while I'm a swindler who lives from day to day. Stooping to my level wouldn't become you. Tell your friends about me to make them laugh, or write about me, but please spare me. For the first time in my life, I have a paying job that I actually like.'

That Suavi made sense also angered me, and I ignored the rest of his pleading. As my father would have done, I spat on my palms and laid into him. This obviously wasn't his first beating. Exaggerating the effect of each slap, he threw himself on the ground squirming. When he could no longer get up, Mahmut broke in and tried to calm me. We got Suavi on to his feet and held him between us. He was scared shitless. Mahmut put him out with a cloth that had been presoaked in ether, and we quickly made our way to the safety wall of the nearby Saone River, where Mahmut threw Suavi over his shoulder, descended the riverbank, and emptied his pockets. Mahmut looked at me and the realisation that this was it, we really were not just going to scare Suavi this time, but kill him, sunk in. Then, tying two rocks he'd brought down there earlier around his ankles, he pushed Suavi into the water. We sat side by side on the wall, and I lit a cigar. After taking another sip of my cognac, I spat on the fake ID in his wallet. I remembered a Chinese proverb, 'If you sit by the river long enough, you'll see the body of your enemy float by.'

When I went to bed and pulled the blanket over me that night, I forgot all about Suavi. Mahmut was reassuring and comforting in his quietness. He had a lovely, autistic daughter who called me Zizi. I don't know how I had been described to her, but she looked upon me as a character, a cross between Santa Claus and the Pied Piper.

After turning forty, I began to feel a stronger sense of belonging. Whenever I caught sight of a car with an Istanbul licence plate in Geneva, the least I could do was to walk over and caress its mirror. I had brought Vakıflar olive oil soap with me to Geneva, and each sniff transported me to an Ottoman hamam. Every summer I flew to Istanbul to stay at Pera Palas for at least two weeks. In the dead of night, I would head off to our mansion, lean on its main door, and wait for dawn. When morning came, I would enter the shrine of Sultan Mahmut II with a basmala and caress the coffin of the great sultan who initiated Western reforms without collapsing under the threats of epidemics and great fires, who never stopped facing enemies at his borders or the revolt of the army, governors and pashas. I would also curse those who ignored him. On explorations of the musty-smelling streets around Istiklal Avenue, which like a chameleon were constantly changing their colours, I would envy the attitudes of those who lived there and refused to take life seriously. Recently, when Mahmut got wind of my illness he mourned, and after he'd lost more weight than I did, his head became a size too big for the rest of him. Once I had returned to Farewell Fountain for good, I signed over my apartment in Geneva to him. But I digress.

I was forty-one years old when I asked our lawyer to tell my father that I had become a professor. Not expecting to be congratulated or forgiven, I only wanted him to know that I had kept my promise.

With a clear head, I turned my attention to Beckett's interviews and memoirs, and tried to clarify his dry and mysterious answers, word by word. By 'memoirs', I mean anecdotes related by people who knew him. When *Waiting for Godot* was first performed in London in 1953 and Peter Woodthorpe was cast as Estragon, he was twenty-two and studying chemistry at Cambridge University. He impressed even Beckett with his performance. During rehearsals, they attended a party and left it at the same time. They were both going in the same direction, so they shared a cab. Woodthorpe said to Beckett, 'Everyone's marching to a different drummer. What's *Waiting for Godot* really all about?' Beckett – who disliked discussing or explaining his plays, and only spoke when he had to – exchanged smiles with Woodthorpe. Then the playwright offered a rare explanation: 'It's all symbiosis, Peter.'

I assume you've never seen Waiting for Godot and don't know what symbiosis means. Briefly, it's a biological term used to express the interaction between two different organisms that live in the same environment. When I read the word 'symbiosis' I was as delighted, for I had solved a riddle that had puzzled people for half a century! Of the two main characters in the play, the commanding Estragon was GOD, and the goofy and ingenuous Vladimir was (idi)OT. In the course of the play, the adjectives switched places. Yes, Estragon plus Vladimir equalled GODOT, but there was no need to wait for him, as GODOT was already on the stage. When the absurd pair joked with each other, they were also setting a trap for the audience.

Except, when Beckett set his trap, he was kind enough to provide the audience with three hints. Estragon's nickname was GO(go) and Vladimir's DI(di). If we look for them in the words, 'god' and 'idiot,' the results are GO(d) and I(DI) ot. Estragon and Vladimir exchange hats several times during the play, and time after time they try to exhibit symbiosis.

Near the end, Vladimir, sure that the trap they've set for the audience remains undeciphered, says, "We're magicians."'

Beckett, surprised when philosophical speculations continued despite his dropped hints, went quiet, retreated, and enjoyed the chaos in silence. Unable to stand it after a group of critics insisted that Godot meant God, he famously turned to actor Ralph Richardson and said, 'If I had wanted to say God with Godot, I would have been content to say God.' Just now, I remembered that during the 1950s the play couldn't be performed in Turkey because the Democratic Party government maintained that Godot stood for communism.

My theory is supported somewhat by the last three lines of the play:

Vladimir: Well? Shall we go?
Estragon: Yes, let's go.
(They do not move.)

Waiting for Godot is the Hamlet of contemporary theatre and if my theory was accepted, I would have been recognised globally. I checked online but couldn't find anything that came close to my idea. I consulted my friends who were theatre experts and followers of Beckett. They agreed with my conclusions. When I became a professor the following year, I sent copies of my paper to leading academicians, editors and authors, as well as to the Samuel Beckett Foundation and the journal it publishes.

An abstract was published in the letters to the editor

section of the Foundation's journal The Beckett Circle, and my theory was embraced by the professor who presided over the board of directors, along with a few editors and academicians. Others, however, didn't even respond to it, although I was surprised when a daily newspaper in Turkey picked it up as a front-page story. I was proud to see the paper mentioned by a serious American investigative reporter in the *Times Literary Supplement*. Otherwise, my discourse made no impact in literature or theatre circles. If those findings had been the work of Jacques Derrida, George Steiner or Harold Bloom, they would surely have earned a place on the agenda. While the media had ignored the discourse of an unknown Turkish academician, at the very least I had come up with an appropriate aphorism for this case: 'Whoever tells the truth also matters!'

Justice and fairness were forgotten inside sacred books as was tolerance in Mevlana's *Masnavi*. And in the twenty-first century, academicians of philosophy, literature and art were rotting in the grip of jealousy and prejudice. This was my first professional breaking point. I'll leave you with one last anecdote about what made me averse to my profession and then never return to my academic past.

A few minutes ago, I said Jacques Derrida's name out loud. Born in 1930, he was a French academician and supposedly a philosopher – the pioneer of deconstruction theory, which is a method of critical thinking. His theory involves a way of reading developed to explain the structural failure of a text, based on inconsistent uses of concepts within that text. I've tried to simplify the definition, but if you're still unable to understand it, I can't say that I blame you. This temporal movement peaked in the 1970s and influenced some disciplines, particularly architecture. If its Don Quixote was Derrida, then its Sancho Panza was the dubious academician Paul de Man.

Paul de Man was the adventurous son of a rich Belgian family. Born in 1919, he fathered his first child at twenty years old out of wedlock – marrying the woman only after he'd fathered two more children with her. A smart and ambitious man who was also a highly confident opportunist, he wrote anti-Semitic articles for a Nazi collaborationist newspaper and later worked for two collaborationist companies, one of which he tried to take over, his status notwithstanding, and failed. Before turning thirty, he established a publishing company with money he'd collected from his father's friends, but was taken to court after their discovery that he was using the capital for personal expenses. As a precautionary measure, he sent his wife and children to stay with his father-in-law in Buenos Aires, where he was due to join them sometime later. But then instead of going to Argentina, he ran off to the USA and never called his family again. After being tried in absentia for sixteen different offences, he was sentenced to five years in prison and served with a fine. His poor father, who was driven almost into bankruptcy while trying to pay off his debt, dropped him completely.

While Paul de Man was working at a bookshop in New York, a French author, Georges Bataille, helped him get hired as a French teacher in Bard College. He was handsome and charismatic, and after he'd got one of his students pregnant, who he then married (despite still being legally married to his first wife), the school fired him. Even though he'd never graduated from university, he was able somehow to get accepted by and to attain success in a Harvard University literary seminar. After filling out a false form saying that he was a graduate of Brussels University, he began to study for a Master's degree at Harvard, during which time he gave private lessons without permission from the university and taught at a foreign language school. In 1955 he left for France because of a visa problem and, thanks to his good relations, gained employment among respectable academicians. Despite the visa problem he returned the USA the following year. His dissertation, largely plagiarized and padded with quotations, was pushed to be accepted, and he landed a job as associate professor of literature at Cornell University. In 1964, without ever having received an undergraduate university degree, he became a professor. At the time Cornell didn't know that he was also being paid a salary by the University of Zurich. In the 1960s he became the leading representative of deconstruction in the Anglo-American world. To be accepted at Yale he needed to have a book, and while he didn't have one, he became skilled at overcoming such obstacles. He somehow found a way to get in and finally rose all the way up to become the department head. When he died of cancer in 1983, his obituaries referred to him as a 'philosopher'. In 1988, a fellow citizen doing research exposed the anti-Semitic essays he had written back in 1941. After that, the rest unravelled quickly in an un-deconstruction-like manner.

In short, a person who wants to become a philosopher and start a movement doesn't need to be a respectable member of a university or adhere to ethical values. All I've told you is what I remember from his biography. I'm sure you often thought about that crook, Suavi, while you were hearing about Paul de Man. This lesson drove me to forsake any of my ambitions of achieving prominence and to decide to become a well-liked and respected academician like my mentor Professor Caron.

I felt as if I had lost a limb when Anatole Bertrand Caron passed away. Except for two distant nephews who lived in Lausanne, he was alone. It upset me that he had burned his diaries before dying, as I thought he would entrust them to me. Before entering the nursing home he sold off his library, but he signed and made gifts to me of four books he cared about. My library wasn't the most well-organised, so when I looked for those books, I couldn't immediately see them. But I found another old treasure instead – a hardback on the highest shelf, lost among reference books. Every page of this twenty-centimetre-long Quran manuscript was knitted like lace with drawing ink and patience, and radiantly embraced by a rectangle hand drawn in liquid gold. Every other page contained colourful motifs that stretched out like a pendulum and were set off with fine details. On the back page I had jotted down two notes: 'July 22, 1982. Thirtieth birthday gift from Refia Hanım' and 'September 19, 1985. We lost Refia Hanım, may she rest in peace.'

I have always kept the books I have been given over the years, which are welcome reminders of our friends when they have passed on. Refia Hanım was a lady of dynasty, she was almost eighty when she passed on. Her face was that of a cherub and she was proud and quiet, with a sad countenance. Forgotten inside the Quran lay a faded black and white picture of a boy, around ten years of age, making a face as if he had been urged to wave. The note on the back said in French, 'Mother, Father and I have missed you very much. Please come back – Nadi Osman, 24 December 1945.' And underneath that: '91(b), No. 3 Bishop's Road SW6, Fulham London.' I had a sudden desire to go to London. If I stopped by the address written on the photograph, maybe I could solve Refia Hanım's mystery; at the very least, I could visit bibliopoles and search for *Induction and Deduction*, a book I hadn't come across anywhere, by the neglected Turkish philosopher İlham Dilman.

Whenever I visited London, I would stay at The Cavendish Hotel on Jermyn Street because Sir Isaac Newton had lived for three years in the building adjacent to it. I owe thanks for knowing the strategic points of the city to Judith Kitchen, an associate professor of sociology I dated for three years but who left Geneva and went back to an old flame when she discovered that I wasn't interested in marrying her. I took the underground from The Cavendish to Parsons Green, which resembles a village train station from a typical British film. The rather bland buildings along Bishops Road were built in the previous century for middle-class families, but because of the area's proximity to the City, the residents there have moved up in the world, judging from the cars parked along the kerbs. The street had apparently taken a siesta, since not a single person had ventured out to be bid a good afternoon. 91(b) appeared to be a closed grocery shop. The brick walls of the three-storey building had blackened and become unwelcoming and a note on the window, which had turned an embarrassed yellow, read 'I'll be right back.'

The name on the top-floor doorbell tab was 'Ferid Ferudun', who must have been a Turkish Cypriot. I touched it gently, offering a basmala. A tired but bold voice came through on the intercom, and when I answered with 'I'm kin of Nadi Osman', I was immediately invited upstairs.

Ferid Ferudun appeared to be about seventy. He was likable and talkative, a slightly overweight brunette who could have been an attendant in a hamam. He most likely didn't know that his first and last names both meant 'unique' in Arabic and Persian respectively, and I wondered how good his English was. As I was showing him the picture in my hand and explaining the reason for my visit, he nodded as if to say, 'I know and will tell you everything.' I warmed to the feel of the house, which imparted neither a Turkish nor British air. The second we sat down his coquettish daughter-in-law Ümmü set out cherry cordials and rose-flavoured Turkish delight. As tea was being served, he gave an oral report about the family. He'd grown up as an orphan, come to London with the help of a British officer stationed in Famagusta, and worked day and night to take ownership of four taxi cabs, two official and two pirate. He worked with his son and son-in-law. Beckett would have felt proud of his brazen telling of the way his wife ran away with one of his former drivers.

Nadi, the boy in the photograph, was Ferid's friend, sort of, and Ferid also knew Refia Hanım's husband, Nasuh Bey. He had a fruitful dialogue with Turkish Cypriots, some of whom considered him an heir, and seized on every chance to convert their reverence for him into money. He was a merchant and a fraud, who had items such as old fabrics, shawls, works of calligraphy, prayer beads and so on brought over from Istanbul that he would then sell as personal items that had once belonged to such-and-such a sultan. He also tutored rich Turkish Cypriots' children, born in London in 'Palace Turkish', for exorbitant fees.

Ferid then told me that Nadi was Refia Hanım's and Nasuh Bey's son. He had been fragile and an introvert, but well-intentioned. After he'd received his degree in business from the University of London, his father procured a job at a bank and married him off to his landlord's daughter.

Nasuh Bey had died when, during a feast, he'd choked on the pit of a plum brought over from Turkey. Meanwhile Nadi lived happily with his wife who was four years his senior, Muhsine. She had been both a big sister and a good wife to him until her death during her second childbirth, which had thrown Nadi into depression. While driving drunk he'd crashed his car into a pole on Putney Bridge and died on the spot.

Muhsine and Nadi's first child, Fahri, became an orphan at the age of ten. His uncle, whose business was suffering a rough patch then, sent his nephew to an orphanage and put his sister's house up for sale. The house became the fateful lot of Ferid, who had been given credit at the bank where Nadi worked. After great difficulty Fahri had graduated high school and forsaking any further education, his uncle took him on at the dry cleaners he owned on Fulham Road, within walking distance from my own present location. Ferid told me the address and I arose at once. Even though I'd told him not to take the trouble, Ferid accompanied me all the way down to the street. He then thought to ask my name. 'Think of it as Mahmut III,' I replied. 'If the Ottoman Empire still existed, I would be its sultan.'

As I made my way along Fulham Road towards the River Thames, the buildings grew shabbier, but the atmosphere took on a colourful dynamism. The restaurant Ferid spoke of as Chinese was actually Indian. Beside it, a blue building identified itself as 'New System Dry Cleaners'. Inside, a battle between chemicals and steam raged, and sullen young immigrants kept their eyes on the time as if they were inmates. Standing beside the window, the long-haired, bearded fellow on the phone must have been Muhsine and Nadi's orphaned child, Fahri Osman. Give him a haircut and clap a red fez on his head and he would look like Sultan Abdulmejid. He was imposing but I liked his soft voice and how he weighed his words as he spoke in street English.

He hung up and smiled at me. Taking on the accents of a gentleman, he said, 'How may I help you, sir?' Introducing myself in Turkish, I said we could be seen as kin. Then I showed him the childhood picture of Nadi and told him that his grandmother and I had been friends. Saying that I was in London on business and that it was my birthday, I invited him to dinner. I remember his reply in middling Turkish that if it was going to be at a fancy restaurant he would not come. Planning as we parted to meet at the lobby of The Cavendish Hotel, I said, 'This is also the 215th birthday of our great-grandfather Sultan Mahmut II', and he shifted his embarrassed glance to the antiquated wooden desk before him. He was tall and thin and projected a mysterious appeal despite the frumpish half-kaftan he was wearing. As I walked out, heading towards Putney Bridge, I anticipated an interesting birthday dinner, and looked forward to learning the secret of Refia Hanım. After I'd crossed over the bridge, it crossed my mind that this might have been the place where Nadi Osman may have committed suicide. I suddenly wondered at what age I would die.

For dinner we went to Franco's, which was on the same street as the hotel. Fahri wore a wrinkled Chelsea jersey and blue jeans. He was a vegetarian and at first found the restaurant odd, but a couple of glasses of wine helped him find his tongue. He recounted his traumatic childhood and days in the orphanage. The savage brats in there called Fahri 'Farty', and it took him two years to come to terms with them. Even in a desperate setting such as that, a Muslim Turkish boy faced racism.

Fahri struggled with his failure to become either Turkish or British. He liked his Uncle Tali but didn't get along well with his disagreeable British wife Hannah. His aunt-in-law disliked children and had none. Fahri was twenty-five years old, and he and his girlfriend Olivia lived in an old barge that was anchored in Putney. When I inquired about his social life, he spoke of the music that he, his girlfriend and her sibling were making in a rock band called Tricks. He knew that his father and grandfather were members of the Ottoman dynasty, but he'd never been informed of its significance. He did at least have a grasp of the Refia Hanım question. After his grandmother had caught her husband kissing her cousin in their home in Geneva, she kicked them both out. Nasuh Bey had denied any involvement with her and apologized, but Refia Hanım would not forgive him. When Nasuh Bey decided to go to London, his son went as well. Refia Hanım was crushed, but she not only refused to share her grief with another soul, she also wrote off both her husband and son. Her pride and obstinacy had brought misery to three generations of her family.

Fahri was a good listener. I introduced him to the Ottomans, who had once ruled the greatest empire on the face of the planet, and he grew as excited as if he was watching a soccer match. I explained that with Mahmut II as the father of two and the grandfather of four of the last six sultans, the dynasty's remaining members could be seen as part of the same family. As a birthday gift, Fahri handed me a 40 para (1 kurush) coin he'd inherited from his grandfather that dated from the time of Sultan Abdulmejid. When I got emotional and stood up to kiss him on the forehead, he invited me to a concert they were giving at a pub garden the following evening. And as we left, he kissed my hand and gave me a gawkish hug.

I had breakfast the next day at Fortnum & Mason, the Queen's deli, located beside the Cavendish. While looking over the weak menu, I couldn't help thinking of the richness of our breakfast spreads in Turkey and pitied the palace attendants. Then I strolled over to Cecil Court to check out a second-hand book shop that sold philosophy books but didn't accept internet orders. After slipping the book written by Professor İlham Dilman – scorned both by the school he had graduated from and his country – into a corner nook, I scanned the other dusty spines lining the shelves as Peter Neal, the owner of the bookshop who I had met through Judith, and I chatted. The ancient shop door opened loudly, and the entrance of a slim older man transformed the atmosphere. He was dressed in an old straw hat, an outmoded shirt, a floral tie, a wrinkled, light-hued suit that he probably hadn't taken off for ten years and crocodile-skin shoes. His eyes beamed brilliantly, as did his smile. Peter, after welcoming him in with a cry, introduced us. That gentleman turned out to be the legendary hunter of the Anglo-American book world, Martin Stone. It was said that while walking along a street he could sniff out any top floor apartment that contained second-hand books. He never went online, and the books he possessed couldn't be found anywhere on the internet.

Peter's praise embarrassed him, and he sat down in Peter's chair and called me over to his side. He inquired about me in a deep voice, and on finding that I was Turkish, mentioned a customer of his from Istanbul, whose name he didn't divulge. He had found a book of poetry titled *Constantinople* written in Istanbul by Vita Sackville-West, for a bibliophile banker who started writing novels after he turned fifty. He surely had things to discuss with Peter, and as I left, I decided that I wanted to become friends with this mysterious man. I went back to the hotel and did some research on him. I was surprised to find that he was only six years older than me, since his photos seemed to show an age difference of at least sixteen years. My surprise lasted only until I found out about his addiction to cigarettes, drugs, alcohol and women. He came from the English countryside and has been captivated by books from the age of ten. He worked as a journalist and was also a guitar player, playing with various groups including the Red Hot Chili Peppers. He made a name for himself as a promising guitar player, and when the Rolling Stones needed a guitarist, his name was near the top of their list. He declined to audition, however, as he didn't want to part from his life with books. He slowly became a respectable book scout and gained a reputation for knowing publishing houses better than their owners. As a vendor he's not greedy or opportunistic and prefers to give books as gifts than sell them. As a result, he was constantly broke. Even though flying terrifies him, he's an adventurous traveller. He knows when to talk and when to listen. He has many famous friends (a familiar name on the list I read was Marianne Faithfull) but doesn't talk about them.

The philosophy of this dignified man struck me. In one interview, he remarked, 'Another good thing about being a bookseller is that there's no retirement date. You can be doing it at ninety, and no one thinks you're too old. ' I understood this as, 'I deal with one thing in this world: books. I don't give a damn about the rest. 'What I had read impressed me, and I jotted down a few tips from him to rework the balance sheet of my life, which had never been balanced.

That evening, I went to join Fahri for the concert at The Three Red Lions pub, which sat at the junction of three streets near Chelsea stadium. We downed a couple of iced vodkas in the bar then moved outside to the concert setting. Sitting beside me was Fahri's sweet assistant Samiye, who spoke Turkish using English grammar with a Cypriot accent. At that moment the five members of Tricks strutted – all except Fahri – on to the stage. I got it from Samiye that Fahri played the bass guitar and was known for his timidity. Olivia, his girlfriend – who wore a patch over her left eye – sang and conducted the group. When they started playing, I was surprised to find that they were actually a really good band. Olivia, with her steamy voice, stood out. Aside from Fahri, the band appeared to have assumed an eye-pleasing rhythmic stance that engrossed the audience. Fahri, unfortunately, wasn't only out of sync but his moves were actually clown-like. While I was thinking of this as another way Fahri see-sawed between the East and West, a man on my left burst out laughing. Holding a beer in in one hand, he pointed to Fahri with the other, and said, 'This kid's moving like a puppet.' He wasn't wrong. Not content to let it go with that, he loudly declared, 'I've got to hand it to him, he makes even funnier moves than a puppet.' I felt as if he was insulting my own son and came close to losing my temper. Spitting twice in my palms, I asked Samiye how to say in English, 'Don't you think that's a little too much?', as I looked daggers at the fellow. I was on the verge of laying into him no matter how he replied, when, changing his tune, the other guy said, 'I'm sorry, sir, is he your son?' I replied, 'No, but he is my nephew.' After he'd apologised once more, I took a step back. Do not judge me; you ought to know that our sultan would fly into rages too. That concert was another turning point in my life. I was opposed to marriage, but I realized that I might be happier if I had a son or daughter to shelter under my wings.

That night I made a decision. I would help Fahri. The first thing I did after I'd extended my London trip for three days was to pay a visit to Judith. She was now the mother of twins and consequently had taken a career break. She was obviously pretending to have a happy marriage. In her opinion, my nephew's best option was the Open University, which meant that he could both work and study. She was impressed to hear that I was about to take on the educational expenses of someone I had known for only three days. I met with Fahri again, and when I started up by saying, 'You're going to vaporise in this gloomy dry-cleaning shop', he flinched. We had a third meeting that was joined by Olivia. Fahri would major in hotel management at the Open University, and I would sell the Quran manuscript his grandmother had given me and send him the money for his educational expenses. Of course, I never sold the holy script, but I sent enough money each year to meet all his needs. He graduated college on schedule and rose to the position of hotel manager at a hotel on Gloucester Road that was preferred by Turks. He and Olivia married and had a daughter whom they named Ziyal, which means, interestingly, long-tailed horse.

For my forties, an aphorism by Elias Canetti is as powerful as a proverb: 'A just person changes forty times a day, but a hypocrite stays the same for forty years.'

6

Ziya Bey

Ludwig Wittgenstein believed that philosophy came into being because for 2,500 years people hadn't been able to understand each other, but Stephen Hawking believed that it was now dead. My own belief is that philosophic possibilities were consolidated in the internet phenomenon to await their entrance into the service of artificial intelligence. I turned down the university's offer of the dean's position. The moment my work at university was done each day, I went straight home. I occasionally suspected that I should have become a historian, then I yearned to hold the position of general director at Martin Bodmer Library. I decided in the end to hang on to my life as an unassuming academician until retirement.

I had fallen into the habit of passing out in the evenings with a cognac goblet in my hand while watching a film or a documentary. Now, at fifty, I lived without ever having known such a common desire as longing to enjoy every frame of my life. As much as happiness, one needs experience; for crying, getting angry, feeling jealous and being sick hold some joy for us, too. I took lessons from each. I didn't feel jealous of anyone else's successes that I believed were deserved, but doesn't jealousy exist even within our own bodies? For instance, apply cream to your face and your hands want some too. I've noticed that every single toenail has its own caprice.

I decided now was the time to create something I could be proud of. Following a suggestion from an ambitious student of mine, I read *Montano's Malady*. In the novel, the overrated critic Walter Benjamin declared in an aphorism, 'The only meaningful work in our time is a collage of quotations and echoes from other books.' I left the house and went down to the old-fashioned stationery shop on my street. For years, I had looked with respect at the elderly artisan inside it and cast around for an excuse to buy one of his embellished notebooks. After going in and eagerly buying three bound notebooks with these distinctive pages, I felt as happy as if I had paid off one of my debts. Following Walter Benjamin's advice, I jotted down the headings to be included in the notebooks. My plan was to fill them with striking aphorisms that were fewer than three sentences; with poetic quotations from works of prose that were fewer than ten sentences; with single lines from poetry that were as powerful as aphorisms; with small but dramatic comic strips, photographs and designs; with tragicomic headlines from newspapers and magazines; and with intriguing names of streets, rivers, mountains, lakes, birds, fish and tribes. I lived on alert like an amateur hunter, one ear always listening for entries worthy of my notebook.

I realized with some shock that so much of my life had passed by between two places: Istanbul and Geneva. Now, I decided to move. When the guitarist and rare books dealer Martin Stone was bored, I heard he used to throw a dart at the map of Great Britain on his wall and go wherever the dart landed. For my thirty-fifth birthday, I had received a fair-sized globe, which I now spun with my eyes closed and reached out to stop with my fingertip. Among the places I pointed to were Manzanillo – Mexico, Ushuaia – Argentina, Abéché – Chad, Daegu – South Korea and Omsk – Russia. Getting the visas for those countries and finding hotels where I would stay was exciting and my welcomes in these countries were always unexpected. Koreans remembered the Turks who had fought during the Korean War more than sixty years ago, and I was embarrassed to be treated as a hero there. Rather than visiting the so-called tourist sites in the countries I visited, I preferred to sit in hotel lobbies for hours watching the human traffic pass, frame by frame, as if I were attending a circus. Evenings, I would lie in wait in the hotel bar for tipsy people who would light up my night with their life stories. I never got tired of listening to the boasts of businesspeople, the regrets of elderly patrons, women who'd been cheated on, and I would reciprocate to each with a different name and life story. I encountered those who felt relief at finding my story sadder than their own and women who went to bed with me because they felt sorry for me. Every night I gloried in the excitement of having a role in a play whose subject I couldn't know. Sometimes, I used Estragon as my alias but told them that they could call me Vlad. I returned from those trips with my fill of Beckett-like skits.

My thoughts also visited Zoe frequently at this time. I watched an engrossing film on a documentary channel about Saintes-Maries-de-la-Mer and the Mistral wind, and afterwards I decided to visit that village and see the statue that paid homage to the poem 'Mireio' by Frédéric Mistral, a relative of Zoe, and to listen for the wind. Mistral was said to blow the hardest during winter and spring. My first visit there was in March. A strong, cold northerly wind blowing from the Rhône valley towards the Mediterranean, Mistral usually lasts one, three or five days, and has an average wind speed of over sixty kilometres per hour. It dries out the soil, cleans up vineyards, and leaves a clear blue sky behind it, blending the fragrances of thyme and lavender as it passes through. The writer Jean Giono compared its sound to 'that of a lion disturbed while eating'. That people would plant cypress trees row upon row to increase the soil's resistance against Mistral, that Van Gogh complained about it while Nietzsche wrote a poem calling it 'My Friend', and that photos showed young people holding onto the tails of special kites and becoming airborne as it raged, all gave one pause to think.

I saw a herd of horses standing in the village square with their closed eyes, apparently savouring the wind; the waves of the sea raging as if they were being directed by an orchestra conductor; heard unlatched doors banging closed with a sound like a cannon shot. The rain waited for evening to come before pouring down. As that rhythmical wave of sound heightened, the curtain of fog parted. Mistral's voice was music to my ears. Compared to natural music, a saxophone's sound is no more than the bray of a zebra – I hope you're not offended. Rico, the hotel's bellboy, claimed that rodents as well as reptiles would emerge from the earth to observe Mistral.

When my first Mistral experience only lasted a day, I felt upset, as though I had been short-changed. When I returned the following year, performing behind a curtain of fog, Mistral established a pastel balance by removing variations, stressing the overlooked nobility of grey, beige and brown.

On my third visit to the village, I tried to start work on my Beckett project, but I was struck by writer's block in the first sentence. For the first time, Mistral lasted five days, and on day three I started to groan, too. I met some interesting characters in the lobby, however. Abe O'Sullivan was a handsome American in his mid-thirties who loved his cigars and cognac. We used to hang out at the bar by the unusable pool. He was the junior partner of an antique shop in New York; his area of expertise was nineteenth-century French bronze statues. A special client had commissioned him to find the statue of Eros that Antoine-Denis Chaudet had cast for the Queen of France. He'd at last come over from Gibraltar. I remember him saying, 'Looking for it was more fun than finding it.' There were also some New Yorkers – a couple called Kate and Nathan – who didn't have a particularly positive outlook, and none of these three knew how to play bridge.

A way to add colour to the fourth day of Mistral came to me. There is a novel by Gesualdo Bufalino called *Night's*

Lies. It is set during the nineteenth century, in a fortress on an unnamed island, where four political prisoners are being held. The members of this group, a baron, a poet, a soldier and a student, face the death sentence for trying to overthrow the Bourbon dynasty. As the scaffold for the guillotine is being set up, they take turns telling their life story. Just as their politically imprisoned personalities aren't real, so are their life stories unbelievable. I presented a proposal to the New Yorkers: we would tell our life stories, blending them with fiction. Right away, Abe said, 'If I can smoke my cigar, I'm in.' After the Coles had agreed half-heartedly, we took our seats around the game table. Abe agreed to begin, followed by Kate, Nathan and myself. Everyone had fifteen minutes to prepare, and no one could ask questions. Abe sniffed his Talisker a couple of times before he took a sip and began:

'The most painful day of my first twelve years took place when I was eleven. My father had killed my mother. The happiest day was when I was fourteen and my father was killed. My mother was a Colombian immigrant. My father was from Boston; when he wasn't bartending, he made a living as a bouncer, a gigolo, or a drug dealer. Assuming on his release from jail that his wife had been involved in an affair with a friend of his, he went and killed them both. On his way back to prison, he entrusted me to James P. O'Sullivan. JP was a professional carer of British descent. The year my father was stabbed to death JP cried for days and then adopted me. JP was a feeble gentleman that my father had slept with for money, and I think he loved my father. He was a model mother and father figure for me, may he rest in peace.

'JP was also the carer for the eccentric American multi-millionaire Scofield Thayer for the last thirty years of his life, a man he saw as an angel without wings and worshipped. Scofield was a handsome and ambitious young man and following his success as an undergraduate in Harvard he was accepted into Oxford. He'd wanted to be an academic, but the culture of gossip and alcohol at Oxford caused him to change his mind. He became a poet and author instead, fell in love with the fine arts, and later became a collector and philanthropist.

'When Scofield was twenty-six, he married the passionate and beautiful Elaine. Scofield's close friend E. E. Cummings wrote a poem for the occasion. Three years later Scofield bought *The Dial* magazine and became its editor. A pioneer of modernism, it made the country aware of Picasso, Matisse, T. S. Eliot and Ezra Pound. While the magazine was passing through these stages, Scofield's wife and Cummings had a fling that resulted in a baby girl named Nancy. As an impoverished poet E. E. Cummings received financial aid from Scofield and was becoming well known thanks to *The Dial*. Scofield detested Cummings for his ingratitude and thought it was shame that drove him to write his initials in lower case. Scofield forgave his wife and his friend and gave their daughter Nancy his surname.

'In 1921, Scofield divorced his wife and moved to Vienna for two years. His symptoms of paranoid schizophrenia led him to become a private patient of Sigmund Freud. For two years he successfully supervised the magazine from a distance and published a pioneering book about art called *Living Art*. During that time, too, he enhanced his art collection with high-quality works.

'After Scofield returned to America and started exhibiting his art collection, his ex-wife Elaine married Cummings, only to divorce him a few months later and marry an Irish banker. All that time Elaine's daughter had assumed that Scofield was her father. Only after she married Theodore Roosevelt's grandson Willard, did Nancy discover that she was Cummings's daughter.

'By 1926 the psychological state of author, poet, editor and aesthete Scofield had deteriorated to the point that he had to be kept under medical watch until the end of his life. His mother took care of him until her death in 1936. He was declared insane in 1937 and was mandated to be supervised by a guardian. In 1950, his archive was turned over to Yale University after his legal beneficiaries had attempted to sell it but failed. His 589-piece art collection was donated to the Metropolitan Museum of Art.

'When he died in 1982, at ninety-two, he had outlived his legal beneficiaries, and his wealth was inherited by distant relatives. He spent the last forty-five years of his life in Bermuda, Florida, his hometown Worcester, New York, and his favourite spot, Martha's Vineyard. JP, one of his trusted long-time carers, never left his side; a special bond seemed to exist between them. I passed my youth in JP's apartment in Brooklyn with his mother. I have no particular memories of the harmless Auntie Mary.

'After the death of Scofield, some friction developed between the executor's lawyers and the caregivers. A gold cigarette case encrusted with diamonds that he had kept on him at all times went missing. JP was insulted to be seen as a suspect, but the case wasn't pursued because of a lack of evidence.

'JP was systematic and punctual. He kept a notebook of things to be done, which he treated as holy script. He listed daily and weekly chores meticulously and happily crossed out the old ones. The fact that he lived a life composed of odd patterns made him happy. JP must have been in his sixties when Scofield Thayer passed away. Afterwards he never worked and remained sunk in depression for a long time. He would leave the house only to take long walks and he wept at night as he drank whisky straight from the bottle. When his mother died, he hit bottom, and one night as he jaywalked across Lexington Avenue, a sports car ran over him. I was a junior in college. Taking JP's advice, I was studying art history on a scholarship at CUNY and intended to write a thesis on Scofield Thayer's collection. I was also working part-time at its library and used the money JP had left me to secure a mortgage. The temptation to take luxury holidays got the better of me, and I defaulted on the payments, and the bank repossessed my house.

'I planned to move in with my girlfriend temporarily. A lot of stuff had to be thrown away, most of it left by JP. A wooden box with the word 'Jagdstaffel' written on the top got my attention. Inside were four platonic love letters, one for my father and another for Scofield Thayer, along with his dear boss's missing cigarette case. It shone like Aladdin's Lamp. I didn't care to ask myself if it had been stolen or offered as a farewell gift. As I hopefully made the rounds of antique shops, I got to know the way the market worked, and I realised that if I tried to sell it in the USA, I'd be in deep trouble. Because it contained a holy African sign, I sold it in cash to an African collector who would take it outside the country. I saved my house and became an antiques dealer.'

We sat in silence, contemplating what Abe had shared. Then I prepared a second glass of vodka for Kate as she fiddled with the wedding band on her ring finger. She went next.

'My father was the head costumer in a Broadway theatre company. Quite a large age difference separated him and my mother, whom I don't remember, because when I was a baby, his wife ran off with an Argentinian on his staff. My maternal grandmother Magda moved in with us to take care of me, and eventually she and my father married. It was Magda's third marriage, and we had a happy family life. When I was a little girl, my father would tell me legends from Greek mythology. I think it was he who benefited most from that marriage. While he was living in a fool's paradise, Magda managed us both wisely.

'I begged my father to tell me the story of Shepherd Endymion and Moon Goddess Selene all the time. It goes like this: a lonely and handsome shepherd whose name was Endymion lived on Mount Latmos, in Ziya's country. His one and only friend and confidant was his pan pipe; he would blow his dreams and troubles into, and out the end of, his pipe. At night he slept on the mountain under a huge tree. Selene, the moon goddess, fell for him at first sight. She started to come every night while Endymion slept and would caress him with her rays, staying at his side until dawn. Some other gods learned of Selene's love for a mortal and told on her to Zeus, the god of gods. Declaring that she had neglected her duty, Zeus decided to take the shepherd's life. On the night when Zeus moved to settle the matter, Selene came and embraced Endymion with her rays as he played a sad song on his pipe. This was an unheard-of kind of lovemaking, with two bodies turning into a single shaft of light. As dawn broke, Selene bid farewell to her lover until they met again that night. Zeus, who observed this scene and didn't have the heart to end their love, shrunk the shepherd down to a minuscule size. Sure that nature would look after Endymion, he placed him in the hollow of a tree to be sheltered there for eternity. When Selene came that night and didn't find her lover, she fell into a depression. Each time she became full, she brightened the earth with her loving rays as she searched everywhere for him; then, after she'd grown tired, she disappeared and grieved. Selene never stopped looking for Endymion.

'For my twentieth birthday my father gifted me a week-long holiday in Bodrum, from which I would be able see Latmos, the scene of my favourite story. Two other college students besides me were in the plane bound for Bodrum. Drake Brown was going there to scatter the ashes of his father, a famous professor of philosophy, which were collected in a jar, on to the ground beneath an old tree in the middle of the ruins of Miletus. While his girlfriend Nora and I didn't care much for each other, we still toured Miletus and Latmos together. Drake explained in an all-knowing manner, as if he were talking to illiterates, that Miletus was in the middle of Arcadia, which had introduced science and philosophy to the world. He also whispered, as if he were revealing a secret, that Thales – who lived in the seventh century BCE – had founded philosophy and taught Anaximander and Anaximandros, and that the physicist Isidore was the architect of Hagia Sophia. He was rather odd but helpful, and I didn't want to fall out with him. Looking down from the ancient theatre on Miletus and its embankment of alluvial deposits was a gloomy sight; it seemed to be slowing sinking, second by second. I feel as if I'm once more looking at the tree standing out there in the centre of it all, alone. I had never seen a tree with that many branches. While Drake and Nora argued about how to go about emptying the jar, the repulsive girl started to cry. Even her tears sounded artificial.

'Later, as a senior in the department of psychology at New York University, I saw Drake in a campus café one day. He had graduated from UCLA the year before and worked for a publisher of course textbooks. He was on campus for business. His friend Nathan, who was accompanying him on the trip, worked as an assistant editor for another publisher. I fell in love with him at first sight. His smooth face, curly hair and big eyes were as alluring as a Greek statue. I had found my Endymion. While Drake and Nathan worked in the publishing sector, they really wanted to be writers. After dating for a while, Nathan and I got married.

As a student, I was a success. As I pursued my academic career at the university, I was frequently called upon to carry out laboratory tests. Nathan had a light work schedule, and he didn't have a high salary, and as his novel proposals were constantly turned down, I was the breadwinner of the house. I was an associate professor when I was diagnosed with breast cancer. While I was being treated with radiotherapy, I had a double mastectomy as a safety measure. As I was recuperating from the surgery, an envelope fell out of the book I had brought with me to the hospital. Since it was an official hospital envelope, I opened it, thinking it contained an itemised hospital bill. Instead, there were two pictures inside it of Nathan making love with the operating room nurse.

'At that time, when I was fighting for my life, I lacked the strength to be shaken by what I had seen. I tried to take it as any psychologist might do. Nathan wouldn't have had sex for a while, and he was a handsome man. In the stressful state brought on by my illness and his occupational crisis, the flirtatious nurse might have seduced him. I decided that after I regained my health, I wouldn't pursue the issue. Eventually, it retreated to the back of my mind. I concluded that a rival or an ex-boyfriend of the nurse must have planted the envelope there as some kind of revenge. When Ziya suggested this game, I recalled those pictures from fifteen years ago. I had never judged Nathan and just wanted to make it known as an odd memory, encouraged by alcohol and Mistral, and leave it at that.'

Tension at the table heightened, as Abe and I exchanged glances and Nathan ground his teeth. Kate excused herself to go to the toilet. By the time she returned, her husband had begun to nurse his third bourbon and refused to make eye contact with Kate. It seemed that a duel was in the offing. He began:

'My father was an army officer, and he saw soldiering as the most honourable profession in the world, which is why our house was on the street nearest Arlington National Cemetery. My big sister was a navy officer and a military and state taekwondo champion in her division. After my refusal to go to a military academy, I was thrown out of the house. My dear maternal uncle lived in San Francisco and was the retired owner of a clown and puppet workshop. He and my father hated each other, so I sought sanctuary with him and studied at UCLA on a scholarship. I wanted to become a writer: to become famous and shame my father. When he was forced to retire before he'd been made general, I had already graduated and moved to New York. My classmate Drake wanted to become a writer, too, and we worked for two different publishers and roomed together for a while. Publishers liked my style but thought my stories were depressing. As I moved from failure to failure, my wife was moving up steadily and making good money. With her savings and warranty, we bought a home and car. When she was diagnosed with cancer, we were in debt to the bank and leasing companies. For some reason a surgery Kate had to have wasn't covered by insurance, and we urgently needed $9,000. Not wanting my wife to know this, I asked my publisher for a loan but was turned down. Drake's mother, who came from a wealthy family and always had money, suggested something to me after I asked her for a loan. Drake knew the details of a project I had in mind that could very well become a bestseller. I fabricated for her the plot of a novel from the first-person perspective that would tell the story of a female detective named Happy, a bisexual woman who was smart and didn't take life seriously. She asked me to sell her my project, on condition that it would remain a secret between us. I snapped up her offer, but later felt as guilty as if I had sold my own child. My dear wife is hearing about this for the first time, too.

'On the night of the surgery, I went to the hospital drunk. On one of my visits to the toilet I saw a young nurse getting slowly undressed through the open door of a staff room. Something in my mind flashed, and I took a few pictures of her half-naked body with my telephone. As I shut my eyes and waited outside the door of the operating room, another subject for a novel came to me. I would photoshop myself into the pictures, so that I appeared to be having sex with the nurse, and then slip the photos in one of Kate's books. I think I thought that I could build a novel around the later developments. Around then I drank often and suffered from erectile dysfunction. After some time, I would explain all this to Kate. However, when I heard nothing, I assumed Kate had never found the photographs, and unsure how to raise the matter, I left it.

'Drake was shallow enough to be a best-selling author.

Through the project he'd bought from me, not only was his first book published but he also received a minor award. In the sequel, Happy's pleasure in making love with a woman without breasts was expressed in explicit detail. This could only mean that my wife had taken her revenge by sleeping with my best friend. I'm glad I ignored the message. Before finishing his third book, Drake was stabbed to death one night on Canal and Mott Street, and the killer was never apprehended. To conclude my little story, I must thank Its Holiness Mistral and Ziya for enabling me to explain how I got even.'

As Nathan killed the rest of his drink in one gulp, his wife covered her face with both hands and once more ran to the bathroom. I was overcome by a dilemma. I seemed to be looking for someone to whom I could offer an apology, but my turn to talk had now come. Things had got out of hand and it was up to me to end this show. When Kate returned, she had pulled herself together and freshened up her perfume. Struggling to smile, she settled down in her seat. I described my friendship with Zoe as I have already told it to you, only I changed her name to Lea. Instead of describing Zoe's mother, I imagined a sister who lived in the States. I knew I would be too embarrassed to describe the lovemaking scene with Lena, who looked very similar to Lea. I described how, four years later, I saw Lena on Bahnhofstrasse in Zurich. She didn't see me, but when the eyes of the three-year-old boy who was holding her hand met mine, I saw everything clearly. He smiled, not understanding that he was looking at his father for the first and last time.

My surprise finale was overshadowed by the intrigue of Kate and Nathan's stories. I can still remember us disbanding quietly as Mistral left the region. I was reading a newspaper in the lobby as Kate and Nathan were checking out the following morning. As they waved from a distance, with no warning we heard automotive clatter and the honking of an antiquated horn. An ugly car straight out of the 1940s rolled up and a fashionably dressed couple stepped out of it. After they'd hugged each other, Kate kissed the theatrically attired woman on the lips, and it occurred to me to check my phone to dig up some information about the Cole couple. Professor Nathaniel Cole was a famous psychologist and Katharine W. Cole was an actor and playwright. As I stood behind them clapping, I asked Rico to open some champagne, and toasted them.

When Abe left, he gave me his fancy business card and told me to call him if I was ever in New York City. Two years later I was invited to a panel at Columbia University, and I flew to that city, which I had visited three times and never grown to like. Meeting up with Abe could have added some colour to my visit, so I called his workplace. The husky-voiced man on the phone told me no one by that name had ever worked there.

If you'd like to know the aphorism of my fifties, it's from Antonio Porchia: 'At night, I sometimes turn on the light to avoid seeing.'

I hadn't found it necessary to think closely of my health throughout my life, and only went to hospitals to take or to see someone there. I was allergic to every kind of painkiller and never took medicine. Once, after helping two elderly American women with their suitcases in Mexico City, a painful swelling arose in my groin, and I had a hernia operation. Otherwise, my head had never touched a hospital pillow. Last spring, following a long period of fatigue, my back started to ache; I was losing weight as well and I saw what seemed to be blood in my urine. The look on Dr Izak's face told me clearly that I had a serious health problem. Dr Izak sent me to see a doctor with gel in his hair, who first announced the good news that seven out of ten bladder cancer cases were treatable. Nevertheless, a long period of examination and treatment ended with him informing me that I had a year to live. I didn't know how my mother died, but my maternal grandmother had died of the same disease. A month later, I heard that Dr Izak had died of a heart attack while having sex with a prostitute young enough to be his daughter. I need not go into the details of what happened, but to try to spare my body and soul undue pain I refused chemotherapy treatment. Later, I changed my mind.

As I left the hospital, now as a cancer patient, I felt as if I'd been caught without a visa on a grey planet and I didn't know when I would be sent back down to earth. Mahmut and I returned home during a gently falling spring shower that brought back to me three key takeaways from my childhood: I had an imaginary girlfriend, Serap, who was a dead ringer for Natalie Wood; whenever I heard the cooing of a dove I thought of grey swans; and that we had a chubby housekeeper, who was mopping the floor one day when a handmade string bracelet broke and its blue beads scattered all around the living room floor, raising a musical clamour that annoyed my mother. If an aphoristic message is buried in these, it may be one best uncovered as I lie on my deathbed.

That night I was alone at home. Mahmut had made me swear that I wouldn't use tobacco, so I finished my cognac and ate bitter chocolate while having a brief reckoning with myself. Had I not fallen ill, I would have liked to have visited the Institución Colombina library in Seville, which had belonged to Hernando Colon, Christopher Columbus's bibliomaniac son. I no longer wished to see any other place. Nor could I think of any books I hoped to read or any museums I needed to visit. The world was growing more and more shallow, with people holding their mobile phones as their confidants, and tomorrow they would become slaves to artificial intelligence. I had no regrets or people who I needed to apologise to. My work had been partially ignored, but others more noteworthy than I, primarily Mahmut II, had also been ignored. I didn't try to be a good person, but only to do what I thought was right. So yes, I might be seen as having duly completed my earthly shift.

As I was nibbling the last of my chocolate and regretting that I hadn't eaten more ice cream and fritters, I drifted off in my chair while watching a documentary. As I made it to bed towards morning, I tried to remember philosophers who had died at the age of sixty and fell into a laughing fit before I found relief in weeping.

When April arrived, I bid farewell to those around me and retired. I decided to leave all I had to Fahri Osman, a distant relative who I had pulled out of a chemical well in London and shown new horizons. After I had invited him to Geneva, mentioning that I was gravely ill, the ungrateful man's response was something like, 'I'm really busy, I hope you have a speedy recovery.' Under his name was written the title 'manager'. I cursed a person for the last time.

One afternoon as I was feeling faint in Park La Grange, the lawyer called to inform me of my father's death, and when I replied, 'I'm about to die, too' he thought I was playing a nasty joke. He passed on to me such an important secret that health issues notwithstanding I had to return to Istanbul. We buried my father in the burial area of the Sultan Mahmut II shrine. I couldn't help carry the casket, and I fell over on my cane as I tried to accompany the pallbearers. Farewell Fountain Street mansion appeared to have been awaiting my return for the last thirty years. As I breathed in its odour, I hoped that a reproachful ney overture would descend from somewhere. The bare silverberry bush and the dry well in the shabby garden reminded me of the principal scene in *Waiting for Godot*. My feet felt as if they were bound in concrete, and I was glad.

The letter my father had left me told of 'a vital matter that I had to address'. While I was reading the letter, I shuddered and apologised to the memory of my father. He had been right, and I tried to gain enough time through chemotherapy treatment to be able to fulfil my responsibility. Although I can't share that secret with you, I can say that I've done everything I could do to resolve it. I'm at peace.

7

Artvin

Ziya Adlan needed four nights to wind up his narration of the events that had shaped his colourful life: two at the hotel and two at the mansion on Farewell Fountain Street, beneath the silverberry bush. He held my attention and seemed relieved to have bared his heart. He was also glad that I had refrained from asking questions and although once he'd finished his story, we did not discuss it again, something in our relationship had changed, and it seemed as though a load had been removed from him. Life continued otherwise as it had before his birthday. The next notable event happened at the end of August, when the three Russians returned to the house. As they left, the one who appeared to be the boss was carrying a briefcase and smiling.

Other remarkable events that month included our watching of *Time to Love*, directed by Metin Erksan. In the film a painter, Halil, falls in love with the photo of a woman, Meral, as he works. However, years later when they meet, the expected love at first sight doesn't occur. Ziya Bey wasn't feeling well and did not enjoy his second screening of the film in forty-seven years. The film's director, Metin Erksan, had passed away on 4 August, and the leading man, Müşfik Kenter, died on 15 August. Ziya Bey slept quite a lot after his final chemotherapy session, which was followed by waves of nausea and vomiting. I withheld the news of Müşfik Kenter's death from him. It felt as though all that was important to Ziya Bey was also dying. I saw death everywhere.

On 27 August, we celebrated my birthday dinner at the Grand Club; likely to be Ziya Bey's last visit there. The average age of those on the club's terrace must have been seventy. They were a decent bunch, but we planned to leave before the live music started up. I felt uneasy for some reason.

I was sure that the little bag in Ziya Bey's hand was a birthday gift. He wanted to share the last of the wine left in the bottle, and then, taking a yellow envelope out of the bag and handing it to me, he smiled as if to say, 'You'll be surprised at this.' I assumed that the envelope contained money. However, two photographs dropped out of it: the first one showed a dead man with one finger in each ear and nostril, and six in his mouth. The second one was of Nemrut Beşir, who I immediately recognized in wide-eyed terror as the man I assumed was behind the loss of my two fingers. I was completely shaken by what I had seen. I walked down to the end of the terrace and tried to order this abrupt and savage message, and what it meant. When I returned and sat back down, a headache came on and I itched all over, so I ran to the toilet to wash my face.

When I returned to the table, walking past the other people at the restaurant and surprised to find them just the same as before, Ziya Bey explained to me what had happened. The three Russian men who had come to the mansion on those two occasions worked for a Russian collector who had approached Ziya Bey, and who had said, if necessary, that he would do anything to get the three Edgar Allan Poe poems. Ziya Bey had kept this in mind and taken him up on the offer to mete out revenge on my behalf. I cradled his hands in mine, expressed my gratitude as we sat at the table, and cried in the car all the way home. As I wiped away my tears, I felt weightless, and that night in a dream a coating of tar silently flowed from my ears, nose and mouth. The next day, newspapers reported that businessman Beşir Kibaroğlu had been killed in Miami by his rivals because of a financial dispute of some kind. I must have been mistaken in assuming that the Russians' arrival at the mansion had something to do with the 'vital matter he had to address'. There must have been something else far more important than that.

I struggled to process the information for days. I should have felt happy that I could now move forward with my life, make plans, return to my own work once my role assisting Ziya Bey was over. Or perhaps I would travel and see something of the world as Ziya Bey had done. But I could not focus on the future. Between moments of relief that revenge had not involved getting my own hands dirty, I felt helpless; like the situation had been taken from me before I was ready and that I had lost something I had thought to be my own. I had planned only to sever my tormentor's fingers, but now he was dead, and I had been denied the opportunity to see him suffer as I had suffered. I felt that the job had been only half completed, though seen to a conclusion beyond what I had dreamed of.

At the end of the month, Ziya Bey summoned me to his room. His health had rapidly deteriorated during this time and now he was able to speak only in whispers. He told me that his confidant Mahmut had just arrived from Geneva and that he had to go back with him to conclude a business matter. As he handed me a bulky envelope, mentioning that in fulfilment of our six-month contract it included my salary for September, he thanked me for carrying out my job perfectly. So, this was the last time I would see Ziya Adlan. It always comes quickly at the end. Moving over to his side, I said, 'Ziya Bey, you are noble and wise. In the five months I've spent with you, I have graduated from another university. How I wish that we had statesmen like you, and that I could grant you thirty years of my own life.' I kissed his hand, and he caressed my hair – I thought he would be pleased by these parting words. Then, closing his eyes, he clasped his hands and laid his head back on the armchair. He was smiling, so he must have been at peace. He looked to be posing for a death mask.

Returning to the outside world, I felt like an inmate who couldn't adapt to civilian life, after living for so long in a cell. Three days after leaving Farewell Fountain Mansion and returning to my uncle's house, I was already missing Ziya Adlan, the house and Farewell Fountain Street. I was also exhausted. My uncle, a self-declared chef since completing a cooking class in Kuzguncuk, was upset with me, I knew. I would half-finish the zucchini patties, the meat-filled eggplant, and the stew he prepared for me, and fall asleep at the table while the poor man brought in cantaloupe and watermelon slices.

Thinking that sex would help me shake off my depression, my friend Cuma angrily grabbed me by the shoulders one evening and asked, 'No juice running through that cane of yours yet?' Also annoying to me in August were those city-dwellers who couldn't escape to the beach or a shady forest and stalked about like zombies. I started visiting Farewell Fountain Street every day, to sit under the shade of the fountain and look at the mansion. When my eyes grew tired, I would nod off beneath a tree in the cemetery.

After my uncle advised me to take a trip, I paid a visit to the wife of Uncle Niyaz, who'd given me my name. Auntie Neveser lived with her sister nearby, in Acıbadem, in a flat above a pastry shop. She was a retired baker. Her sister Sündüs Hanım never left her spot by the window, where she sat cross-legged on the sofa counting out her ninety-nine beads and focusing on the traffic flowing by, as if she was watching a live broadcast. Auntie Sündüs, on seeing my fingers, exclaimed, 'Whoever did this to your fingers, may God punish him fully', and gradually a new idea began to form in my mind. I had learned much from Ziya Bey about how to live as a full-blooded man. I knew that a return to academia full-time would not satisfy me at present, not when this other work had been only half-completed. Ziya Bey might have exacted revenge on my behalf with the man who called the shots, but I was going to track down the man who had struck the blow and confront him face to face. When it was time to depart, I was itching to go, and I felt lighter. I had direction. I slept well that night.

I wanted to ask Ziya Bey what he had done with his notebook – I wanted to find it and add my own aphorisms. I remembered a quote ascribed to Thales of Miletus 2,500 years ago, 'The most difficult thing in life is to know yourself.' It was true, but at least I knew what I had to do.

I began first thing the next day. I contacted Selim, the trumpet player, and he agreed to meet with me at Café Gezi, beside Atatürk Cultural Centre. It wasn't yet noon, but Selim asked for vodka with lemon. He turned to me and said, 'My hands shake if I don't drink, Arto', and then he glanced apologetically at my left hand with its three fingers. When I asked him for information about Nemrut Beşir's organisation, without asking me why, he rang up an acquaintance from Eve's Evenings and jotted down notes on a paper napkin. He told me that after Nemrut was murdered, his partner bought up the remaining shares. He had also fired Nemrut's staff. Now, Maho, Nemrut's driver who did his dirty work, lived in a wretched hotel in Tarlabaşı – Hotel Baş on Peşkirci Street. It was owned by one of Maho's relatives, and the old driver was sick.

So, my next move was to find Maho. A dozen questions circled through my mind. I think Selim guessed what I was up to. And attempting to help, he advised me that if I was going to go through with this, I had to be prepared to shell out cash. As we bid our farewells, Selim said, 'If you've got it on you, could you loan me 500, Arto?'

Around noon the next day I went to seedy Tarlabaşı and located Hotel Baş. Looking out of the five-storey building, which appeared ready to collapse at the first opportunity, the unbroken windows vied with one another for the title of filthiest. I walked curiously inside. The lobby had the look of a phone booth with a couple of fat cats sleeping inside it. No one inquired about my business there. Strange, beggar-like men looked at home in the lobby and paid no attention to the mixed scents of tobacco, alcohol and urine. Some were napping, while some others were enraptured by a coarse comedy showing on the television. I looked closely at them all. One scrawny man with a boil on his nose, who was sitting alone by the window, fit Selim's description of Maho. With each cough, he took another drag or two on his cigarette. Standing before him, I said, 'Peace be on your head, Maho' as I showed him the gun inside my jacket. He couldn't have known it was loaded with blanks. 'Come on,' I said. 'Let's have some tea and a chat in the coffeehouse next door.' Without resisting, but with difficulty, he stood up, wobbling. 'Are you a cop?' He asked.

'Worse, Maho,' I replied. 'I am a man with no job to lose', and I showed him my left hand.

I had to hold him up by the arm to get him over to the coffeehouse in the neighbouring building. I covered my nose with my right hand to ward off the reek of tobacco and sweat as he leaned on my left arm. He must have been driving the car used in the butchering of the fingers on my left hand. I didn't doubt that he was also the scum who'd put me under from behind with an ether-soaked rag. From that moment, he was a walking dead man.

In the dimly lit coffeehouse on the ground floor, old men were quietly playing cards at two tables. Maho stopped at the table nearest the door that was reserved for smokers and swore as he kicked out a young man. First, he had me ordering two sausage sandwiches for him from the snack stand across the street, saying, 'Tell them to toast the bread good.' It was clear he had nothing to lose, either. As he tucked into his sandwich and slurped his tea – which was served in a water glass – he let me know that he'd retired at the lowest grade, as if I'd been the cause. Half of his retirement pension went to the hotel; with the rest he bought food and a pack of cigarettes each day. In the morning he ate a simit and drank tea, and in the afternoon, he had a pastry and tea, smoking a cigarette every half an hour as he awaited death from lung cancer. As Maho tried to get my sympathy, I humoured him and heard him out. He came from the town of Mut, and his last name was Çekilmez, meaning 'unbearable'. Even though he looked to be in his eighties, he was only sixty-two and had worked with Nemrut Beşir all his life. 'We made loads of money,' he said, 'and blew it as if it had to be all gone in a week.' He'd had a wife who died from some disease he'd forgotten, and he had no one else. He didn't mind not getting any new clothes for two years, but he'd racked up a total debt of 600 million to the simit vendor, pastry shop and snack stand. He disregarded the six zeros that had been removed from the currency six years before, and he was prepared to talk for a fee. I raised the pitch of my voice. 'Look Maho, know first off that I was the one who got Beşir killed. I have a few questions for you. Give me accurate information and I'll pay off your debt; but let me see you make any wrong moves and I'll take your life before the cancer can.'

On hearing that I was connected with Beşir's death, he flinched and his hand began to quiver. He looked all around and tried to reach for a cigarette, but I snatched the pack away from him and flicked his nose. Pulling a cigarette out of the pack, I held it up to his mouth and then immediately yanked it back.

'First, you piece of shit, tell me who cut off my fingers.'

'Lokman from Pozantı took care of all Beşir Bey's dirty work,' he answered.

I went to give him the cigarette, then jerked it back again, startling him. 'How can I find this Lokman? What does he look like?'

'They say that after Beşir Bey died he got on as a bouncer at a nightclub on Balo Street. There's a lot of drugs there. Lokman had been into the drugs business for a long time and was a friend of the club's owner from back when. He's in his fifties and has long hair and a knife scar on his cheek.'

'You don't know what the nightclub's called?'

'It has an infidel name that I forgot the minute I heard it. It's on the part of the street that's closest to Tarlabaşı Boulevard.'

'Where does this Lokman live? Does he have a wife and kids?'

'He used to live in Tarlabaşı. I don't know the address,

though. Probably within walking distance from the club – he doesn't drive. His first wife died and the second one ran away; then he paid 10 million as a bride price for this young girl from his village. He had a little daughter with her. I don't know much about his situation lately. Anything more I say might be a lie.'

As he looked at me, I pulled two cigarettes out of the pack and stuck them up his nostrils, and then took out two more and stuffed them in his ears. I had never done, or seen done, such a thing before but it felt natural to me. I had got enough information and was sure that he wasn't lying. 'I hope I don't have to look you up again,' I said, and threw a couple of hundred dollars in front of him. His eyes lit up. On my way out, I asked him what Maho was short for, and he said with a scowl, 'Mahmut'. I raised an eyebrow at this coincidence, that both Ziya Bey and I had a Mahmut in our lives.

I was hungry for something. I walked up Istiklal Avenue and stopped at historical Hacı Bekir for a kashar cheese sandwich and lemonade, and then had profiteroles at İnci Patisserie. Then I walked over to Balo Street. Half the shops on the street were shuttered, and I wondered if it was only pre-evening quietness. The signs were mostly for clubs, snack stands and hotels. I did a double take when I saw an Irish pub called The James Joyce, then I ducked quickly inside and downed a couple of beers. It was strange, after months of assisting Ziya Bey, to roam around as I pleased, considering only myself. While I was there, a disenfranchised member of the navy told me the name of a club popular among the gay community. He told me that the place was known as 'Club Sexchange'. On finding the place at the end of the street, it looked as though the club was on the ground floor of an otherwise derelict building. A neon sign read 'Club Exchange'. Its business hours were from 9 in the evening until 4 in the morning, but it was clear that it was not the sort of place where just anyone could enter. I had achieved more than I had expected to that day.

The next evening at 8 pm I checked into a hotel that had a second-floor room with a sideways view of the club. When I told the receptionist that I wouldn't be staying the whole night, he took 50 lira and didn't ask for an ID. I had brought along a powerful set of binoculars and set myself up to watch the club's entrance. My suspicions were raised when Lokman failed to show up by 9 pm. Only two people had arrived at the club, who had both snuck cash to the doorman. I went downstairs, put on my sunglasses although it was dark outside, crossed the street, slipped 20 lira into the doorman's pocket and asked him when Lokman would arrive. He asked in a raspy voice if I needed some weed, and I replied, 'And how!' The doorman said that he would come around 10.30 pm and leave between 2.30 and 3.00 am. So I returned to my hotel room and sat there, becoming more awake as the sound of faked and real orgasms and laughter came through the walls from the adjoining rooms.

Finally, Lokman arrived at the club, prayer beads in hand. After pausing to greet the people hanging around outside, who laughed long and hard at a joke he appeared to have made, he stepped inside. At times he came back outside with customers, who he sent on their way after glancing around furtively. The couples who'd made their eager exits disappeared into the hotels nearby, and to my own hiding place, with its foul bouquet of mildew and urine. At about 3 am the coffee in my Thermos ran out, and Lokman made another appearance. After chewing out the new lookout on duty, he ceremoniously puffed smoke as if his fingers held a sacred cigarette and swayed gently. Then he glanced around and then began walking slowly down the street. I made a quick exit and took off after him.

Heading down Tarlabaşı Boulevard, we moved almost in step towards Taksim Square. While the operation in itself was thrilling, tailing a junkie through those dismal streets was tiring. After a while, we crossed the boulevard and headed down Pelesenk Street. I took note of the streets where, in the darkness, we turned first right and then left, as I planned to return the following morning to chart the route. As a precaution I had taped Cuma's red-handled switchblade below my right knee. I had taken Cuma into my confidence and told him what I had planned before I left that evening. I knew it would appeal to him, and I knew that, as my best friend, he would help me out.

With great difficulty Cuma had made it through middle school, and his family had sent him off to military service, hoping this would make a man of him. I don't know which was funnier: him learning from his uncle in Poyrazköy how to use a rifle to save him from embarrassment during his military service or the fact that I had accompanied him there. Surprised by my marksmanship, his uncle set it down to my work as a musician. Mother Gülriz might have considered it ironic that I would settle accounts with the man who had ended my musical career with the marksmanship that my musical talent had improved.

When I returned the next morning in the daylight to retrace our steps, Tarlabaşı's lively streets with their sweet names gave me a sense of relief. Clotheslines drooped with freshly-laundered clothes, strung between careworn buildings that hadn't seen a drop of paint in over half a century; narrow streets shook with rickety vehicles and megaphones advertising vegetables and blankets; portable kebab shops radioed seductive smells; small children shouted together in four different languages; and tragicomic graffiti decorated the buildings' walls – it all made me feel as if I were lost in a Fellini film set. I settled on a spacious intersection where three roads met at Kapanca and Doğramacı Street as the right place for the ambush. My plan was to stop Lokman by holding him up with a gun; Cuma would then approach from the rear and knock him out. I would lay him face down and fire three bullets each into his index and middle fingers.

It was reported that Turkey contained five million unregistered weapons and two million registered ones. Sourcing a weapon wasn't a problem. For $2,500, I bought a lightly used Walther PPQ pistol: a silencer-equipped weapon with a fifteen-bullet magazine. The man who sold it to me assured me that hammering a nail into a piece of wood would make a louder sound, a statement he'd surely repeated to countless others before me. The fact that my uncle was at that time enjoying a holiday in Bodrum with a woman he'd met online made my job easier. I had plenty of ammunition, and after tracing the outline of the fingers on my right hand on to a homemade target that I set up in my uncle's garden, I shot at the index and middle fingers from an appropriate distance until I was sure of my aim. Whenever I held the Walther, my hands shook. As I rehearsed my meeting with Lokman, the thought that he might fall on his knees and beg forgiveness left me feeling confused.

Downtown, just below the boulevard, life had been set back some thirty years. The people, vehicles and stores had resolved among themselves not to progress beyond the 1980s. I wondered what Ziya Bey would have to say about this observation I'd made. With him on my mind, I wondered about his last business matter in Geneva, and whether it had been a success.

When I was heading back, my attention was taken by a group of boys and girls, all around seven years of age, who were playing on the street. I couldn't make out what sort of game they were playing as they ran about, to the left and right, screaming in Turkish and Kurdish. Among them, as smart as a whip, was a brunette girl with almond-shaped eyes and a snub nose. She seemed to be enjoying the game the most, and I envied the father of this happy child. I had plenty of time to spare, so I went into the nearest grocery store and bought some vanilla-filled chocolate wafer bars. I handed them out to the children, and met the brunette girl, whose name was Nihal. She told me proudly that she was five-and-a-half years old. Although one of the younger ones, she was clearly the leader. When I asked them all what they wanted to be when they grew up, Nihal stepped forward first, then hid her hands behind her back and giggled, 'What's it to you?' Then, seeing that I was a bit put out, she commanded me to bend down and yelled very clearly into my ear, 'I'll be a mother, of course!' I noticed some of the children looking at my left hand and noticing as they always did my missing fingers. Children are so much more observant than adults. Nihal wasted no time in asking, 'Abi, were you born with missing fingers?'

'No, Nihal,' I said. 'A bad man cut them off and very soon God will punish him.' As I was leaving, she and the other children waved goodbye.

The upper part of Pelesenk Street was full of buildings with nameplates saying, 'suite' and 'residence', which looked to be under repair. While I was wondering which of these weren't brothels, from the doorway on my right burst a man tugging the arm of a scrawny young girl dressed in sweats. Kicking open the door of the adjacent 'suite', he shoved the girl inside. As he leered at me, on impulse my hand reached down to the cuff holding the switchblade. Whatever that pimp on Pelesenk thought might happen to him, he ducked back inside.

I had planned to take a tour of the back streets of Tarlabaşı. It seemed wise to plan a route through back alleys to get down to the Golden Horn, after we had carried out the ambush. The streets were quiet. I grew more and more used to the sounds of mussel shells being washed in old machines and prepared for stuffed-mussel production. I joked around with the kids playing ball on the street and asked migrant grocery-store keepers for directions. Speculators had bought up the buildings where middle-class Armenians had once lived and started restoring them, so construction was underway everywhere. Were the elderly inhabitants of dilapidated buildings, seen through the curtainless windows of basement apartments as they lay stretched out on bunkbeds, awaiting death or trying to hang on to life in Tarlabaşı?

All the kids in Tarlabaşı were out on the street in the evening heat, and I saw the girl Nihal again, with a doll in her lap, sitting on a doorstep with a friend. She held out her hands, expectant for another chocolate bar.

'Alaaddin Abi, are you our neighbour?'

'No. I do not have a house right now.'

'You can stay with us until you find one,' she replied.

I relented and bought some more wafer bars for the girls from the grocery store before heading south. Since I had plenty of time, I walked from Unkapanı Bridge to Cibali before taking a breather at a coffeehouse on the shore. The fishermen were talking heatedly back and forth and the scene reminded me of a famous series of photographs by the iconic artist Ara Güler, taken there in the 1960s.

Backtracking by taxi to Balo Street, I went into the James Joyce pub for dinner. I took a table beneath a photograph of Joyce, and while waiting for my hamburger and ice-cold beer tried vainly to remember who came up with the line, 'If James Joyce hadn't existed, academicians would have made him up.' My thoughts returned to Ziya Bey, and what had happened to him. When I finished the hamburger, I sipped two Irish whiskey doubles over the course of an hour then asked for the bill. Attempting to imitate Ziya Bey's sweet curse Suavi, I told the waiter to deduct the price of the nuts I hadn't eaten, but when he replied, 'We don't charge you for those anyway', I felt embarrassed.

At around 8.30 pm, I decided to do a practice run. I waited in the designated space as Lokman approached the spot where I planned to ambush him on his return journey later that week. Like a minute hand, I was certain to move in a specified direction at a specified time, but I still enjoyed every minute that I passed doing this.

The next evening, Cuma and I followed Lokman for a practice together. During the whole routine Cuma whispered prayers, and when I finally turned to him and said, 'Look man, you don't have to do this', his torrent of curses broke me up. The following evening, a holy Friday night during the first half of September, with an elegant crescent moon reigning in the sky, we finally carried out the operation.

Heading the country's news that day was a report of the twenty-five soldiers who died and the fifteen injured in an explosion at a military ammunition depot in Afyonkarahisar. I buried the gun and the silencer under dirty clothes in two separate bags, and shortly after 2 am I was squatting beside the building at the intersection of Kapanca and Doğramacı Şakir Streets. No one was around other than some stray cats. I put the silencer on the gun, felt relief wash over me as I swallowed a pill the man who I had bought the gun from had also sold me, and put on my glasses, gloves and a red 'Cirque de Soleil' cap. I was also chewing gum and humming Van Morrison's 'Days Like This' to stay calm. I focused on the narrow building right across the way with its main entrance door outlined by tiles that had been made to look like book covers. When I had asked about it earlier, a local grocery store owner said it belonged to the Aziz Nesin Foundation. Noticing just then a dim light on the first floor, I imagined, sitting inside it, a writer scribbling in a lined notebook, in pencil, a novel with the title Farewell Fountain Street. The protagonist was the philosopher Ziya Adlan, but the writer was unable to come up with a suitable role in the story for Artvin Taner, who, after losing two of his fingers, lacked even the ability to make jokes with a waiter.

At 2.45 am Cuma called me. Lokman had left the club. When I stood up, my chest felt tight. He called again ten minutes later to say that Lokman was coming down Pelesenk Street. I moved up to the intersection and lay in wait with the gun still in the bag. When I saw Lokman approaching, I pulled my gun and shouted, 'Hey, stay right where you are!' He continued walking confidently towards me, and shot back, 'What the hell are you talking about?' With the gun clearly visible in my right hand, I showed him my left hand. I said, 'You cut off these two fingers, and you'll pay for it now.' He looked at me, amused. I knew my voice sounded thin and weak and was all too aware how amateur I must look and sound to Lokman. Cuma was nowhere in sight. When Lokman said, 'What the fuck you beardless twat?' I realized that I'd neglected to put on my ski mask. Swearing at my mother, he reached inside his own jacket. I lost it and put three bullets in his mouth and three in his chest. When he fell, I put the gun in his mouth that had insulted my mother and kept on shooting until the magazine was empty. The gun dealer was right; the gun's sound was no louder than that of a nail being hammered into a piece of wood. After emptying the magazine, I tried to get a grip on myself as I looked down at his shattered face, which appeared to be smiling. I lost it again, and picking up a rock from the roadside, brought it down on his face with both hands. Then Cuma arrived and stopped me, muttering in his Laz accent, 'That's some grudge you have there' as he slapped me a couple of times to bring me back to myself. I guess it was a blessing that he'd stopped to clean his shoe. Lokman's jacket pocket contained a gun and two envelopes holding the takings of the day stacked separately as dollars and euros. I removed the bills and dropped them into my bag with the pistol. Cuma and I then parted ways, the only part of the operation that was carried out as planned.

I made my way through the back streets to Unkapanı Bridge. While I was walking, I started to breathe more easily. It was hard to know how I was feeling, but adrenalin was pumping through my veins and I felt that I had got even with life. I felt back in control again. Choosing a moment when there were no cars in sight, I threw the gun and silencer separately into the waters of the Golden Horn. Feeling at peace, I stopped in at the same coffee house I'd called in on a few days before. Those who weren't sleeping with their heads on the table were smoking. The tea vendor, who remembered me, said, 'You look like you've taken care of an important business matter.' I said, 'You're right, my friend. Half an hour ago, I killed a man', which made everyone laugh. They assumed I was joking, of course.

This time around, after further inspecting the faded posters and pictures on the wall and hearing the comforting sounds of snoring and farting from the other tables, I fell asleep without needing pills. After a breakfast of tea, simit and kashar cheese, I whistled as I walked along in the early morning, making my way to Üsküdar. Cheerfully boarding the Üsküdar boat as the sea flirted with the sun, I thought of Endymion and Lokman Hekim, who had lived for a thousand years as he sought a remedy for death, and finally Ziya Bey, who was awaiting his own death.

For two days Cuma and I scanned the newspapers, and although relieved, I wasn't surprised to find that Lokman's death was not reported anywhere. Since I'd gone to Tarlabaşı three times before the ambush, I thought suspicion might be aroused against me if I didn't show up there at least once more, so I bought some sweets for the children I knew would be there (and who would ever suspect of murder someone armed with chocolate wafers?) and headed down to Doğramacı Şakir. The street was quiet but for a small girl, who was skipping. When she came running towards me, her slippers flew off her feet. She told me that her friend's father had been shot and that everyone was inside because they were scared. I closed my eyes and for a moment felt myself spinning around like a character

142

in one of those TV series I despised. I asked her what her friend's name was, and she said 'Nihal'.

Taking hold of her hand, I asked her to lead me to Nihal's house. I planned to pay my respects to Lokman's widow and although I wasn't thinking straight, thought I should give them whatever cash I had on me, as well. From the spot where I had left his body, we turned towards Taksim Yağhanesi Street. On our way there, I wondered what I would say. Surprisingly, the girl took me to the most charming building on the street; it was clean and well-kept. I just couldn't picture Lokman inside it. Nihal opened the steel door slowly. Shockingly, she did not appear to be at all upset. She said, 'Alaaddin Abi, they killed my father and stole his money.' Then she took my hand and led me to the living room, from where I could hear voices. The beauty of the place with its striking simplicity surprised me; how nice it was not to see a lace doily draped over a state-of-the-art smart television. Sitting inside were three women with their heads covered. They must have been the last party of mourners to come by and offer their condolences. A beautiful brunette with long legs stood up to welcome me. Her face left no doubt that she was Nihal's mother. She introduced herself as Esma, and she didn't appear upset either. She had a calm voice, and she weighed her words before speaking. As I extended my condolences, I made my decision.

I suggested taking Nihal and her friend out for some fresh air if that was helpful, and surprisingly, Esma readily agreed. On our return an hour or so later, Esma made tea and invited me to stay for a cup. She told me that she had been expecting something like this to happen since day one; that her husband's death was in 'the nature' of his affairs. Far from my worries that my actions had made life worse for Nihal and her mother, I came to congratulate myself on the better life they could now lead, rid of Lokman. The following weekend I stopped by again. And the next. I'd given some thought to converting the currency I had stolen from Lokman into Turkish liras and giving it to Esma without offending her or arousing any suspicions about my intentions; however, it transpired that she and Lokman, and now Esma only, owned the entire apartment building in which they lived. I congratulated the late Lokman for not leaving his wife and daughter destitute, so prudent and unlike Maho's approach. As we were drinking our tea, Nihal put on her pyjamas and then came over and lay her head in my lap. I stroked her hair. As Esma and I chatted, keeping our sentences within the proper limits, I saw her looking at, but not asking about, my two lost fingers and thanked her silently because I did not want to lie to her. Later, after she'd taken Nihal off to bed, I kissed Esma. The day we started sleeping together was also a Friday.

The game Ziya Bey and the three Americans played as they waited for Mistral to blow over didn't seem very plausible, and at the time I had certainly entertained the possibility that Ziya Bey himself had made that whole tale up. Yet the internet confirmed what I'd been told about Scofield Thayer. My own life was responding to strange but symmetrical rules like a game within a game, and it felt stranger and more coherent than any novel.

8

Artvin

The envelopes that I took from Lokman's pocket contained 10,000 dollars and 8,000 euros. To convert all that into liras, I had to visit three exchange bureaus. Over Cuma's objection I donated half of it to the orphanage that had cared for me as an infant, and Esma and I gave the rest to needy families on Doğramacı Şakir Street. The wife of my victim thought my victim's money was an inheritance of some sort from a relative. She prayed for my loss in this period of bereavement, as I pretended to pray for hers.

Now I had tied up the business that had been so preoccupying me for the best part of the previous year, I was ready at last to go to Artvin and visit the grave of my Uncle Niyaz. Sitting beside me on the flight to Trabzon was an elderly Armenian gentleman. He was on his way from California to his late father's home in Artvin. He sported a handlebar moustache, and I wasn't surprised by his broken English after he told me that until his mother passed away, they'd spoken Turkish at home. His name was Aram Karaoğlanyan but he said I should call him 'amca', which is Turkish for uncle, and when he learned that my name was Artvin, he hugged me and kissed me on both cheeks. His father used to own a grocery store in Artvin, and he himself ran a real estate business in Fresno, which he had signed over to his son-in-law after he retired. The more he sighed like an Anatolian, the fonder I grew of him. The friendship that Amca Aram and I had formed continued all the way to Artvin. His excitement grew as we neared downtown. He'd find their old house and store and eat eggplants stuffed with ground beef and cracked wheat pilaf; then, after having his fill of Artvin, he'd head back to Fresno with a handful of soil. The last Armenian couple in the city were waiting for him. I did not ask him their age.

The rental car driver was a retired primary-school teacher and knew the region. 'Artvin is our only city with no soccer team because we lack enough flat area to build a stadium,' he said. I told him that the Ottoman traveller Evliya Çelebi had noted on his trip in the seventeenth century that he 'couldn't find a place flat enough to set my glass on in this city' and we laughed. The rugged terrain made farming or animal breeding in the area impossible. The only hope a young person from Artvin with aspirations had was to go to a public boarding school and become a civil servant. Along with their high literacy rate, Artvin residents were known to be decent and modest. With its pristine nature and fresh air, Artvin was the paragon of peace; remembering Mother Gülriz's claim that the farther away from Istanbul one moved, the greater the kindness ratio, I felt like giving my name a kiss. Reaching

Artvin as we did, by driving through the mountains and along the River Çoruh, passing thousands of migratory birds who had stopped there for some respite, it really felt like a remote, natural haven. When we asked for directions, people were as discreet as if they were offering condolences. One of Amca Aram's two suitcases that I took out of the car was patched; I was sure that his father had carried it with him when he left Artvin.

As we neared Şavşat, the size of the trees and flowers decreased as their appeal increased. Green stood up to autumn, and I felt as though I was only now starting to grasp that colour's allure. With a population of just 5,000, the place resembled those one-street cowboy towns. After eighty years Amca Aram had returned home, and I fell in love at first sight with a dream town. As I stepped out of the car at the hotel, the driver said Aram Karaoğlanyan had taken care of the fare earlier, during our comfort break. When I chided him for agreeing to it without asking me, he brushed off my rebuke, saying, 'He said "please" so sincerely that if I had refused him, he would have cried.' On the way up to my room, which smelled strongly of soap, I remembered a poem by Melih Cevdet Anday:

If I went there as a guest
If they prepared a clean bed for me
If I slept and forgot everything, even my name ...
If I awoke and my bed still smelled of lavender
If they fixed me a breakfast of olives with thyme

If I didn't remember where I was
And even forgot my name.

On awaking the next day, I felt at ease in my mind, as if my sins had been partly redeemed. For breakfast I had, one after another, bişi – a local pastry. I got a call and chatted with Esma and Nihal, who scolded me and wanted to know when I would return. A car as old as I was and Mücahit, its driver who was somewhat younger, arrived to carry me to the bleak village of Çavdarlı. Noticing my hesitation, Mücahit, slightly embarrassed, said, 'This black donkey knows every inch of the road to Çavdarlı.' The route was so scenic, it was like an exhibition of summer and early autumn photographs. Soon, we entered the bleak village of Çavdarlı with its thirty houses. The young people, escaping to cities – the sources of depression – had left this untouched natural beauty in the care of its elderly inhabitants. Adopting a census taker's air, Mücahit pointed out that the village cemetery was more crowded than the village itself. The tombstone of Uncle Niyaz Tezcan, the martyred public prosecutor, displayed a setting crescent moon. I went over and wept as I hugged the milky, white marble tombstone. A breeze from the mountains had picked up the fragrance of flowers and left it there on the tombstone like a gift. As I hugged the crescent and breathed in the fresh array of scents, my life flashed before my eyes, and I saw myself settling accounts with the monumental man I thought of as my godfather.

Rather than having lunch I ate some bişi along with ayran

in the restaurant where I'd had breakfast. At the hotel I read Beckett and napped. In the afternoon, I ascended Efkâr Hill, the symbol of Şavşat. I was so keen not to miss the view that I had to remind myself to blink. I could hear the music of silence. While the author Fakir Baykurt was working as a teacher in Şavşat, he wrote a memoir titled *Efkâr Hill*. The book I had brought from Mother Gülriz's library, dated 1960, opened with a description of Efkâr Hill:

Oh, my. Green, green, ever so green, you just wouldn't believe it! When you look at it, everything you see, dark green. Walnut trees fused with pines, pines with shrubs, and shrubs with oaks, and the greens fused with more greens.

Master Sefer the Barber says: 'Dear sir, this here is like Swedzerland. You can find such woodland, such graceful scenery only in there, just look at this!' speaking as confidently as the villager who brags about the oats he's grown. If you asked him where 'Swedzerland' is, he could not even point to it on the map. But in fact, the land you see here is no different from the 'Swedzerland scenery' the mind creates. In Mount Qaf they shot the fairy giant, then skinned his green hide and stretched it out here. Big creek, trees everywhere. Trees, flowers! Be a beekeeper here. Set up the hives in two lines, call up the bees. All the bees in the world, asleep, at rest, in flight, if they don't come, count me out! The green in springtime drives you crazy. All that creepy crawly, that smell, that buzz; as if we had all that stuff you find in the old storybooks right here ...'

The thought of Switzerland drove me back to Ziya Bey. Was he now dead? I remembered the sixty fully lived years that he managed to fit into those brief aphorisms, and that he didn't state his aphorism for his final decade. I wouldn't live long either; I wasn't able to fully live out my life and I was worn out. I'd settled my account, got even with the world and had no new goals. When the time came, all I needed now was a friend I could call on to honour my request: 'Bury me beside Niyaz Tezcan.'

Each October I remembered what Mother Gülriz had explained to me about the 1925 switch from the Hijri calendar to the Gregorian calendar. The Turkish names of five months (February, April, June, July and September) were borrowed from Mesopotamian civilisations and three months (March, May and August) were imported from Europe; however, four months (January, October, November and December) were all ours. September and October were enjoyable months in Istanbul and I had returned part-time to my academic work and was now in the habit of stopping by the university twice a week. Two days a week, I visited Esma and Nihal. On Thursdays, I gave English lessons to a man in Kuzguncuk looking to upgrade his language skills. Kudret Bey was a widower living in a small mansion with his German shepherd dog and his carer. Despite being past the age of seventy, he had decided to move to America. He offered me bribes to keep the lessons short and avoid giving him homework, and whenever

I raised my voice, his dog, Rip, would snarl. I couldn't bolster the English skills of Kudret Bey, but thanks to him, I got to know the Kuzguncuk area and make Çınaraltı Café my haunt.

İcadiye Avenue, the main artery of the neighbourhood, reminded me of a film set erected for some sort of happiness commercial. Sloping gently, it ran between a line of miniature stores facing it on both sides. It also hosted a book dealer, an art gallery and some design and chocolate shops. Locals patronised coffeehouses and packed cafés like sardines. Stray cats and dogs that respected the ambience of the avenue and its monumental trees were treated as individuals in their own right. Also meaningful was the fact that the mosque, church and synagogue sat side by side. I noticed historical buildings on the side streets that ran up from the main road but felt too lazy to have a look at any of them.

Çınaraltı Café lay beside the sea, beneath a sycamore hunched over like a comedy character from a traditional Turkish shadow puppet play. It was a bohemian hangout favoured by poets, authors, artists, sculptors, actors and journalists. There was a dry Ottoman fountain in an empty corner of the café. I thought of Farewell Fountain Street each time I saw it.

The outdoor part of Çınaraltı Café overlooked the sea from a break between two wooden buildings, from there, there was a fine view across the water, and glimpsing a passing vessel would have the same effect on me as a newly hung painting. One afternoon I was sitting on the makeshift pier, sharing my sucuk sandwich with the seagull that was part of the cafe's permanent staff and getting slowly high on the vodka in my flask. Behind me, two painters Yusuf Abi and Sali Abi were arguing enjoyably about who knows what, and I was asking myself which of the skyscrapers crowding the horizon I would prefer to live in if I could choose only one. Just as I'd picked the white cylindrical one that looked as if it could take off into the sky at any second, a woman appeared beside me. With her hair done up finely and wearing bright lipstick, she clung tightly to her coat as she looked around, then suddenly threw herself into the sea. Having just begun to drink, I was still fully myself, and, kicking off my shoes, I jumped in after her while shouting, 'Yusuf Abi, Sali Abi, help!' The water seemed warm, but the suicidal lady's water-laden coat pulled her down. When I at last got her to the surface, she looked confused, as if she'd been awakened too early. She began talking to herself, and I remember that the two artists never stopped their furious arguing as they dragged her out of the water.

When the woman was being dried off in the roofed-in area, which could have been thought of as the lodge of Can Yücel, the famous poet, she started to cry and then suddenly, fainted. The psychologically troubled Leman, who appeared to be in her forties, lived in a mansion in the hills of Kuzguncuk and was a member of the Ottoman dynasty. As her neighbours arrived to take her home, she pointed her finger at me as if to ask me why I had dared to meddle in her business. And Cuma, who came in the bakery truck to bring me dry clothes, scolded me for not catching hold of her before she jumped.

After drying off, I hurried away to Tarlabaşı. As I hugged Esma, who had answered the door, I told her apologetically that I had saved a life.

Ruhsar Hanım, Leman's mother, invited me to come to dinner that weekend. I may have upset Leman Hanım by saving her life but starting that night I almost regained my own joy of living. I watched Agnes Varda films and got together with my musician friends for dinner and drinking each evening that week. None of them would ever become famous or important, so we joked about that fact and raised a toast to it.

Ruhsar Hanım's Ottoman mansion was situated on Meşruta, a street tucked away on one of Kuzguncuk's affluent hills. The first two floors had been rented out. I warmed up at first sight to Ruhsar Hanım and her house with its Bosphorus view. She seemed to be about seventy-five, with white hair, fair skin, and a poise that radiated charm; she was more chic than she needed to be. Like the palace ladies described by Ziya Bey, she was elegant and prudent in every possible way. When she spoke, her tone of voice was impressive, as sweet as if it might break into song at any moment. Ottoman items filled the living room and its walls, and I imagined the amazing Ottoman living room that might be designed with everything that Ziya Bey had crammed into storage. She described her family to me, mentioning her daughter's mental problems, which were much like those of her late husband, and said that she had once more been sent to a nursing home. On the other hand, her son had graduated with honours from

Stanford University and moved up in the ranks of a software company in California. Her prayers let me know that he was the one taking care of his mother. Eleni, her middle-aged Armenian maid, wore spectacles and a uniform, and their way of conversing in French was amusing.

Ruhsar Hanım and I soon warmed up to each other. Two days later, I invited her to Villa Bosphorus Restaurant for lunch and felt honoured when she held on to my arm as we entered. Once she found out that I had a girlfriend, she asked if Esma and Nihal would join her for breakfast at her home the following morning. They were delighted to hear that an Ottoman princess had invited them to dine with her, and we went together to buy special clothes and discussed how they should behave. This was my first visit to the mansion in the daytime, and on the high garden wall of the adjacent derelict building I saw lines written by local poets. At the very top was a line by Gülce Başer, a poet whose work I didn't know: 'You find me. If I look for you, everyone will know.' This in and of itself was both a poem and an aphorism; I couldn't tear myself away from it, as it seemed to have been written for me. I reached up and felt alive inside as I touched each letter. During my next visit, Ruhsar Hanım insisted that the following summer we go together to visit her son in San Francisco.

On 28 October Ziya Adlan's lawyer Saim Bey called; he would expect to see me at Farewell Fountain Street the next morning. Thank God no bad news about Ziya Bey had appeared in papers that publish obituaries. I ironed the suit that I had worn the first time I went to meet him and turned in early. After my back and cheeks started itching, I got up, took a sleeping pill, and read Beckett until I fell asleep.

In the morning, I explained to my uncle why I was dressed in a suit. He took offence at my refusal to have any of the walnut jam he'd placed before me. So, I quietly counted to ten and set out from Doğancılar Avenue, which was decorated with Turkish flags, as warplanes put on an air show overhead. It was the eighty-ninth anniversary of the foundation of our Republic. The taxi driver, whose cab had a bumper sticker saying, 'Don't worry!' had no idea where Farewell Fountain Street was located. The young man had come from Sinop, and I suspected that he didn't know anything about his fellow citizen Diogenes, either. He'd only just completed his military service and begun to work as a cab driver. He was full of self-confidence, and I liked the way he said, 'We'll learn by going back and forth.' I got off at Farewell Fountain Street, which was as desolate as ever. As I walked towards the mansion, I felt as if I was returning to a cell that I regretted ever leaving. With its repaired and repainted walls, the mansion looked as if it had taken a step up the social ladder. It must have been sold, I thought to myself. On entering the yard, I saw construction labourers hard at work, despite the holiday. If the new owner was renovating the building, then why had I been asked to come here? I greeted the mansion's long-time employees at the door, but they hurried away. On the way up to Ziya Bey's study I felt relief, thinking I'd been invited to pick up the books and memorabilia that were offered to me as the mansion's furnishings were being liquidated. I would ask for Cuma's help moving things, which would result in another load of swearing, and I smiled.

The mansion's interior was like a three-ring circus. I made my way through the noise coming from hammers and hatchets and past the smell of paint and the shouts of workers. In the room where I had stayed, a young man with a high-pitched voice was murdering a bizarre song: 'He's a soldier now / What could he want, who knows / In my sleep, dear Lord, / Show him to me.' These lines cheered me. I walked past and on to the threshold of Ziya Bey's room where I could hear more noises but was not pleased at what I saw inside. Saim Bey – wearing his usual outfit, of course – had settled down behind Ziya Bey's desk and made himself at home there. His wife, again clad in tracksuit bottoms, gyrated her hips in front of the window as if she was trying unsuccessfully to mimic twirling a hula hoop. A box had been placed under the green-brocaded velvet coverlet in the middle of the table. I took a seat in my usual chair, and we greeted each other brusquely. He handed an envelope over to me, saying, sceptically, 'This is for you.' It contained a letter that Ziya Bey had composed for me. My palms began to itch as I read:

Dear Artvin,
When I summed up my life story to you on my last birthday, I had to skip the final part. Now is the time to fill in that gap. After I had returned to Istanbul for my father's funeral, Saim the lawyer gave me the letter my father had left for me.

I told you that years ago, after my last fight with my father, I slept with the young maid Naile. Four months later, Naile quit her job and returned to her family. She was pregnant and didn't want my parents to know about it. They believe that she thought that I would try to find her. At last, she gave up on me and ran away from home just before it was time for her to give birth. When Naile's uncle related all this to my father, he contacted a retired chief of police that he knew. Thinking of Naile's depressed state, they kept a watch on all the hospitals, police stations and mosque courtyards in the area. Naile left her baby at Doğancılar Police Station, then she threw herself in front of a city bus in Bağlarbaşı. To avoid scandals my father kept an eye on all these developments from a distance. When he had positive feelings about Gülriz Hanım, who wanted to adopt you, he provided her with all the financial assistance she needed, and the two of them kept everything to themselves. My father had planned to reveal this secret to me one day after I had apologized to him. When that didn't happen, he left me a short letter to be delivered after his death. That letter, which was filled with spelling mistakes, bore Gülriz Hanım's address and other necessary information, and your grandfather Asaf Bey seemed to have managed the crisis well. The final matter I had to deal with before I died was to find and get to know you, which is why I put up with the stress of chemotherapy. Before I hired you, I had dozens of photos of you taken. Your face looked like that of your mother, so I thought your character would resemble mine. Our only similarity was the large mole we both had on the right side of our forehead. To keep from tipping you off, I put Band-Aids on both sides of my forehead when you were with me. The DNA test I had done on the hair taken from your bed proved that you were my son.

Even though I was nearing the end of my life, knowing that I had a son made me happy. I observed you with great pleasure, tested you, and gave you messages. You are a knowledgeable young man, and you are self-made. I could probably explain your falling apart after the loss of two fingers by saying that you took after your emotional mother. If you've taken after me in any way at all, you will probably find whoever chopped off your fingers and get even with him for doing it. Vindictiveness is a noble trait; it was in Sultan Mahmut II's character, too.

I have left you all I had; you can close out the legal dealings with Saim Bey. He also possesses a copy of the DNA test. If you would like for a new test to be done, a lock of my hair is ready for it. The mansion is undergoing a major makeover, so furnish it to your heart's desire and enjoy your life there. Before taking my last trip to Geneva I dictated this letter to Saim Bey and signed it. Underneath the green velvet coverlet, which my mother would drape over her legs when she got cold, is a jar holding my ashes. Mahmut was told to bring it to Istanbul after my death. Sprinkle some of the ashes on the branches of the silverberry bush and spread the rest of them around it.

I was once upset because my Godot theory had been ignored; now I am happy to leave this world as perhaps the only person aware of its secret.

I used to think that my life's aphorism would come from a Western poet or philosopher, yet my choice is a statement that originated in the East and is debatable as to whether it's a verse or a proverb: 'Everything evil contains some goodness.'

All the best to you, my son.

Your father,

Ziya Mahmut Adlan

By the time I finished reading the letter, my whole body was shaking, and when I looked at Saim Bey, both he and Saniye Hanım tried to keep from looking me in the eye. I quickly reread the letter, then stood up and paced the room until I felt dizzy. When I looked out of the open window at the Farewell Fountain, it seemed to be glowing. Then I remembered the line, 'You find me. If I look for you, everyone will know', and mumbled to myself that life is indeed stranger than fiction. As I pondered how to explain all this to my uncle, foulmouthed Cuma, and Ruhsar Hanım, I stood proudly before the painting of Sultan Mahmut II with my feet planted firmly on the ground and my shoulders raised. And while I was facing my great-grandfather squarely, I felt lighter. Looking down at the stumps of my two severed fingers, I decided that now I had two goals: I would keep Esma and Nihal protectively at my side, and I would devote my life to promoting the great but largely ignored Sultan Mahmut II. I began to caress the jar lying beneath my grandmother's coverlet, but I did not cry. When Saim Bey suggested that I change my last name, I said, 'No, let's add to it – Artvin Taner Adlan'. I asked for the construction crew's foreman and was introduced to a man who looked like a wrestler. As I scowled at him and said, 'What's the earliest time that I can I move into my house, chief?' I even scared myself.

GLOSSARY

Abi: Colloquial use of 'ağabey', meaning older brother, often used as an honorific title for men.

Ayran: A drink made by mixing yogurt, water and salt.

Basmala: the Islamic phrase (which translates as 'in the name of God, the merciful, the compassionate') frequently recited by Muslims to elicit God's blessings on their important actions.

Bey: a respectful term of address used after a man's first name.

Bişi (pişi): A bread-like fried dough typically eaten for breakfast or as an afternoon snack.

Büyükada: Literal meaning 'big island', Büyükada is the largest of the Princes' Islands in the Sea of Marmara, near Istanbul.

Çınaraltı: Literal meaning 'under the sycamore', Çınaraltı is a famous café in Istanbul's Kuzguncuk neighbourhood.

Doğramacı Şakir: Literal meaning 'Şakir the joiner', this is a historical street in Tarlabaşı, Istanbul.

Efendi: A title of respect or courtesy, equivalent to the English 'sir' – literally 'lord' or 'master'.

Efkâr: Sorrow.

Hanım: A respectful term of address used after a woman's first name.

İcadiye: With the root form *icat*, meaning 'invention': a street in the neighbourhood of Kuzguncuk, Istanbul, famous for its mixture of various ethnic and religious groups.

Iftar: The evening meal that breaks the Ramadan fast.

Imam: A prayer leader and director of other services in a mosque, who may also take on a larger role in providing community support and spiritual advice.

Kalima shahadat: Literally 'words of evidence' in Arabic; the person who recites kalima shahadat with conviction and a clear understanding of its meaning thenceforth becomes a Muslim. ('I bear witness that none but Allah, the One alone, without partner, is worthy of worship, and I bear witness that Muhammad is Allah's servant and Messenger.')

Kashar (kaşar): A type of cheese, made from the milk of sheep, goats or cows, or blends thereof, which is often served for breakfast or used as a topping on oven-baked meals.

Kurush (kuruş): A monetary unit of Turkey, the 100th part of a lira, also known as 'piaster'.

Laz: An indigenous ethnic group primarily inhabiting the southeast corner of the Black sea's shores and the dialect spoken by its members.

Meyhane: A restaurant with meals that include mezzes (small dishes similar to tapas) and alcoholic beverages.

Mukhtar: A chief official in a village or a district in Turkey, elected by consensus.

Ney: An end-blown reed flute that is commonly used in classical Turkish music and that serves as a primary instrument in the music of the Mevlevi Sufi rites.

Para: A former currency of the Ottoman Empire.

Pastırma: Salt-cured, air-dried beef similar to pastrami that was developed by the Turks of Central Asia.

Salep: A drink made from the starchy, dried roots of certain orchids, prepared with hot milk and usually sprinkled with cinnamon.

Simit: A traditional loop-shaped bread covered with sesame seeds that is commonly sold by street vendors. Often eaten for breakfast.

Sucuk: A dried, spicy sausage made of lamb or beef and flavored with garlic, cumin and red pepper flakes.

Tughra: A calligraphic monogram, seal or signature of a sultan affixed to all official documents and correspondence.

Yenge: Literal meaning 'sister-in-law' or 'aunt-in-law', yenge is a term of endearment, at once respectful and congenial, which refers to the wife or significant other of a respected person.